Standing STRONG

Diane Reeve

with Jenna Glatzer

Health Communications, Inc.
Deerfield Beach, Florida

www.hcibooks.com

Events detailed in this book are a product of court transcripts, journal entries, and the author's best recollection of events and conversations. To protect privacy of individuals, certain names, locales, occupations, timelines and dates have been modified or are compilations.

Library of Congress Cataloging-in-Publication Data
is available through the Library of Congress

© 2016 Diane Reeve

ISBN-13: 978-07573-1902-0 (Paperback)
ISBN-10: 07573-1902-5 (Paperback)
ISBN-13: 978-07573-1903-7 (ePub)
ISBN-10: 07573-1902-0 (ePub)

HCI, its logos, and marks are trademarks of Health Communications, Inc.

Publisher: Health Communications, Inc.
        3201 S.W. 15th Street
        Deerfield Beach, FL 33442–8190

Cover design by Larissa Hise Henoch
Interior design and formatting by Lawna Patterson Oldfield

CONTENTS

ACKNOWLEDGMENTS

If I thank everyone I should thank, this acknowledgment would be longer than the book, but I hope you all know who you are and how much you mean to me.

I especially need to thank my dear Mom, who never wavered in her support. And my daughters, Stacy and Megan, who stood by me from the darkness all the way into the light. If I've done nothing else right in this world, I've raised two intelligent, kind, honest, and steadfast women. And thanks to Carol, who has been with me through the three most difficult times of my life. She has kept me alive on more than one occasion. I owe her a lot.

Thanks to the entire Frisco PD, particularly Tom Presley and Tonia Cunningham. God put you there the day I walked in and it has made all the difference, not only for the sisterhood, but for hundreds of other women. Andy Kahan and Houston attorney Andy's friend worked tirelessly and ended up helping so many. Gratitude to prosecution team Lisa King and Curtis Howard. They listened when we thought we had an idea, gave us the truth, and knew when to tell us to let them do their jobs. Thanks to my friends in the health department. You took steps to get a predator off the streets despite great risk to your livelihood.

A special thanks to Shana Druckerman, the ace producer at ABC who produced the bombshell program on our case that was impeccably accurate, compelling, and gut-wrenching. Thank you for helping me find the courage to come forward and disclose my status on national television. Thanks to Elizabeth Vargas and Oprah Winfrey for being thorough, professional, gracious warm and kind.

Thanks to my black belts, who cried with me, propped me up and held my school together when I was almost too sick to move. And for all my students and parents who stayed, unafraid and unashamed.

Bottomless thanks to my black belt, office manager, confidant, counselor, advisor and best friend, Debbie. Everybody knows you are the one who really runs my life. Much of the credit for what I have accomplished belongs to you, my friend. You are the wind beneath my wings.

My utmost gratitude to my ghostwriter Jenna Glatzer for listening to my story and reliving it with me a bazillion times, and for her uncanny and incredible ability to capture my voice. To my agent Sorche Fairbank, who is as diplomatic as she is brilliant, thank you for believing in me. Also, a huge thank you to my editor, Allison Janse at HCI Publications for her sharp eye and limitless enthusiasm for getting this story out there in the world. And to her colleagues Lawna Oldfield, and Kim Weiss, a big thank you.

And finally and most importantly, a huge thanks to the sisterhood. For women who in most cases would have been at each other's throats, even if we did give into occasional minor squabbles, we never let it get in the way of our sisterhood or of our mission. To Britney, thanks for having the courage to come forward. I wish you health and wellness. To Nina, our fighter, I admire your strength and your courage. Rhonda, our guardian angel, thank you for your sweet mothering spirit that helped us see the good in all of this. Laura, who was the most hurt by all of this, I am so proud of you! Sophia, our counselor, you helped us all get in touch with those raw and painful emotions by showing your own vulnerability. Your support and encouragement has meant the world. Maddie, the peacemaker, thanks for being the glue that held us all together. We would have all come apart at the seams had it not been for your ability to reason and your superior sense of humor. Finally, Susan, my alter ego of the Cagney and Lacey team. Thank you for having the courage to listen, to evaluate, to dump the rat bastard, and then to get tested. And thank you for having the kindness and the forethought to make sure I was notified. I would not be where I am had it not been for you. Thank you for being quiet when I was loud, thinking when I was acting, staying calm when I was crazy and holding it together when I was falling apart. And a thank you to all the women we contacted. My greatest fear was that someone would alert Philippe to our plans, and not one of you jeopardized our lives or our end game. I applaud you all. We made one hell of a team—all of us together—STANDING STRONG!

At any given moment,
you have the power to say:

This is not how the story is going to end.

—*Christine Mason Miller*

CHAPTER 1

Black Corvette

That son of a bitch.

It's not like I didn't know. In my heart I knew, but I had to be sure, which was why I was sitting in Philippe's driveway dressed to the nines at 11:00 PM with hot tears ruining my perfect makeup.

It was the night of my daughter's wedding, for goodness' sake. He had come with me to the ceremony and cake and champagne afterward, but then there was a break before the reception. I was feeling run-down, so I went home to take a nap, which was interrupted by the ringing phone.

"Sweetie, I don't think I can make it to the dinner tonight. I'm just not feeling well," Philippe said.

"What do you mean, you're not coming? It's Stacy's wedding dinner!"

"I just can't. I'm too sick to go."

"You're sick? What's wrong?"

"I don't feel good. I need to just stay home."

My sleep-haze lifted as I tried to process this.

"Seriously, my ex-husband is going to be there with that evil bitch. Don't make me go there alone. I am not going to be the odd man out."

"Sorry, I can't go," he said again.

What else was there to say?

1

I hung up and stared at the caller ID for a second. He had called from his cell phone, and the lack of specifics really made me suspicious. He didn't say he had a headache, or that he was nauseated, or that he had a fever, just this vague "don't feel well," when he had seemed completely fine just an hour earlier when congratulating my daughter on her marriage and offering words of wisdom for her future.

I called his house phone a few minutes later and got no answer. Where exactly was this "sick guy" resting? A hard knot formed in my stomach.

You've got to be kidding me, I thought. After four and a half years together, he was bailing on a day this important? But I couldn't spend my energy thinking about it too much—today was about Stacy and her new husband. I went to the reception dinner, feeling self-conscious about the fact that now everyone would see that my boyfriend had ditched me, and I smiled and toasted and did all the things that a good mom should when her daughter has just gotten married. I even felt them. But then I drove right over to Philippe's house to "check on" this poor, ill man.

It was no great surprise that his car wasn't in the driveway and the lights were off—and yet it still punched me right in the gut. I felt so stupid. I'm afraid it wasn't the first time. Earlier in our relationship, he had left me for two months for an ex-girlfriend who supposedly thought she had cancer, and then there was the time I nearly caught him with another woman. He apologized like crazy and swore it would never happen again, and I let him sweat it out for a few days before I chose to take him back. If anything, I thought we might become closer because he had come so close to losing me.

Despite such incidents, our relationship had been really good in my view. He was so focused on me when we were together, so attentive. He made me feel strong yet protected, desired, and cherished. We traveled well together—the universally accepted test of a relationship. We swam and climbed mountains and kissed under stars and mistletoes. We'd gone to Vegas six times and sang along at a Cher concert. Wherever we went, he had his arm draped around my shoulder, and I felt safe with him. And he was *always* in a good mood. Even when he lost his job, he had such a positive attitude. It made it easy to be his girlfriend. I could remember only two arguments, aside from the ones about the other women, and even those were quickly resolved. How had it come to this?

Rain fell on my windshield, the most clichéd backdrop for my tears. I tried calling his cell phone again, but there was no answer. I sat in his driveway for an hour, feeling hurt and miserable before the hurt gave way to a more powerful and ultimately more helpful emotion: anger.

His cell phone was in my name because I'd added him to my plan a few years back. Some quick thinking led me to call customer service and pour on a little Texas charm.

"One of the kids got ahold of my phone and somehow changed the password on the account," I said. "Now I can't get into my voice mail. Can you tell me what it is?"

"Well, I can send you a text message with a link to let you reset it," she said.

"Oh, that would be just fine. Can you send the text message to my other phone? The one I'm calling from now?"

"Sure can. Thank you for being a good customer for the past twenty years. Is there anything else I can help you with?"

"No, dear, that's all."

A minute later, I took a breath before committing one of the cardinal acts of distrust: I broke into his voice mail. There were two new messages, one from Friday and one from that day.

"I'm so sorry I couldn't meet you tonight," a woman said. She sounded pouty. "I had to get diapers for the baby."

The bile rose in my throat. We were both in our fifties. He was seeing a woman young enough to have a baby?

The voice in the second message was more matter-of-fact: "Yeah, Sunday afternoon sounds really good! I'll see you then."

Not only was he out cheating on me the night of my daughter's wedding, but he had also made plans with two different women for the night before and the afternoon after. Then I realized that whoever he was with now was neither of those women, so he was already on to a third. It made no sense. We were a loving, committed couple. We were in the process of *buying a house* together. This was supposed to be my last true love. I felt so gullible for having ever believed in this man. So gullible, so alone, and so ready to rip his balls off when he got home.

I was going to wait as long as it took—all night if necessary. I was totally prepared to sleep in the car to ensure that I got my opportunity to see his face when I ended things. Finally, around midnight, his black Corvette turned the corner . . . and then drove right on past as soon as he noticed my car.

Oh, it's not going to be that easy, I thought, and I threw the car in reverse and chased after him down the block. He took off like a rocket, speeding right past the police department. I couldn't keep up with him even as I approached ninety miles per hour, but I kept him in my sights as he got onto the tollway.

"We can do this all night. I have a full tank of gas," I said under my breath.

It had taken me years to control my hot temper. Martial arts had helped a lot, as I worked to stop myself from burning bridges and letting things fly out of my mouth that probably shouldn't have. "You can't unring a bell," one of my friends once told me.

Nowadays, most people would describe me as calm and even-tempered, yet here I was, ready to blow that right out of the water with a bona fide car chase, straight out of a movie. Down wet highways and dark side streets, I chased after him with an unshakeable determination until he gave in and pulled over. He got out of his car and approached as I rolled down my window.

"You checked my voice mail, didn't you?" was the first thing he said.

"Hell yeah, I checked your voice mail."

"You're invading my privacy."

"I pay for your cell phone. It's not your privacy."

"What do you want from me?"

This wasn't how I pictured it going. He was cold and remained distant, even as things heated up. It was hard to believe it was the same man who earlier that afternoon had held me close and toasted my daughter's happiness with warmth and love.

"I listened to the messages, Philippe. I know you've been cheating on me again. Not even with just one woman, but two? Three? How many?"

He just stared at me combatively.

"This is the last straw. I'm done," I said.

"Look at why this happens! You're meddling into my affairs and following me around like a crazy woman. This is your fault."

"Don't try that bullshit on me, Philippe. You're not going to twist this around. I have been faithful to you for four and a half years, and I had every right to listen to those messages after the way you lied to me about being sick tonight of all nights, you sorry sack of shit!"

"Stop harassing me!" he said, looking increasingly unhinged. I thought I was just getting started—I wasn't *nearly* done unloading on this jerk—but then things took a weird turn.

My car was a convertible, and I had the top up because of the rain. He began hammer-fisting the top of the car until it shook, and kicking the side of the car by the wheel well, repeating, "You're harassing me! You're harassing me!"

I was a black belt in karate and the owner of a martial arts studio, but he was a martial artist as well. And I was also fifty-four and barely five feet tall. I can't pretend he didn't scare me. The way he was kicking and punching my car made me think that if things escalated any further, it was going to end bloody—or at the very least, I was going to need a new top for my car.

"We're done, Philippe. I'll get my stuff, you get your stuff, and that's it," I said, suddenly more tired than I'd ever felt in my life.

"Oh, we're *done* all right," he said.

I threw the car into drive and peeled out. I don't know how I got home that night, but I know I cried the whole way. I was never going to be able to forget this night, June 17, 2006; it would be forever linked with my daughter's wedding.

∽∾

It was a miserable time trying to put myself back together again over the next few days. I didn't want to get out of bed or do much of anything, but I had my annual ob-gyn visit scheduled two days later, and I made myself go. I had no idea that my terrible week was about to get a whole lot worse.

"You have cervical dysplasia," the nurse told me over the phone when the lab results came back. "There are abnormal cells on the surface of your cervix."

I swallowed hard. "What stage is it?"

"Well, it's not cancer—yet. It's a precancerous condition, caused by your HPV."

"My *what*?"

I knew from my years as a nurse that HPV was the human papillomavirus, and I also knew it was a pretty common sexually transmitted disease that usually didn't show any signs. I'd never had it before, though, and Philippe was the only man I'd been with for years, so it was pretty clear where it came from. Worse, the nurse said it was the "bad kind"—there are more than one hundred strains of HPV, and around thirty of them are known to cause cancer. Mine was one of them.

"You're going to need a procedure to remove the abnormal tissue so it doesn't advance," she said.

That asshole, was all I could think. Not only did he cheat on me, but he gave me an STD, and now I'd have to have surgery soon, or I'd wind up with cervical cancer.

While I was stewing about it, I realized something: There were at least two other women out there who were at risk of the same thing—and I had their numbers. At least 90 percent of the reason I decided to track down the women Philippe was sleeping with was out of this altruistic desire to help. Okay, fine—70 percent. The rest of it was just the *smallest* bit of rightful vengeance. It didn't escape me that the women would be unlikely to want to go out with him again if they knew he was spreading STDs, and that maybe they would give him the chewing-out that I never got to finish. It seemed a better use of my time than trying to confront him directly about it. And seriously, didn't they have a right to know?

I sat at the kitchen table poring over the pages of cell phone records—two months' worth of his outgoing calls. Some were numbers I recognized, like my own or the studio's, but there were dozens of others. It was daunting, but I knew there was no point in rehearsing it in my mind over and over—it was time to just dive in and make a call.

"Hello. My name is Diane Reeve. You don't know me, but there's something important I need to talk to you about. May I ask if you've dated a man named Philippe Padieu?"

"Yes . . . ?" came the response.

"Okay. Well, I don't know what your relationship is like, and it's none of my business, but I was with him for four and a half years, and up until last week, I thought we were exclusive—so that's something you may wish to consider. But the main reason I'm calling is that he gave me HPV, and now I'm fighting a pre-cancerous condition because of it. I wanted to warn you that the same thing could very easily happen to you, so it's important to get a Pap smear soon and to make sure you get one every year."

I hoped I had said it gently enough.

"*When* did you break up?" she asked.

"Last week."

"Last week! We've been together for six months . . . we're supposed to move in together in October."

"Well, that's funny, because we were buying a house together. I wonder how he was going to make that work."

"What a jerk!"

This is going well, I thought. I hadn't known what it would be like to call my ex's many mistresses and deliver news like this, but I knew it was important. And in an odd way, I felt less alone. So, over the next several weeks, I went through every phone number in his records and dialed each unfamiliar number.

Often, it was something innocuous, like a bank or a store, and if a man answered the phone, I just hung up. But if it was a female on the other end of the line, the odds were that Philippe was sleeping with her.

I crossed out numbers and wrote in names throughout the records so I wouldn't call the same woman twice. One woman with a thick accent I couldn't place, Nena, screamed at me to leave her alone, saying that she didn't need to hear this, and then slammed the phone down on me. It was so confusing to me—why was she mad at me for trying to warn her? *But people are weird*, I reminded myself. You just never know what goes on in another person's head.

One woman I called, Susan, agreed to meet me in person.

It's hard to explain why I felt the need to look good for this meeting, but I made sure to dress just so, including a great-fitting pair of jeans and my best high heels, and fix my hair and makeup just right. Even though we were all in the same boat, I guess I hoped to be better and prettier than the others. Ours was the "alpha relationship," and I felt like I was in an unasked-for competition to prove that he hadn't cheated on me because I was hideous.

Susan and I met at a local upscale jazz restaurant, where she was already waiting at the bar when I walked in. I knew immediately who she was, just by the way she was sizing me up. She was about my age, with short, strawberry blond hair, and was dressed in sharp business attire. I wondered if she had dressed up for me as I'd dressed up for her.

"You're so beautiful," she said, which caught me totally off guard. I had no idea how to relate to this woman as a potential friend; she was still my competitor in my eyes. And yes, I was impressed with her, too.

We had a little small talk while we ordered appetizers and drinks, and I learned that she was the vice president of a financial group. When I told her my story about Philippe, my aim was to be matter-of-fact, even though I still had plenty of anger coursing through my veins. She listened politely and attentively but didn't react as strongly as I expected. Unlike me and many of the other women, she didn't believe she was in an exclusive relationship with Philippe. She hoped they were getting serious, but they had never discussed it, and she had seen other guys as well.

Next to me, Susan had been with him the longest. Whereas he spent Mondays, Wednesdays, and Saturdays with me most weeks, he was with her on most Tuesdays and Thursdays for the last year and a half. The pattern quickly filled out: on Fridays he would pick up women at a bar, and Sundays were his swing days—he might be with a neighbor, or meet someone online, or any number of other places. At this point I understood that there was someone in his bed *every night*, and he'd created his entire schedule around it.

"I think he feels you've pulled the rug out from under him a bit," Susan said.

"He's told you about me?" I was floored.

"Well, yes. He said that he never told you it was an exclusive relationship, and that now you've been trying to really mess up his life because you're upset."

"Oh, no. I promise you, he told me we were exclusive, and we were about to move in together."

"Okay," she replied in a noncommittal voice.

She described a man who was down and out, which made me deliriously happy. I have to admit that I'd called the unemployment office to rat him out when I found out he was working off the books while collecting benefits, so now he was just about broke and without any real prospects for a job. She looked at me like I should feel bad about that, but I didn't. I felt really good about it. Not quite as good as I would've felt had she told me that he was living in a cardboard box in a flood zone, but good nonetheless.

At the end of our meeting, Susan thanked me and said she would "watch" Philippe and decide what to do. She didn't say she'd break up with him; she just said she'd think about it. "I just don't think I want to abandon him right now. He's very down. I'll probably end things eventually, but I don't know if I'm ready to do that yet."

I was disappointed but figured I'd done my job, and I wasn't sure I'd ever see her again. I had no idea that our paths would cross again a few months later for a much darker reason—and that this time, she would be the one to share a deadly warning with me.

CHAPTER 2

How It Began

Truth be told, if I wasn't desperate when I met Philippe, then it was something close to that. I was twice divorced, had just turned fifty, and had spent two years unsuccessfully navigating the online dating world, mostly because a friend of mine told me that I should.

"You're too young and too vibrant to give up on love," she said, and enlisted the help of a neighbor to snap some photos of me and put up a profile on a singles site before I had much of a chance to protest.

I found the process exhausting. Inevitably, if I *was* interested in the guy, then he never called again after the first date, and if I *wasn't* interested in the guy, he did. And then came Philippe.

There was nothing particularly memorable about his online approach—just the typical, "Hi. Liked your profile. Write back if you're interested" type of introduction. But he immediately stood out because of his handsome photo, which looked like a professional headshot. He had dark hair and eyes and seemed upbeat and adventurous. I remember thinking that if his profile photo was current, then he really looked great for his age, which he'd listed as forty-five. I wrote back. If there was anything in my life that I'd like to take back, it was the moment I hit "send" on that first e-mail.

We had a bit of a back-and-forth and exchanged the basics (born in France? How cool!), but also wrote about martial arts, which I avoided talking about with most potential dates because it usually led to some moronic variant of, "So you can kick my ass, huh?" But he didn't seem to be intimidated or patronizing about it; in fact, he seemed genuinely interested. He signed every e-mail with "XOXO," a quirk I found endearing. Then we talked on the phone. I had strict rules in my mind for how online dating would work: always a few e-mail exchanges before I'd give out my number, and if we were to meet, then we'd meet somewhere in a public spot. No coming to my house or picking me up. But Philippe managed to bend my rules from the start.

"I'd love to see your studio," he said.

My martial arts school. It was the joy of my life and my second career, after twenty-three unfulfilled years as a nurse. What had sparked my initial interest was the *Kung Fu* television series with David Carradine. When my older daughter, Stacy, was in the second grade, I signed us up for an all-ages karate class at the YMCA. I loved it; she less so. After she progressed to an orange belt, she turned to me one day and said, "I don't want to go to karate tonight."

"Why not?"

"I don't really like hitting people."

"Well, I understand that. But Mommy really *does* like hitting people, so I'm still going to go, okay?"

It was a heck of a way to release stress, and it improved my temper and taught me discipline. I'd been a nurse since I graduated from college, but as I'd moved up the ranks to become a nurse manager, I no longer felt like I was helping anybody—I was just hurting myself with a stressful job I'd grown to hate. It had been a long time since I'd felt any passion for my work. Getting into martial arts felt very empowering, and before long, I was there three times a week instead of just the once-weekly beginner class.

I had to squeeze it in amid home life—meal planning, cleaning, my daughters' school, help with homework, day care, Girl Scouts, art classes, and ballet—so there wasn't time for it to become an obsession yet, but everything in me was shifting inside. I became more balanced and stronger physically and mentally. I was much more toned and self-confident.

There weren't many other women in the school, but I watched them with a sense of competition. In my third year of training, I held my breath, hoping that none of them would make it to black belt before me; one by one, they dropped off. By the time that year had passed, I had outlasted and passed all of the women who had started training with Master Yates before me. I was now a brown belt, and his highest-ranking female student.

When he blew out his knee with a self-defense technique, he asked me to substitute teach while he recovered. It was the coolest thing—I taught children's classes and sometimes stuck around to help teach the adults, too, and I got to watch positive transformations right before my eyes: shy kids gaining confidence, standing taller, and women getting in touch with their own power. *This is what I want to do with my life*, I thought. *This is how I can help people.*

That's what flipped the switch for me: finding a way to combine my new love for kicking butts with my passion for helping people. I couldn't wait to be invited to test for a black belt, but that's the thing in martial arts: you're not allowed to ask to test; you have to wait patiently until your instructor says you're ready. When mine did, I barely slept for the six weeks until the exam. All the major high-ranking black belts in the area were invited to sit on my exam board, and more than twenty-five of them showed up.

Barely healed from a broken nose, I sparred against many of them and some of the other students who were also belt testing that day, and then I had to take on three, four, and five of them at once. When they finally announced at the end, "Diane Reeve, first-degree black belt!," I about fainted from the excitement. I'd made it: I was officially a member of the Badass Bitch Club. And next to being a Disney princess, that's what I had always wanted to be.

I was up to a third-degree black belt when I opened my own studio in Plano, Texas: Vision Martial Arts Center. For a year, I continued working as a nurse while I built up the school, but it became my sole career in 1996. Becoming my own boss was a fitting change, because I liked getting things done without having to run anything by a committee. My first marriage at age twenty-one had been abusive, and I had tolerated it until I was pregnant seven years later and realized that I never wanted my child to witness that.

My second marriage was entirely different. Rusty was my best friend. We got along well, did projects together, and he supported my goals. But toward the end of our eighteen years together, things started unraveling, and I escaped to the martial arts studio for peace more and more often. When I hit the mat, nothing else in the world mattered.

The final straw was a chore that he hadn't completed—I can't even remember what it was anymore, but it sure seemed important then. First I went white-hot with rage—"After two months, you still can't get one simple thing done?!"—but then something shifted. The rage turned into its polar opposite: apathy. I had short-circuited. The love was gone.

He was at the kitchen table when I stared right into his eyes and said in a voice barely above a whisper, "I want a divorce. I'm going out."

Did I make a mistake in not working harder to save my marriage? I've second-guessed it a thousand times. You know what they say about hindsight. I mostly hung around with guys because that's the vast majority of the martial arts training population. I didn't have married female friends to tell me that "unfinished chores" was a problem in *most* long-term marriages; maybe I should've kept that in perspective, considering everything else that was good about him.

Staying with Rusty sure would've been easier and less deadly than the path I chose instead. I was happy with my martial arts school, happy with the fact that I hadn't stopped at black belt, as so many who look at it as the end of a journey do, when really, it just means you've mastered all the basics of the discipline. But I was lonely, and part of me had never let go of the idea of a prince coming along on his white horse and riding off with me into the sunset. So when Philippe came into my life, I hoped he would be the one to fix my broken pieces.

Originally, we were supposed to meet at Chili's for dinner on a Friday night, but he called at about 5:30 to cancel.

"I'm sorry. I had a terrible day at work and I got into a fight with one of my coworkers. I'm still angry about it and I would be terrible company."

I had mixed feelings about it; a last-minute cancellation on a first date didn't sound very promising, but I told myself that his reason for it sounded legit, and I appreciated honesty.

"Can we go out tomorrow instead?" he asked.

Well, that was reassuring. He wasn't just blowing me off. I said yes and he told me he'd pick me up at the school. I said I could just meet him at the restaurant, but when he pushed the issue, talking about his enthusiasm for martial arts, I agreed to let him pick me up there. And thus began a series of times when I caved in to Philippe's wishes despite my better judgment. You can get away with a lot by being charming and attentive.

The next day was a sunny Texas Saturday in February, and my heart raced just a little faster than usual during my workout. Before long, I was changing out of my uniform and into a nice, fitted pair of jeans and red high heels.

When his gorgeous black Corvette pulled into the lot, I peeked out the window to see how prince-like he might or might not be. Online dating photos never tell the real story.

He was a few years older than his profile pictures, but that was par for the course with online dating. Aside from that, he was tall, well-built, and wearing a crisp, white button-down shirt with dark jeans and black cowboy boots. I admired his full head of wavy dark hair and his easy smile. He definitely passed my inspection. *A French cowboy?* I thought. *This could be interesting.*

"I'm Diane," I said. As if he didn't know. "Do you want a quick tour of the place?"

"Of course!" he said.

My classes had just ended and some of the students were still hanging around, so I introduced him and we chatted about martial arts as we walked around the place.

His French accent only comes out every now and then, I thought. His dialect was more Midwestern, with a few twangs of the southeast coast. I didn't know how to make sense of that, but I figured I'd ask him about it eventually.

Conversation was easy because he talked about himself so much that it was hard to get a question in. It wasn't off-putting to me; most of the guys I'd gone out with had to be probed and prodded to share information, making the first few dates seem more like an interview. It left me exhausted and a little put out that I was doing all the interview work, so this was a refreshing change. He was so open and interesting, and in his car, I mostly just sat back and listened.

When we got to Chili's, he came around and opened the car door for me. That's where I noted up close his meticulous grooming: impeccably clean-shaven, neatly trimmed fingernails, and a light, manly cologne that just slightly wafted by me as we walked into the restaurant.

We ordered chips and salsa to start with, margaritas to wash them down, and before I knew it, more than two hours had elapsed. *But he's not giving me "The Look,"* I worried. I knew right away that I was interested in him, but I couldn't tell if he was attracted to me. We were talking more the way that friends talk, not really flirting. A lot of our conversation centered on martial arts. I wondered if I'd chosen the wrong outfit or if I just wasn't his type. I fretted over the fact that I was heavier than I wanted to be; growing up with Twiggy as a sex symbol meant that I was perpetually on a diet and messing around with how I looked.

Then he asked, "What do you like best about karate?"

"Well, I like sparring, but my favorite thing, really, is working on my forms."

"I'd like to see your form," he said with a wink.

Oh, he *was* interested!

Always leave them wanting more, I told myself. That was one of the most important rules about dating. I liked to be the one to end the conversation first, and that's what I did on this date. I made some excuse about a prior commitment for the evening and he held the car door open as I got back in. Our great date ended with an unexpected and heavy make-out session—again, against the rules I had made up for myself.

"This is our first date. We can't go any further than this," I finally said.

"Why not?"

"Because then you won't call me tomorrow."

"I will. I promise I will. You can trust me."

How I wanted to hear those words. I wanted so much to feel these feelings again. It was exciting and dangerous and wrong and right all at once. My older daughter had been out on her own for a while and my younger was a teenager who was very immersed in her own life at that point; on this night, I abandoned so much of my good sense in favor of feeling alive again. This handsome man, four years younger and sexy as hell, made me feel desirable . . . irresistible, even. I let him take the lead, all the while worrying that I was coming across as too "easy."

He's going to get what he wants and then that'll be it, I told myself, and yet my impulses wouldn't back down. He was such a good kisser, and in the midst of pushing him away and fighting my own urges, I realized he was going to kiss me until I gave in. It was *on.* If I gave condoms any thought, it was fleeting, because I was too busy being kissed, and it had been a long, long time since I had felt passionate about a guy. Besides, I had zero worries about pregnancy at that point.

It was hard to sleep and hard to breathe afterward. I was so worried that I was going to get my heart broken and he wasn't going to call.

"Hi, sweetie," he said on the phone the next day, his voice warm and full of promise. "When can I see you again?"

I exhaled. Things were going to be different. This was a man I could trust.

CHAPTER 3

The Saddest Story

Philippe was born in Paris to a mother who didn't want him. She was nineteen and fresh off a three-month affair with the privileged son of a plantation owner from the French Caribbean islands of Guadeloupe. The affair ended as soon as she found out she was pregnant, and the man had come to see baby Philippe in the hospital just once. After that, he vanished. Philippe never saw him again.

"What a shame," I said. Each time we saw each other, I'd learn another piece of his background, and it added up to something tragic and gripping.

"She told me his name was Marcel Marceau, only spelled differently from the famous mime."

His mother handed her baby to her mother and then left to be a barmaid in Bordeaux. Philippe didn't have kind words about his mother, but he did smile when he spoke of his grandmother.

Post–World War II France was largely rubble even ten to fifteen years after the war had ended. So many bombs and so much destruction had yielded an enormous backlog of rebuilding work and displaced thousands of people whose homes were leveled by the war. One of those families was Philippe's grandmother and step-grandfather, so his first memory of home was a shelter, or "camp," as he called it, set up by the social services of France on the outskirts of Paris.

"We had dirt floors," he explained. "My grandmother used to go into the fields and gather up dandelion leaves to make us salads. And I had a pet rabbit, but it disappeared one day. That night, we had meat in our stew."

He laughed when he told the story, which surprised me. *Maybe that's how you have to get through that kind of sadness*, I thought. Disease and malnutrition abounded in the camps, and there wasn't much for kids to do in such squalid conditions.

"I was a handful for my grandmother. I was always getting into trouble for being selfish and hitting the other kids. Sometimes my grandmother would be so tired of all my energy, she would promise me an éclair if I was good. I would be good all day just to get that éclair."

When he said word *grandmother*, he would leave out the "d," running the word together in a slur. He also emphasized the "er" at the end: *granmothER*. It sounded exotic, one of the few remnants of his native accent.

"So that's why you like éclairs so much," I said with a smile.

He nodded. "The ones she bought me at the little bakery were like nothing you've ever tasted."

Scavenging for food and hoarding his few toys had kept him at arm's length from most of the other children in the camp, so he was alone a lot. And then *she* appeared.

Her family had just moved into the camp. She had wispy pieces of blond hair that framed her tiny face and highlighted her light blue eyes—a perfect contrast to him with his jet-black curly hair and dark brown eyes. The first time he set eyes on her, he fell in love, her image forever burned into his psyche.

He did everything he could to win her over, including allowing her to play with his precious toys and sharing with her whatever meager scraps he had to eat. Every day, he looked forward to seeing her in the common area of the camp, and he spent most of his time following her around like a little puppy dog.

She was smaller than he was. Malnutrition had left her frail and thin. He wanted to protect her and to make things right for her, but all he could do was follow her around and offer his toys. He would do anything for her, even though she was too sick to reciprocate his attention or kindness. All her strength was used to fight for her life; she had nothing left over. But her fight didn't last long.

"She didn't make it?" I asked as gently as possible.

Philippe shook his head and continued, with tears brimming. If he'd turned his head in either direction, they would have fallen, but he stayed still and tucked them back.

"I think she starved to death or something. They never told me. One day, she was just gone. I really loved her."

My heart ached for him. It was one of the saddest stories I'd ever heard, and I just wanted to comfort him. I think this was the moment that I knew I could care deeply for this man. He was working so hard not to cry. "Philippe, I am so sorry," I said.

He squared his shoulders and seemed to snap himself out of it. "It was a long time ago," he said—maybe just to remind himself. He shook his head as if to shake away the sorrow, and then we moved on to other subjects, but I never forgot the way he looked when he told me that story.

This is a man who knows what love means, I thought. And I fell a little deeper under his spell.

◈

Philippe's tough beginning got even tougher when he turned six. That's when he was caught eating out of a trash can and social services removed him from his grandmother's care.

"So they put me in a foster home in Switzerland. I lived with this Swiss couple for about a year and it was very good . . . they wanted to adopt me and I wanted to stay, but they had to get my grandmother to give up her rights permanently. She refused. And so I had to move on."

That started the cycle; he'd be moved from place to place over the next four years, never staying in one spot for very long.

By age ten, he attended a Catholic school. There, he befriended an older boy whose father was the Vietnamese ambassador to France in 1965, right around the time the war in Vietnam was cranking up. The boy was a martial arts enthusiast who gave Philippe his first lessons.

Meanwhile, his mother was still working as a barmaid when she met an American soldier. He was a military cook stationed in France, and he wanted to take her back to the states with him when his deployment was over. He wanted to marry her and start a family with her—but she had no desire to have kids.

"That's when she remembered I existed," Philippe explained. "She thought if she could get me back, that would satisfy him enough and she wouldn't have to have another baby. So she grabbed me out of Catholic school and brought me to where her new husband was from: Detroit."

Their house was in the inner city, as depicted in the movie *8 Mile*. Except that they lived on 6 Mile—"two miles closer and two miles worse," he said. The matchbox-size houses were right on top of one another, and there still wasn't very much to do. He didn't speak English and he was smaller than most of the kids his age, but he still tried to make friends. The neighborhood kids would play baseball, so he joined in. He'd never seen the game played before, so he tried to get the idea by watching first.

What he noticed was that whether they got a hit or struck out, the batters always threw the bat down afterward. He interpreted it as a sign that the important thing wasn't whether or not you hit the ball, but how you threw the bat afterward that mattered—so he made a point of throwing the bat hard.

Once he'd picked up some English, he realized that what the kids were saying was, "Watch out for that French kid. He throws the bat."

Detroit wasn't kind to Philippe. He was picked on at school quite a bit for his then-small stature, his language problems, and—not the least of it—the color of his skin. His neighborhood was almost all black, and so was his stepfather, but Philippe and his mom stood out. When they drove down the street, people would often throw garbage at their car. Philippe remembered a time when two boys chased him all the way home.

"I got to my front door and pounded on it so I could get away from the boys. My step dad took one look at what was going on and locked it. He left me out there to figure out what to do."

"So what did you do?" I asked.

"It was winter, but it wasn't cold enough for the water to freeze yet, so I turned on the hose and sprayed them with it. They ran away screaming."

"Inventive."

"And you know, I'm not mad about it. He taught me to stand up for myself. It was a good lesson."

Philippe also signed up for the free trial classes at every martial arts studio he could find. Most offered a free first month for new students, so he would just go from place to place learning different disciplines, though never earning any belts. Often, he had to walk to the schools in the snow—which he said made him mad. The longer he walked, the madder he got, so he showed up ready to fight.

Over the next few years, Philippe learned English and had a growth spurt. He had his first semi-long-term martial arts training with a man named Master Kim, who himself spoke very limited English. When he got frustrated with someone, he would say "Goddammit you!"

As Philippe's confidence grew, he got more and more hell-bent on revenge on the boys who'd picked on him. He joined a gang and frequently got thrown out of school for fighting. He also joined in when the gang held up a McDonald's and made off with about $100 ("Just change," he said).

Another time, when he was walking down the street on 6 Mile with a black friend named Clarence, they were mistaken by the police as suspects in a high-profile criminal case. The whole city was looking for a "salt-and-pepper team." A squad car slowly pulled up beside them, and when the window rolled down, Philippe saw the barrel of a gun pointed directly at them. As he stood there, petrified, he heard an officer say, "It's not them," and then the gun slowly slid back inside and the window rolled up. It gave me goosebumps just listening to the story.

If he'd learned anything from that event, though, it's that guns give you power. I knew Philippe hadn't been an angel as a kid, but none of his stories really gave me pause until he told me the one that follows.

When he was in high school, he was arguing with one of his gang members. The fight escalated and the kid did some damage to Philippe's car.

"I grabbed him and threw him into the front seat of the car," said Philippe. "Then I got into the back of the car and I held a revolver to his head. I pulled the trigger . . . just once. He was so scared! I let him go after that and he never messed with me again."

"Were there any bullets in the chamber?" I asked.

"One. I'm really lucky I didn't kill the guy."

My God, I thought. He was that close to killing somebody. Was it really just meant as intimidation—a warning to this kid? Or had he pulled that trigger in a fit of rage?

I told myself to file this story somewhere to think about later. The man before me seemed so kind and genuine and gentle; it was hard to imagine that he could ever have done something so horrible. It was a long time ago, I told myself. He was just a teenager who'd never known a parent's love, a boy who'd been picked on and uprooted so many times. Of course he was messed up for a while. The important thing was that he *hadn't* actually killed anybody, right?

But his next big story would test the limits of my understanding.

CHAPTER 4

You Knew I Was
a Snake

There were lots of tales Philippe told me that seemed a little questionable, at least in retrospect. For instance, he told me that when he was seventeen, a female friend of his was pulled into a hippie van and gang-raped, resulting in a pregnancy. Because this was 1972, her teen pregnancy would be seen as a shameful act on her part—even more so if she couldn't name the father. So Philippe offered to let her put his name on the baby boy's birth certificate. Afterward, he would visit with Tommy ("T," as Philippe called him) every now and then.

Soon after this, he was thrown out of school for fighting—again—and this time, his mother kicked him out of the house, too. He hooked up with a woman who needed someone to care for her baby while she was at work; they had an affair that ended pretty quickly, but he told me this was okay because he was turning eighteen and had to serve in the French Navy. Two years of service was required of all French citizens, he said.

It raised my eyebrows a bit because I didn't understand how they would've tracked him down in Detroit, and because he never again mentioned this factoid, despite telling me that he'd gone back to France for two years to serve in the military there.

What isn't in question is that he really did serve in the U.S. Navy and was stationed in Virginia Beach. Why the change of location? He never said, but it did explain the bit of southeastern twang I'd noticed when we first met.

If military life is supposed to straighten you out, it failed spectacularly in Philippe's case. He spent more time in the brig than out, mostly because he kept going AWOL. He also participated in some boxing matches, which they called "smokers," on the USS *Nimitz*.

"And once they saw I was good, the sailors would cheer me on. But they would say it like this: 'Pa-doo! Pa-doo! Pa-doo!'" he said with a laugh. Regardless of the mispronunciation of his last name, he seemed to be delighted that someone was finally on his side. He had so often been the odd man out. If it caused a bit of trouble, then I guess it was worth it to him.

He met and married a Filipino woman, only to divorce within two years; they both had numerous extramarital affairs. He told me her name was Lucy, though I found out later it wasn't. I don't know why he changed this detail.

Eventually, he was discharged from the Navy. He stayed in the area, though, and made some friends. He fell in with a group of Puerto Ricans who liked to go clubbing every night, and he became serious about his dancing skills. His archrival on the dance floor was a man named Pablo, and it galled him that people would get them confused because they looked so much alike.

"You speak Spanish?" I asked.

"No, but I could understand almost everything because Spanish and French are very much alike."

"They don't sound much alike to me, but what do I know? I just speak Texan."

He smiled at me then—such a smile. Whenever we talked, his eyes would focus on me so intently, like I was the most fascinating woman on Earth. It was a heady feeling. Before long, we were seeing each other two or three times a week and traveling together, too. I enjoyed his colorful tales and his attentive company.

It had been so long since I'd felt fireworks the way I did with him. Not only was this relationship an emotional reawakening for me, but a sexual reawakening, too. It didn't matter that I was in my early fifties; he made me feel like a twenty-year-old again, except more self-assured this time around.

∽

We'd been dating for a few months when he dropped the big bomb.

One of his new friends after he was discharged from the Navy was a man nicknamed Flaco, the Spanish word for "slim."

Philippe was unemployed and getting desperate for money when Flaco let him in on a plan—they knew Fridays were pay-days at the Navy base, so they'd wait around for an officer to emerge with his recently cashed paycheck, jump him, and steal his money. I don't know how often they did this; it might've been several times or just once, but it didn't go according to plan this time.

One late afternoon, they'd hidden out and jumped an officer, stealing his whole paycheck. But they were chased down and barely made it off the base, the two running in separate direc-tions. Philippe kept on running, knowing he'd be in big trouble if he got caught.

Since the robbery had taken place on a naval base, it was a fed-eral crime, and the FBI took over. Before long, they had identified Philippe and visited his then-girlfriend. At first, she pretended to have no clue where he was.

"Then they said they would have social services come and take her children away, so she dropped a dime on me."

Dropped a dime? It was an expression I'd heard only in the movies. But that's what he said, and not in a joking manner. I sat glued to my chair in anticipation of what was coming next.

"Flaco always had a knife. Not me," Philippe said. "I had no weapon. But they arrested me anyway and charged me with aggravated assault. I got twenty years because they said I had a knife. I was set up."

"My God, Philippe. Then what happened?"

"I got to choose which federal prison to go to, so I chose Milan because it was the closest to Detroit. But that was a bad call, because some guy planted drugs in my cell right away and then ratted me out. And another guy tried to shank me for no reason."

Look, I know it's really uncool to admit this, but in addition to feeling shock at this latest story from his past, I was the tiniest bit turned on by the "bad boy" stuff. I didn't like what he'd done to get into prison, and I had no interest in dating someone who was into criminal activity. But a *reformed* criminal was a different story. It meant he had an edge—a dangerous side—but that he had learned from his mistakes and had become (from what I knew) an upstanding citizen with a respectable job: a network security analyst for an information technology equipment and services firm, preventing hackers from getting into their data. Surely they did background checks for a job like this. It had been close to twenty years since he'd been in any trouble, and given his upbringing, I figured it was understandable that he'd had a rocky path in his teens and early twenties.

When you looked at this guy, no one's first thought was, "He looks like an ex-con." He looked sophisticated. Warm. The stories he told seemed to be from a past life—something that had happened so far in retrospect that a lot of it was funny now. It amazed me how matter-of-fact he could be about those years, telling me stories about the old cons and the new cons, what prison food was like, how they spent their days. He didn't seem angry about any of it.

He talked a lot about "Big John," a burly blond-haired man he lifted weights with, though he made it a point to tell me that he'd never had sex in prison because he was "strictly for the ladies." I did wonder just a bit about how such a sexually charged man had made it through years with no sexual outlet but quickly dismissed the thought, as he exuded masculinity.

While in prison, he took advantage of a program through the University of Michigan and earned a college degree: he proudly showed me his BBA certificate (bachelor's degree in business administration).

During his incarceration, his mother visited him only once— "And only because her church ladies shamed her into it," he said. "They came around and picked her up and brought her to see me. Just that once."

Terrible, I thought. Whatever your child does, you're still supposed to be a mother. A total lack of guidance and foundation seemed to account for so much of his trouble, though he pretended not to care. He seemed to shrug it off, as if to say, "Ah, well, what can you do?" They still spoke on the phone in French, though sometimes I wondered what in the world they had to talk about.

I couldn't imagine what life would be like knowing that your own mother didn't really want you, and that no one else could be bothered, either, except for a paycheck. Yet here he was today, happy and successful. What resilience. What a good example of how people really can change. I so admired him for that.

In the end, he served one-third of his sentence: six and one-third years. He told me that was because he had researched the law and managed to get the time whittled down, but I think it was just standard: because of prison overcrowding, few people serve their entire sentence.

"Want to hear a joke?" he asked.

"Of course."

"A convicted criminal is standing before the judge waiting for sentencing. The judge pronounces his sentence: 'Twenty years in the state penitentiary.' 'No, no!' exclaims the perpetrator. 'I can't—I can't do twenty years!' And the judge replied, 'Just do what you can, son. Just do what you can.'"

I laughed awkwardly and wondered why he thought it was so funny. Would I have been able to laugh at prison jokes if I'd been there, too? It seemed like it *should* be more of a sore spot than it was.

Looking back, of course, I should've been scared off by his criminal history—but it didn't seem that way to me back then. In addition to the "reformed bad boy" aspect, I also admired that he had used his time to earn a degree, and that he had a good attitude about the years he had lost. And I was honored that he was so open and honest with me. As far as I knew, he'd never told another woman about his history the way he'd told me. I felt special—like he knew he could trust me to be open-minded and know that he deserved another chance.

I just wish I hadn't been so open-minded that my brain just about fell out.

Another story he liked to tell was a variation of Aesop's fable of "The Farmer and the Viper."

"Did I tell you the one about the old man and the snake?" He didn't wait for me to respond. "There was an old man who was walking down the road, and as he was walking, he passed by a snake that had been injured by a passing car. The old man felt sorry for the snake, so he picked him up and carried him home and nursed him back to health. In the process they became good friends and the snake would go everywhere the man would go.

"One day after a long journey, as they sat around the fire, for no apparent reason, the snake bit the man. Since the snake was poisonous, the man very quickly began to die. And as he was dying, he cried out, 'Why did you do that? I saved your life! I cared for you. I treated you as a friend.'"

Invariably, as Philippe said the last line, he smirked. "The snake replied, 'You knew I was a snake when you picked me up.'"

"Isn't that funny?" He would ask, as if it really were. I never did understand why he found it so funny—it was a lesson, not a stand-up routine. I had no idea how prophetic it would turn out to be.

CHAPTER 5

Exclusivity

I looked forward to my dates with Philippe more than anything. We didn't talk every day, but I told myself that was okay—more than okay. It was healthy. We were both adults with developed lives of our own, and I needed my space to run my school and have time with my girls. He coached a men's soccer team on Tuesdays and Thursdays, so I knew those days were off limits. Three days a week together was just the right balance. Mondays, Wednesdays, and Saturdays we'd meet up after work, often go out to dinner somewhere fancy, and spend the night together at either his place or mine.

This is the healthiest relationship I've ever had, I told myself. *We're not codependent. We're not jealous. We don't fight. How did I get so lucky the third time around?*

We hadn't yet used the "L" word, but I couldn't help but think that we were heading that way. After so much worry that I'd never find love again, this felt like a tremendous gift. Not only did I find a great guy online, but he was more than I had dreamed of—so optimistic and good-natured, always with a big smile. So handsome, so spontaneous, so everything. I was sure he could have just about any woman he wanted, and I was flattered that he chose me.

I was pretty sure we were an exclusive couple, though we hadn't ever discussed it outright. Four months into our relationship, though, he gave me a perfect excuse to bring it up. Oddly, it was our first argument.

We had just finished making love at his apartment and I was walking around naked while gathering up my clothes.

"I know what you're doing—don't leave your panties," he said in a smart-ass tone.

I didn't know whether to take the comment seriously or not, but I didn't like the implication.

"Oh yeah?" I responded angrily. "Well, I'd have no reason to leave a pair of telltale panties if we're not seeing other people. I'm not seeing anyone else . . . but if you are, we'll start using condoms right now."

I picked up the panties in question and threw them at him, hitting him in the chest.

"I'm not seeing anyone else, but you better never throw anything at me again!" There was a bit of pause while he took measure of what to say next. One of his Detroit expressions came out: "Aight?"

The ferocity of his reaction took me by surprise. He had successfully maneuvered the conversation away from my concern about condoms to the offense of my throwing things at him.

Even though I was uncomfortable about the fight, I was also pleased that he had confirmed we were exclusive. I ignored the little voice in the back of my head that was trying to warn me that something wasn't quite right.

We hadn't used condoms before then because I didn't think there was a need to. My tubes were tied and I was fifty, so I was obviously not worried about pregnancy, and despite my training as a nurse, I was just sort of naive about sexually transmitted diseases (STDs). I figured that was in the purview of teenagers in the backseats of their parents' cars and promiscuous young adults in clubs. At my age, I just didn't think it was something I had to worry about anymore. I knew about things like herpes and genital warts, but assumed two middle-aged, middle-class people were not in the danger demographic. And to me, HIV was still a gay men's disease. It just wasn't on my radar at all. The only afflictions I thought were even a remote possibility would mostly just make me itchy. Seemed a fair trade for the intimacy of condomless sex with the man I loved. Besides, I figured, nobody uses condoms in an exclusive relationship!

I knew that Philippe had a storied sexual history, but that was long ago. After he got out of prison, he went a little girl-crazy—making up for lost time, as he explained it. He didn't talk about any of it as one-night stands, but short relationships. The first one was with a psychiatric nurse, which raised my eyebrows. That was at least the second nurse he'd mentioned dating, not counting me. Although the women he dated came from all walks of life and didn't share many physical characteristics, he obviously still had a "type."

Nurturing, I guess. Maybe making up for the mother he never really had.

They were just dating a few months when the nurse got pregnant. They had already broken up by the time she gave birth to twins: a boy and a girl.

"They live in Detroit with their mother. I see them whenever I can," he said. That was good to hear—he hadn't run away from them even though it wasn't a serious relationship. He never explained what happened between them, only that it ended and that he spent most of the next ten years going from woman to woman.

He wasn't shy about telling me all about them, even when I didn't want to hear all the details. I got the feeling he was showing off a bit, letting me know how many women wanted him.

There was the college girl in New York who just wanted to have fun with him until she graduated, the nurse who worked too far away for them to get serious, the administrative assistant who went on Caribbean cruises with him, and the fling with a much older woman in California (twenty years his senior) who lavished him with the good life—plus a black BMW. He played the role of her boy toy for a year and a half, but then went right back to Detroit.

"The hard part wasn't leaving her . . . it was leaving the BMW," he said.

There was just one woman who he talked about with real love and pain in his voice, and that was "Princess." That's really what he called her, even now. Could you just throw up?

Princess was a statuesque blonde he met in 1999 on a dating website. According to him, they fell madly in love and he secured a transfer to the Plano office of Electronic Data Systems (EDS) to be close to her since she was living in Dallas.

She had grown up as the daughter of a prominent physician in Texarkana and was accustomed to a certain standard of living. Sometime during this time, Philippe started driving a sleek black Corvette, though I never found out if he bought it or she did. They actually moved in together, and he thought all was well until a couple of months later, when she stunned him by showing up with a $20,000 engagement ring—she had just agreed to marry the vice president of a major corporation. The turn of the century was a bad turn in Philippe's life.

"She was the love of my life," he said. It stung a little because, to me, Philippe was the love of mine. I wasn't real fond of this Princess character. I hoped she had very bad crow's feet and creaky knees by now, or maybe some hairy moles on her face.

By my math, his longest relationship had been just under four years, but I was determined that we would change that. This was my last chance at true love, as far as I figured it. He was just about everything I had ever hoped for, and I was too tired to start over again. This one, I planned on keeping. I would do whatever I could to keep his attention squarely on me. I'd always been a perfectionist about my appearance—I got Botox before Botox was cool and collagen injections starting in my midthirties. "Aging gracefully" wasn't a concept I understood. I can't tell you how many years I was thirty-six.

I particularly wanted to look good for the trip we were taking in June—my youngest daughter, Megan, was graduating from high school in May 2002, and I had promised her a trip to Cancun with a friend.

Now that we'd gotten through the exclusivity talk, I thought it was the right time to take the next big step forward in my relationship with Philippe.

"Do you want to come to Cancun with us?" I asked him.

"Of course!" he said, putting his arm around my waist. "Will you wear a bikini the whole time?"

"Even to breakfast."

I called my travel agent and had her add a guest to my package. It was thrilling to me to think about spending five whole days in a row with Philippe—waking up with him every morning, going to bed with him every night, totally uninterrupted time together, far from the responsibilities of everyday life. As soon as I hung up with the travel agent, I started counting down the days.

∽

Megan and her friend had their own room and mostly wanted to go off on their own—we would meet up for dinner and some activities—so Philippe and I were free to have our first romantic vacation. We were greeted with glasses of champagne at the Beach

Palace hotel, which I sipped happily en route to our room, feeling my stress fizz away into the air along with the bubbles. The glasses were not the typical long-stemmed crystal flutes; they were heavily faceted glasses that looked like ice-cream sundae dishes. It struck me as so unique and elegant that it started an illicit tradition in me: Instead of returning the glasses downstairs, I wrapped them in a couple of T-shirts and placed them in my suitcase. I knew it was wrong, but I justified it by saying to myself, "Everybody does it!"

Philippe laughed as I packed the glasses and said he could've predicted I was a thief.

"You have a little petty larceny in you," he said with a smirk. He seemed a bit proud of me for that. Should I have felt flattered or chagrined?

After settling into the room, we went down to the hotel bar. He excused himself to go to the restroom and I waited patiently for about fifteen minutes, then I started to get alarmed. I got up and began looking for him, wondering if he'd gotten into a conversation or got sidetracked somewhere, but there was no sign of him. Eventually I resorted to standing outside the men's room until someone came out.

"Could you do me a favor?" I asked. "My boyfriend is in there. Could you just ask if he's okay?"

"There was no one else in there," the man said.

Huh.

Panic crept in. Was he somewhere on the phone? Or had something horrible happened? I wasn't sure if I just kept missing him as I wandered aimlessly or if it was something more ominous.

Finally, I spotted him walking through the bar.

"Where were you? I was so worried!"

"I was in the bathroom feeling sick the whole time," he said. "But a guy told me the bathroom was empty."

"No, I was in there."

"Are you okay?"

"Yeah, I'm fine now. Probably just the drinks on an empty stomach."

He casually draped his arm over my shoulder in a possessive yet protective kind of way. It gave me an addictive adrenaline rush. The forty-five minutes were erased from my memory just as if he'd zapped me with a neuralyzer from *Men in Black*.

◈

The next morning, after we made love as always, Philippe made the bed. It cracked me up that he always did this, no matter where we were.

"Make the bed in the morning and the day starts out right," he'd say. I'd never really cared if the bed was made before, but I liked his disposition so much that I tried adopting as many of his good habits as I could. Really, how much time did it take? When I was alone, I slept curled into a little corner of the bed, so it would take all of about thirty seconds to fix the sheets and covers. And it did make me feel a little better about the day.

"It's a beautiful day in the neighborhood," he sang in his best Mr. Rogers voice on his way to brush his teeth.

It was. Of course it was. It was Cancun!

In no time, we were strolling the beach arm in arm, soaking in the sun and the sights. We watched as a parasailer took to the sky, rising, rising higher over the blue water.

"Let's do that! Let's go parasailing," Philippe said.

"I really don't know . . ."

"You'll be fine. Besides, it's fun!"

My palms got sweaty just thinking about it. I understood why people would do it—the chance to see the pristine beaches and crystal clear water from the expansive view that only parasailing could afford. But the idea of being up that high with my legs dangling precariously, supported only by a string and a canvas seat, was enough to make me hyperventilate.

Look, I'm no chicken. I can handle the sight of blood and guts, I can kick significant butt in the studio, and I'm not easily rattled by spiders. But heights? Heights are near the top of my list of Things I Could Certainly Do Without, Thank You Very Much.

Terrified as I was, I looked into his pleading eyes and I knew I would suck it up. I wanted to be his everything: the fun and adventurous woman, the spectacular lover, the spunky redhead, the accomplished martial artist, and the savvy businesswoman. I also wanted to show him that I trusted him enough to overcome my fears.

"Go ahead. Book the trip," I said.

"Yes!" he said, then took off like a kid running after the ice-cream truck.

It was a clear and balmy day when we took our ride together. The workers strapped us into the parasail contraption with me in front. We were in two separate seats, but I was practically sitting on his lap. I squared my jaw, preparing for a stomach-dropping thrill ride, but it was nothing like that. The boat took off and we glided up, up, up, gracefully and effortlessly across the water.

"Here we go, here we go!" Philippe called out. It was the first time I'd heard him say that, but it became a hallmark of our adventures; each time we greeted a new experience together, there it was: *Here we go, here we go!*

The ride was so peaceful and pretty, the breeze gently washing away my fears. At the end, I was so proud to have done it and surprised by how much fun I had.

The rest of the trip was phenomenal, too, both the natural beauty of the place and the resort. We rode horseback on the beach, took moonlit strolls, indulged well at the daily all-you-can-eat-and-drink buffets, took a bus ride to the Tulum Monument, and relaxed in the big Jacuzzi in the middle of our room. The darn thing was big enough to swim laps in.

So don't ask me why, in the middle of all this ecstasy, I chose this time to do the dreaded thing: I checked his online dating profile. I'd deactivated my account as soon as we'd been dating for a few weeks, and these many months later I hoped he had done the same. Unfortunately . . . he hadn't. It broke my heart to see his smiling face still there, just the same as when he'd first contacted me.

I called him out on it right there on the beach that night.

"Why, Philippe? I thought we were exclusive. Are you still looking for another woman?"

"No, sweetie! I just haven't taken the time to go back on there and close my account."

I accepted it. I wasn't thrilled, but I chose to take his answer at face value and we continued our vacation without tension. Actually, it was one of the best times of my life. When we landed back in Dallas, I had a suitcase full of souvenirs and a camera full of pictures, but I was sad that we would go back to our three-day-per-week routine. It had been so nice having someone to wake up to every day.

I had paid for that trip because I had invited him, but it was just the beginning of what would be—to me—one of the best parts of our relationship. Megan started college in the fall, and for the first time in my adult life, I was footloose and fancy-free, ready to explore the world with my new love. We were both doing well financially, and I had established the studio well enough that I could leave it for a week at a time to go on trips, so we took lots of them. I felt like I was making up for lost time; Rusty and I hadn't done a lot of exploring together because our kids were little. Philippe was a great and enthusiastic travel companion, up for just about anything I suggested—and I was up for whatever he suggested, too.

We would split the costs of the trips roughly equally; sometimes I'd pay the airfare and he'd pay for the hotel, or vice versa. We weren't keeping score. I'd buy a piece of jewelry as a souvenir at each of our destinations.

He brought up Jamaica and Paris, I suggested New Orleans and California. It was all just a dream come true! I had finally arrived at the place I'd been waiting for in my life: I was still young enough and in good enough health to travel actively, I had the money and freedom to do it, and I had finally gotten it right in choosing a mate who loved life and wanted to see it all with me.

About the only time he turned me down for trips were times when he went to visit his kids in Detroit, which was pretty frequently—at least every few months. When he went to see them, he wouldn't call me. I understood; I figured he needed to focus on being a father, and I didn't worry too much about needing contact. I knew he'd call me when he got back to town, and we'd be right back to our usual fun.

He didn't share a whole lot of detail about their time together or about his family in Paris, but there were stories here and there. Little things. One time after he came back, he kept saying "Yo!" and I cocked my head to the side and asked, "Yo?"

"Oh, my son says that," he explained.

We were in the midst of planning a big vacation to Europe when he went to Detroit to visit his kids, and then came over afterward ranting and raving about how he'd gotten into a big fight with his cousin for not inviting Philippe to the wedding.

"We're not going to visit my family when we go to Paris," he said. "If they don't want to invite me to their wedding, then we don't need to see them!"

Poor guy, I thought. It must be hard to have so little family, so few connections. He seemed to be hurting badly over the missed invitation.

"It's okay. We can just do our own thing when we're there. Who needs your cousin?"

Truthfully, I had been looking forward to meeting his extended family, finding out more about where Philippe came from. He was already pretty well entwined with mine, though my daughters remained detached and not particularly vocal about their feelings about him. They didn't seem to mind his presence, but they didn't light up around him, either. I figured they'd seen me get burned before and were probably cautious about Mom's defective man-picker. He'd win them over in time.

Just a few days before we were set to leave for Paris, Philippe got laid off from his job, along with another colleague. He didn't seem worried, though; he started applying elsewhere right away. I again admired his positive attitude—this was just a blip, and he was confident he'd find work soon.

The scary part for me was that he thought he might find it in Paris.

EDS had a branch in the city, which he thought would be great. On the other hand, I thought it would be a disaster. He had talked about it so casually, and it took all my willpower not to beg him to stay in Dallas. Following him to Paris would've been impossible for me. Luckily, they apparently didn't have any openings. We had a wonderful vacation, and he remained unemployed. I'd never been so happy to date someone without a job before.

I hired him to teach at the school on our days together, Mondays, Wednesdays, and Saturdays. He taught jeet kune do, a mix of disciplines that went with Philippe's scattered training. After some time, he also added a tai chi class. Neither class was wildly popular, but they did bring in a little money; I scheduled them late at night when we didn't have any other classes anyway. He also found some odd jobs to do here and there.

I wouldn't find out for years that the real reason we didn't see his family on that trip was that when he told me he was visiting his kids in Detroit, he was actually in Paris with another woman—and he introduced *her* to his family. He could hardly go back just two or three months later and introduce them to a different woman—thus the concocted story about the fight over the cousin's wedding.

But I had no idea. To me, everything was going so well. I was happy—genuinely happy—for the first time in a long time. A few months later, that happiness would be tested in ways I'd never imagined.

CHAPTER 6

The Highs and Lows

About all Philippe knew about his mysterious father was that he was originally from Guadeloupe. By then, his mom had fessed up that his name wasn't, in fact, Marcel Marceau. At one point she said his last name was Mariceau, and then a number of different iterations that were sort of close to that. It was all pretty questionable. Knowing that Philippe had always hungered for more of a connection with his father, I booked us a trip to Guadeloupe as an early Christmas present.

We left for a ten-day trip on December 1, 2003, when we'd been dating just shy of two years. The salmon-colored Club Med was practically deserted, and not as luxurious as I had hoped—more like a dated apartment complex—but the resort wasn't the point of our trip anyway. We were there for outdoor adventures and some genealogy sleuthing.

Our search for Philippe's dad began in an Internet café in a small town that was across the bay from Napoleon's fort. I hadn't realized that Napoleon had made such far-reaching exploits, but it was interesting to see the old cannons and look at other memorabilia from that time period.

The fort was located on a little island south of Guadeloupe's main island that you can reach only by ferry. Our day trip included snorkeling, but I'm not so much of a snorkeling gal.

"You go ahead," I told Philippe.

"Come join me!"

"Nah, I have a thing about breathing through my mouth."

"Don't worry—it'll be great!"

"I know you got me to parasail, but I'm sitting this one out."

"Goddammit you!" he said in his old sensei's accent, which always made me giggle.

I watched him from the ferry deck. He looked so strong and muscular as he swam, drops of water glistening on his broad shoulders and emphasizing his black curly hair.

After lunch, we rented a car and drove to the courthouse. Philippe went inside while I walked around looking at shops and such, but he came back empty-handed. Nothing came up from the names we were searching for. But it had been such a fun and relaxing day that it wasn't a total bust.

That evening during our all-you-can-eat buffet at the resort, we met another American couple and struck up a dinner's worth of conversation with them. They told us they had been to Guadeloupe before and suggested that the local volcano excursion was a day trip not to be missed. Since it was a dead volcano, there was no risk, only idyllic scenery to behold. We decided to make it a couple's trip for the next morning. I'm not much of a hiker, but the couple assured us it would take only thirty minutes from the parking lot to the top of the volcano where the view was incredible.

⁂

We set out late in the morning and drove as far up the volcano as the road would take us. When we reached the end of the road, there was a parking lot full of cars and a few tourist buses. It was a little cool and cloudy, and I didn't have a jacket. *Suck it up*, I thought. *It's only thirty minutes to the top.*

Philippe and I took the lead, with the other couple close behind. It was fun at first because the scenery was lush—much more tropical than the sandy beaches of the resort. The walk was pleasant and not very steep, with a lot of switchbacks.

"Oh my gosh," I said. "That's the waterfall we've seen in so many pictures of Guadeloupe!"

We happily chattered away and, before we knew it, an hour had gone by—but we were nowhere close to the top. The path got steeper. There were a couple of places where Philippe had to help me up the steps because my legs were too short. After another half hour, my mood was no longer chipper. I decided that this woman and her story about the trip up the volcano were full of it. I was starting to get tired—the air was thin up there—and cold. More clouds were rolling in and cooler winds had kicked up.

"Hey, do you maybe want to call it a day?" I asked.

"Sure, if you're not up to finishing. Doesn't really matter to us—we've seen it before," said the woman. But Philippe wasn't ready to quit.

"How about if Bill and I go up a bit farther and see how much longer it really is to the top?"

"You go right ahead. I'm gonna sit right here," I said—and I did. If it was just a few more minutes of walking, fine, but if it was more than that, I was over it.

After about fifteen minutes, Bill came back alone. He said that he and Philippe had agreed to turn around because the summit was still too far away to keep going, but then Philippe had evidently changed his mind and decided he wanted to continue by himself. So we all waited for another ten or fifteen minutes, by which time the sun was setting and the temperature had really plummeted.

My frustration level rose as I felt a light mist on my already-damp shirt. I was fed up with the whole deal. This idiot woman and her tales of a thirty-minute hike had turned into a half a day of climbing in the cold and wet. Not only was I anxious to get out of this place to somewhere warm and dry, but by that time, I had been waiting well over half an hour. Patience is not a virtue I'm very familiar with.

I started to worry that Philippe had fallen or that something else might've happened to him. So I began yelling at the top of my lungs, "Philippe! Philippe!" But there was only the emptiness of the damp mountain air.

I was emotionally spent when he finally returned almost forty-five minutes from the time we had parted. My nerves were shot and I just wanted to get back to the room. Philippe, on the other hand, was in a heightened state of exhilaration. He tried to make me cheer up by issuing commands like a drill sergeant.

"Soldier, you are not cold! Soldier, you are not tired!"

His efforts to perk me up with humor worked only a little. I was mystified that he could be in a good mood after a day like this. Just as I started to cry, he scooped me up in his arms. Without complaint, without question, that man carried me halfway down that mountain and all the way back to the car.

What an indescribably delicious moment in time that was. It was one of those experiences that stays burned in your memory in a crystal clear picture. My hero, my knight, had rescued me from the darkening forest and carried me back to safety. That, combined with the way he had remained so level-headed—even jubilant —made me fall in love with him even more at that moment.

He's never bitter, I thought. *He's a damn saint. This guy really has it all together.*

After I had changed and gotten warmer, we all went to dinner, had a few drinks, and it was all better.

Our return trip had layovers in both San Juan and Miami, so instead of a really long one-day trip, I had booked a hotel in South Beach for a night to round out our trip.

At the San Juan airport, there were two lines for customs coming back into the country: one for U.S. citizens and one for noncitizens. Since Philippe had never gotten his citizenship, we went to two different lines. I finished first because the noncitizen line was much longer. As soon as you get through customs, you're led down an escalator to the baggage return, so that's where I went to pick up our luggage. I picked up a cart big enough to carry both his and my luggage and loaded it up, then waited.

When I finished and he was still not around, I got a bit concerned—but I was in a pickle. I couldn't get back up to the customs area on an escalator with the luggage cart. Eventually, I asked a nearby stranger to watch our bags so I could go back up to search for him. It was becoming a recurring theme in our relationship —him disappearing and me desperately trying to find him.

At the top of the escalator, Philippe was nowhere to be found. Thinking I must've missed him, I started to head back down, but a uniformed officer appeared, seemingly from nowhere, and grabbed my arm. He was dressed in a crisp white shirt with gold tabs on the shoulders and navy blue pants with matching gold thread. He was very official-looking and wore a badge that said "U.S. Customs." I caught my breath as he approached me with a scowl and said, "Are you with the French guy?"

I blinked and gulped, my heart already racing. "Yeah?"

"You need to come with me. We have your boyfriend."

I was stunned. My heart went into my throat and it felt like I could barely breathe.

"I can't come with you because my luggage is down the escalator and it's being watched by a stranger," I said. This was so confusing! I couldn't fathom what was happening. *Maybe it's just a scam*, I hoped desperately.

"We'll take care of your luggage, lady; just come with me," he commanded with an ominous tone. I was scared, but I was angry also. He treated me as if I were a criminal and he was holding all the cards. I don't take kindly to abuse of power.

I followed him silently, my head spinning, to a door with wood along the bottom and a frosted glass window stamped with "U.S. Customs." By this time I knew it was something serious and terrifying. I followed the officer into a cold, small office with a desk and two hard chairs. And there was Philippe, sitting forlornly.

He was pale, with that "deer in the headlights" expression that told me he didn't understand any better than I did what was happening.

"We're going to keep your boyfriend with us for a while and we're going to give you five minutes with him and then you have to leave," the officer barked. He walked out the door and my heart stopped.

"What the hell happened?" I asked, too stunned to really think.

"When I went to give my passport to the agents in line, they took me off to the side for questioning," he said matter-of-factly. "They asked me about my conviction . . ."

I didn't get it, and I was unraveling. My voice became shrill with mounting panic and anger. "What does that have to do with anything? We've traveled many other places and this has never come up!"

Philippe's demeanor changed—he turned on the now-familiar charm and said, "I'll take care of this, sweetie. Don't you worry about me."

All I could think was *Geez, how can he be so cool and confident at a time like this?*

I tried to think. "Do you want me to take anything back with me?"

He shook his head. "They've taken my wallet and keys, so you just get my luggage."

I told him I already had it, and we stood looking at each other in that freezing room, not knowing what else to say. We stared at each other a moment longer in silence and then the customs agent returned and ordered me, "Now you go catch your plane to Miami, lady." Philippe and I held each other tight for the briefest of moments, and I caught the customs asshole scowling and leering at the same time.

He practically pushed me through the door, ushering me back through security with my luggage, and sent me into the waiting area for the next plane. I had already missed my connecting flight, so I had to schedule another one quickly. I was amazed that I got that done, considering my disarrayed state.

∞

The instant I sat down in the waiting area, I picked up the phone and called Jane Logan, the best person I knew to talk to—a lawyer. Jane had been my friend for a while. She and her four boys had trained with me for years. Every once in a while, I had the faintest suspicion that Jane and Philippe had been fooling around, but when I confronted her, she pooh-poohed me. "He's just my friend, Diane," she said with no emotion.

Not totally satisfied, I asked him the same question. "I would never do that fat, nasty bitch," he said.

Okay, I thought at the time. *Guess I got that one wrong.*

Right now, I needed her as both a friend and an advisor. I raced through the story of Philippe's incarceration to her.

"I don't understand how they could hold that against him. He served his time and he hasn't been in trouble since. WTF, Jane?" I cried out for an answer, hoping against hope she could give me the one I wanted. But she said just two words that totally finished me off: "He's gone."

She said it with such certainty and finality that it caught me way off guard.

"What do you mean?"

"Don't go there. You just need to write him off."

I sunk into an immediate despair. There was no chance of fixing this right now. I had to travel home without Philippe. *Oh my God, how can I do this?* I thought. *I'm alone and he's in custody.*

My hero of the mountaintop—the French cowboy I desperately loved—was ripped away by an immigration system at attention since the 9/11 terrorist attacks. But how could the system deport an upstanding and reformed individual, a caring teacher who owns his own home, pays his bills, and, most important, someone who loved me?

I found out later that a 1996 law ruled that any noncitizen convicted of a felony was to be deported. But at that time, before 9/11, the computer systems from different government agencies didn't communicate with one another effectively, so even in 2003, Philippe and I were able to travel in and out of the country without a problem—until the computers caught up with him.

The long flight to Miami gave me an opportunity to solidify my mission. I would save him just like he saved me on that mountain.

The taxi ride to the hotel was draining, and carrying two sets of luggage that reminded me of who I was missing just added to my overall despair. In the hotel room, I slumped on the bed while waves of nausea overcame me until I fell asleep from physical and emotional exhaustion.

Once I made it home, I got up early to call the detention center in Puerto Rico. "Hello. Can I speak to Philippe Padieu?" I asked, not quite understanding that where he was in detention was pretty much the same as jail.

That fact was brought home to me by the guy who answered the phone. "Lady, this is a prison. We don't just call these guys to the phone." He didn't have to add the word "dumbass" to his declaration; I could hear it in his tone of voice. And it ticked me off.

"Another wannabe cop asshole," I said to myself as I slammed down the phone. I felt like reaching right through that phone, ripping his lungs out, and stuffing them down his throat. Yesterday's despair was turning into anger and determination.

I gathered up my closest friends and invited them over to babysit me on Monday night. The thought of being alone again was just too much for me to bear. While they were helping me drown my sorrows in a bottle of wine, my cell phone rang unexpectedly. I couldn't believe my ears—it was Philippe!

"There might be some hope of me getting out, sweetie," he said excitedly.

"What do you mean? Have you heard something?"

I saw a glimmer of light. Everyone was hushed all around me in a protective and excited huddle. What followed was a stream of consciousness report from a man who was just as distraught as I was. "They left me in that room all night—I didn't have anything to sleep on and the room was freezing—they even left on the lights." He spilled out the words as fast as he could, knowing our time to talk was limited.

"Also, they took me to another place called Guaynabo—they checked me into the detention center and I'm running out of time on this call. I just want to say I hope now that I'll get out of this, so don't give up on me."

He hung up the phone. Even though I had no clue how this was all going to turn out, just hearing his voice and knowing that he felt hope put me on top of the world.

The next day, my older daughter Stacy, a whiz kid at Internet research, helped me locate an attorney in San Juan who might be able to help: Gerald McAfee, Esq. McAfee was a weird name for a Puerto Rican immigration attorney, but he got good reviews online, and I trusted my gut and hired him on the spot. He was very confident and said he had a ton of experience with cases like this. I spent the remainder of the day gathering up and wiring the $2,000 retainer he required to start work on the case. He also told me he would go to the detention center in Guaynabo the next day to see Philippe. I was so eager to hear what he would learn.

Philippe called again and told me that most of the meals were beans and rice, and the lights were on all the time. Plus, it was brutally cold. I wired him fifty dollars so he could get snacks and toiletries for sale at the prison.

During my multiple conversations with Jane Logan, I finally convinced her that the immigration lawyer was going to be successful.

"Okay, you've convinced me he's coming back. Now we need to get the guns out of his house. If immigration raids his house and finds those, it can't be good," she said.

"So how are we going to get into his house?"

"I have a key," she said nonchalantly. She might as well have dropped a bomb on my head.

"How do *you* have a key? I don't even have a key," I said suspiciously as bile rose from the pit of my stomach.

"Oh, I do some computer work for him while he's working during the daytime." The first big question in my mind was *Why does a network security analyst need computer help from a bank-ruptcy attorney?* Not only this, but Jane ran her own law practice; how did she have time to visit his house during the day for free computer support?

Even with the overwhelming evidence that something was amiss between the two of them, I made a conscious decision to compartmentalize that fact so I could focus on the task at hand. I was on systems overload. I just couldn't handle one more crisis right at that minute.

We teamed up and found the gun that I had purchased and the ones he had before we met. We also had the forethought to begin searching for any papers and documents relating to his family. I came upon his briefcase and had a stomach full of knots as I flipped the latch open. The first thing I spotted inside was the quintessential little black book filled with names and addresses of a multitude of people. I stuffed it in my purse.

There were so many women's phone numbers in that book I couldn't help but worry that there were more "Janes" out there. But as I rifled through the briefcase, there was something I was elated to find. It was the birth certificate for Tommy—Philippe's "son." This was key because McAfee's strategy was to prove that Philippe had strong family ties in America and therefore his deportation would create a considerable hardship.

I wasted no time the next day trying to find any information I could about Tommy from Detroit's 411 directory assistance, but no luck. I was stonewalled, and the best I could hope for was that McAfee would have more luck.

Next, with the little black book in hand, I started calling every name in the book one by one: Frieda Ratchett, Margaret Thomas, Emma Jenkins, Candace Wilkins, and a multitude of others. Frieda was the mother of Philippe's twins. She was the first on the list. I had never met her, and it was heart-palpitating to pick up that phone, but I had to follow every lead.

"Hello. Is this Frieda Ratchett?" I tried to be polite.

"Yes, who is this?" she asked sharply.

"This is Diane Reeve. I'm seeing Philippe and he's in trouble with immigration and I was hoping you could help me." I spit the words out quickly. "Do you have any legal document that we could use to associate him to a legal citizen of the United States?"

There was a short pause. "He's not even on the twins' birth certificates and I couldn't care less if he rots in prison or is sent back to France!"

"Oh," I said, reluctant to hang up but not able to think fast enough to keep her on the line.

Whew! Obviously no love lost there. My heart sank as one more door to Philippe's freedom slammed shut in my face.

After Frieda, I contacted Margaret, who turned out to be an old flame of his in Michigan. Margaret was pleasant enough on the phone and left me with the advice not to lend him any money. It was an ominous warning I wish I had heeded.

Then there was Emma Jenkins. She had nothing but great things to say about Philippe, and also told me that she had recently spoken to him about me. She said he had told her all about me, which made me feel a hell of a lot better about all those names in the black book. *Maybe they're just numbers from his past*, I tried to convince myself. The doubts were pushed farther back into a corner of my mind, but they didn't stay there long.

Candace Wilkins, next on the list, sent shockwaves through me.

"Hello. This is Diane Reeve. I'm looking for information regarding Philippe Padieu. I'm his girlfriend and your name is in his little black book. Can you help?"

"*You're* Philippe's girlfriend? *I'm* Philippe's girlfriend," Candace spat out. There was an awkward silence, and then we started trading information back and forth about who was *really* his girlfriend.

"I've been with him for two years," I boasted.

"I've been with him for two and a half years," Candace volleyed back.

"No way!" we both said together.

"We need to get together and talk about this, I think," I said.

Amazingly, she agreed, and we decided to meet up at a local restaurant to discuss who was who and what was what with Philippe. He had become almost a secondary thought in this pissing contest.

We met for drinks at Terilli's, a cozy little Italian restaurant in nearby Frisco. Candace was a tall blonde who towered over me, and I began to feel a bit troubled. Maybe she was more competition than I had bargained for. Once the conversation started, I felt a little more comfortable. After all, we were both in the same boat, and we easily found common ground talking about Philippe.

It turned out that Philippe had a regular schedule with both of us, from which he almost never deviated. With me, the regularly scheduled times to be together were Monday, Wednesday, and Saturday. This was because he taught classes with me at the school, so it was natural for us to leave together. For almost two years he had told me he was coaching a men's soccer team on Tuesday and Thursday, when in fact he had been with this woman. I realized I didn't even know where the soccer team practice was because he had managed to avoid talking about it to a large degree.

Now there was confirmation that Philippe was having a long-time affair with another woman—yet that didn't dissuade me from trying to get him out of prison. You'd think it might, but no. I wanted to give him a piece of my mind, but I also loved him and wanted to be with him forever. The other reason I had wanted to meet Candace, even after discovering his indiscretion, was that I still wanted to find out if she knew anything that could help me with his release. Unfortunately, this was another dead end; it turned out that she probably was as in the dark about Philippe's life as I was. We were surprisingly civil toward each other, I thought, and by the time the check came, Candace told me that she was through with him. The conversation ended amicably, but I really felt like I had just faced the competition. Rather than reducing my resolve, it only increased it. I was a woman on a mission, and I had to get him back. I again compartmentalized the incident and hoped at some point I would have an opportunity to confront him.

Finally, a glimmer of hope emerged about ten days into the ordeal while I was explaining to McAfee that I'd found Philippe's birth certificate, which listed only his mother.

"Wait, is his mother a U.S. citizen?" McAfee asked.

"Well, I think so . . . why?"

"Because if she became a U.S. citizen before Philippe turned eighteen, and he was in her custody at the time, then by default he is automatically a U.S. citizen. If that is true, then this is our best bet to get him back to the states."

Could it really be that simple? As easy as getting her citizenship papers?

"I have her number. What do we need from her?"

"I'll need the original paperwork she filed and received for her citizenship application and acceptance. That's it!" Even the attorney was starting to get excited.

As we hung up the phone, I was flooded with hope.

Please let her have become a citizen before he turned eighteen. Please.

"Hello, this is Diane, Philippe's girlfriend."

We'd never spoken before, though she knew about me. I explained that her son was stranded in Puerto Rico and facing deportation.

"Oh? Okay."

She seemed rather nonchalant under the circumstances. I thought that maybe that was just an effect of age or because she didn't quite totally understand. But then we got to the good part: she had gotten her citizenship in 1970, when Philippe was only fifteen.

A home run in the World Series!

"What do you need from me?" she said.

"All I need is just for you to send us a copy of your citizenship papers. With those, we can appeal Philippe's detention and get him home."

"I'm so sorry, but those papers are back in our condo in Las Vegas, so I don't have access to them."

Say what?

"So when can you go get them?"

"Oh, I am so sorry. My back is so bad and it is hurting all the time. I could not possibly go on the airplane to retrieve them."

My mouth flew open in disbelief. I couldn't have heard what I just heard. His own mother had the key to his release but her back hurts? *Seriously?*

What kind of mother wouldn't do whatever it took to get her son out of prison? *But we're not talking about a real mother*, I remembered. *This is different. She sucks.*

I tried to reason with her, but her attitude was that it wasn't her problem, and she surely didn't have the time or money to help him.

"So you're just going to let him rot in jail?"

"I'm so sorry. I have to go now." And, the mother of my love, the woman with the keys to the kingdom, hung up the phone. I sat in stunned disbelief and plunged right back into the abyss that had engulfed me for the past twelve days.

Her back hurts? *Her back hurts?* I had more thoughts than that, but most of them were just strings of four-letter words. And "bitch." Bitch has five letters.

Luckily, McAfee had an idea about how we could do an end run around his mom: I had to find immigration archives that had the original paperwork she had filed for her citizenship in 1970. The immigration office was in Chicago, so I pleaded with a local attorney to retrieve the documents for me. For a fee of "only" $700, she would go to the building, retrieve the document, and FedEx the original to McAfee—who also needed another $800 for court expenses. It was six days to Christmas, and I was heart-broken thinking about what Philippe was going through.

True to her word, the Chicago attorney sent the papers right away and we got a court date set for the following day. Then it was pushed back another day, then another. Christmas, of course, was a wonderful excuse for court delays.

Please let him get home in time for Christmas, I prayed.

But everything shut down for the holiday. Even the ever-cheerful Philippe began sounding depressed on the phone. I sent him more money and told him it *had* to be soon now.

We were supposed to be in Las Vegas on December 26, but I optimistically rebooked the Vegas trip for January 1. And then I waited.

On December 29, I got a phone call from the attorney.

"Did he call you? He's out."

My palms went sweaty. Was this for real? Would there be yet another emotional roller coaster?

"What?! No! I haven't heard from him!"

"If he calls, it's important that he knows he has to be in court at nine in the morning for all this to go through."

"Oh my God, thank you!" I said, talking to both McAfee and the Lord at the same time.

It turned out that Philippe had been dumped outside the detention center with no money or passport, just his driver's license. McAfee got him a hotel and agreed to pick him up for court the next morning, and then take him to the airport.

The flight was due at 11:59 PM on December 30, but I was so anxious that I was already at baggage claim an hour early. Of course, that meant that the plane was late. As the passengers started to deplane after midnight, I eagerly searched the crowd for that beautiful mop of thick, black, curly, French hair. First there was a mom and her screaming kid, then a woman with her cane, and lots of families coming home from the holidays. With each passing person, I felt a wave of disappointment. And then, to my horror, the pilot walked out. *Oh my God, he didn't make it.*

Just as I was about to fall apart, that thick, curly, black hair popped into view. Underneath was a thinner, paler version of the man I knew and loved. But finally he was home.

"Where were you?" I wailed, though I didn't wait for a response as we kissed and held each other like we might never let go again. It was a reunion worthy of the movies. After three weeks, more than $4,000, and what seemed like years' worth of anguish, I had my lover back!

You have no idea how much I wish now that I'd left his sorry ass in jail.

Vegas 2004.

Paris 2003.

CHAPTER 7

The Morning Light

Vegas was a train wreck of a city on January 1. It reminded me of the aftermath of a teenage party when parents are out of town. There were broken bottles, trash, and confetti lining the streets. It was a sorry sight. And it looked exactly the way I was feeling.

We'd made it to Vegas! I had him back! But . . .

But Jane had a key to his house and Candace thought she was his girlfriend, too. The compartmentalizing could only take me so far. Once the emergency was over, it gave me a little time to think about how screwed up my situation was. The love of my life was cheating on me and had been for the duration of our relationship.

If I were in my twenties, I would've broken up with the guy and that would've been that. But now? Now he was my last-ever shot at true love, I thought, and I wasn't about to let that go. I also had a bit of sunk cost fallacy, like when your dream car has found its way to the bottom of a lake and you have tunnel vision about getting it out. Nothing matters in your mind as much as not losing the considerable investment (time, money, effort, love) you have made. So instead of just cutting your losses, you try everything to salvage it—pouring in even more time, money, and effort. No matter how much money you spend trying to repaint it and fix it up, it's not going to run . . . but some people—like me—need to learn everything the hard way. This was the human version of throwing good money after bad.

We went through that whole trip doing wonderful couple things, without my ever hinting that anything was wrong. I'd bought fifth-row tickets to a Celine Dion concert because she was his favorite, we went to a Moulin Rouge cabaret and had a professional photographer take our picture . . . it was a trip filled with high points despite my unrelenting, quiet anxiety.

I'm not going to let him get away with it, though, I reasoned. *I have my dignity.* I practiced and practiced what I would say—a no-nonsense, cutting statement—sure that I would find the perfect moment to confront him. And the perfect moment would be . . . just before we had to get on a plane ride home, where he'd be stuck sitting next to me for hours with no place to hide.

"You have to know that in my all-out effort to help you, I ran across quite a few women's names in your address book. I had quite an interesting conversation with Candace Wilkins."

I raised my eyebrows and took a deep breath. His blank expression never changed. I studied his face for any sign of anything: remorse, embarrassment, rage, humiliation, or indignation. There wasn't so much as even a tiny tic. My heart was racing, yet I'd bet his heart rate didn't even change. I'm not sure if it was a "deer in the headlights" response or maybe just ho-hum "another one bites the dust" that was on his mind. At the time I just chalked it up to the shock factor.

"I also want you to know that I have forgiven you this first and *only* time. I have no intention of discussing this now or ever for that matter, and I will not bring it up again. Now let's go home, *sweetie.*"

All the way home on the plane I agonized about whether or not we had a future and how this would all play out. There was a palpable tension between us. Sitting side by side on the plane, we made little more than polite conversation as we buried ourselves in our magazines, pretending everything was okay. It wasn't.

Was he grateful for everything that I had done to get him released? Did that make a difference in how he felt about me? Had I done enough now to prove to him that I was the one he was meant to stay with?

And then I'd realize what I was saying—that I was trying to "earn" his loyalty. To be good enough so he wouldn't cheat on me anymore. I'd been a fighter and a scrapper for so long in my life that I'd worked too hard to turn it around—I'd let the pendulum swing too far the other way. The situation certainly warranted more than a little bit of screaming. But I was afraid if I let one more sentence escape, all my pent-up hurt and rage would spew out like an overstuffed, exploding trash compactor. And then he would leave for sure.

It was this deep-seated insecurity that had led me to "over-prove" myself in so many areas of my life; it was the reason I couldn't stop at just one black belt. No, I needed to achieve black belts in tae kwon do, weapons, Kenpo, *and* Aiki-jujitsu. And I needed to be the perfect girlfriend to be worthy of his love.

But what that conversation really taught him wasn't that I was perfect; it was that I would put up with *anything* and not even say much about it.

⚭

We went back to our routine: leaving the school together three times a week and having dinner, watching *Jimmy Kimmel Live!*, and making love every morning. We still didn't see each other or talk much on the other four days, and that kept me suspicious. I often took the opportunity to mess up the routine to test him—like the time I got us concert tickets to see one of his favorite jazz bands on a Thursday night.

"Great, sweetie! I'm looking forward to it," he said.

If he were cheating, there would have been some hesitation, wouldn't there? I thought. *He'd have to figure out a way to get out of his other date.* The fact that it never seemed to be a problem when I scheduled something on our "off" days gave me more confidence that things were over with Candace.

For the whole next year, we continued traveling and living it up, though I paid for a lot more now that he was just sporadically working. That was okay with me because my business was doing well, and I was sure he'd find his footing again soon.

I knew we were really moving closer when we went to see his family in Detroit in early September 2004. I had bought a cute jacket to wear just for the trip, but on our way to dinner with his family, I noticed that the magnetic tag was still attached. Somehow the alarm system hadn't picked it up on my way out of the store.

"Let me see that," he said gently, gripping both sides of the tag.

"Nobody can get those things off," I said. "Don't rip it. I'll take it back when I get home. The store will remove it for me."

He didn't respond or look at me—but like magic, he pulled that magnet apart in seconds with his incredibly strong fingers. My mouth flew open. While I was grateful that I could now wear my new jacket to dinner, that was one of the very few times during the relationship that I ever felt afraid of Philippe.

Crap, I thought. *If he could do that to a magnet, what could he do to my throat?*

Then came the second thought: *What?! Why would you even think that? What a ridiculous thing to think about. This man loves you.*

His mother and stepdad had split up and she lived in Florida with her longtime partner, but I met his stepdad and his aunt, his sister, his nephew, old friends from the neighborhood, and even Philippe's sort-of son, "T"—a very likable and friendly guy who was now a banker in his thirties.

It was a completely different story when we got to the twins' house.

I was elated that I'd finally get the chance to meet Philippe's children. We stood at the door ringing the bell, and although I didn't know what to expect, I didn't anticipate what happened.

Frieda's apartment was in a run-down neighborhood. She filled the doorway with her imposing frame, hair pulled into a severe bun and a scowl etched across her face.

"What do you want?" she said, the words thick and crackly with venom.

"We were in town, so I was hoping we could see the twins."

Looking at this woman, it was all I could do not to shout "Abort mission! Abort mission!" and go running out of there. Her look told me that she might just have a shotgun a few feet away from that door and we might just be on the wrong end of it. I really didn't want to meet my doom on a doorstep in Detroit.

"Kayla is out and Kyle is in the back," she said. Then she turned and hollered, "Kyle, your *father* is here!" The word "father" dripped with sarcasm.

I heard something unintelligible murmured from the back room and Frieda translated with a hint of glee: "He says he doesn't have a father."

Philippe left his business card with Frieda in case the kids ever wanted to contact him, but I don't think they ever did. It confused me in light of the number of times he'd told me he'd gone to visit them—why were they so angry now? And didn't they already have his phone number? I might've asked these sorts of questions, but I felt bad for Philippe—he was unusually somber on the way back to the hotel, and I didn't want to make things worse.

Both on this trip and the one that followed to San Francisco, there was an odd dichotomy happening: I got to meet more and more people from his life, yet I felt like he was getting quieter and more distant, like his mind was somewhere else. Maybe he just needed some cheering up, I hoped. Sadness about the twins, maybe wistfulness about his broken childhood—that had to be it.

"Where's one place you've never been that you've always wanted to go?" I asked.

"Hawaii," he said. Cool! Put me anywhere with an ocean and I'm happy, but especially in the middle of a dreary winter. I scheduled a ten-day trip just before Christmas. We were to leave early on a Saturday morning.

Friday night, the phone rang just as I was drifting off to sleep.

"Hello, Diane, this is Candace Wilkins. Is Philippe with you?" There was no hesitation between her last name and the next question —it was all one sentence. She slurred her words like a college kid at a keg party. I didn't know what the hell to make of it. Was she faking me out?

Before I could get a word in, she continued. "He was supposed to be here by ten and I'm starting to worry about him . . . oh, hang on. He's at the door now."

This can NOT be happening!

I sat there in stunned silence, not having said a single word yet beyond "hello." Then, just when I thought things couldn't get more surreal, Philippe took the phone away from Candace.

"Look, I wanted to tell you this for a couple of months, but I just didn't know how," he said.

"What?" The contents of my stomach began to burn the back of my throat.

"In October, Princess called me because she thought she had cancer. She's divorced from that guy and she didn't have anyone to talk to." My mind fired in a hundred directions. He was at Candace's house. He was talking about Princess (whose name was actually Patricia). What the hell was going on?

"So, you know," he continued, "she's always been the love of my life . . . and I just can't go to Hawaii with you." *The love of your life?* I thought. *Then what am I, motherfucker?*

"Oh my God, Philippe, I don't believe this. First it's Candace who calls—then you tell me you're going back with Patricia and you give me six hours' notice? You are bailing on our trip to Hawaii, the place you always wanted to go? You can't do this!"

I strung every sentence together without a single second of hesitation. I said it like it was Hawaii that mattered, instead of me.

The tears fell. I took a breath. "You can't do this! She dumped you the last time for a richer man, and you know this time won't be any different. She'll dump you again, just like she did before." I fought to keep the panic out of my voice.

We argued—relatively calmly—back and forth until almost one in the morning. Finally I proposed a compromise: "Look, just do me a favor. Just sleep on it tonight and call me at five in the morning and tell me you've changed your mind."

The Paul Simon song "50 Ways to Leave Your Lover" played in my head. ("Why don't we both just sleep on it tonight, and I believe in the morning you'll begin to see the light.")

"I'll think about it." He hung up before I could say another word.

The thing with Patricia was so huge to me—the love of his life? I didn't even have the mental space to consider how Candace -effing-Wilkins played into all this.

For the next five hours, I melted down. I was still awake and gasping for air when the phone rang at 4:00 AM.

"Hello?" *(Oh please, please tell me you've changed your mind.)*

"I'm not going, Diane." It was one of the few times he didn't call me "sweetie." "I just can't."

I held the phone until there was a dial tone.

CHAPTER 8

The Bomb

It's because I'm fat.

That's what I decided. I looked through all our photos—weren't we happy then?—and decided I had gained about fifteen pounds in our nearly three years together, and that must be why he was looking elsewhere. Plus, I was looking old. My deep-set eyes were too sunken in. I wasn't pretty enough. This stupid Princess probably still looked like a model.

I managed to get nearly a full refund on the Hawaii trip and impulsively used the money at the plastic surgeon's office instead: a brow lift and liposuction. That, combined with the fact that I was so emotional I couldn't keep any food down, meant that I was soon thinner than I'd been since I was training for my black belt.

I could've fired Philippe, of course, but I didn't. He continued teaching classes three days a week. I told myself it was because the classes were at least a little profitable and I didn't want to lose the money, but the reality is that I was hoping to win him back, and having him hang around and see my transformation was a strong step in that plan.

And he did notice. I caught him staring at the "new me" many times over those next couple of months, though we didn't say much to each other.

Finally, he made an excuse to stop at my house after work one day in February. It was a scenario that had played out in my fantasies a million times. The words I had been waiting for tumbled out.

"Things aren't working out with Princess. We're having a lot of problems."

What he didn't say was, "I am so sorry; I made a huge mistake and realized that you're the only one for me. I'm not worthy of your love, but I'll spend the rest of my life making it up to you if only you'll find it in your heart to forgive me," but that's what I thought I heard anyway.

Although fireworks were going off in my brain and all I wanted to do was hug and kiss him, I played it cool—for about an hour. I just nodded and gave noncommittal *mm-hmms* until he was about to leave. Then . . . *quick! Think of something!*

I made some ridiculous excuse to go change into a bathing suit, telling him I was going into the hot tub after he left. I couldn't stand having that new body and not showing it off. The minute he spotted me in that bathing suit, I knew I wasn't making it to the hot tub, and that was just too cool for school, as far as I was concerned. We were back together just in time for our three-year anniversary. Every couple had some "off" times, right? To me, this was a growing experience—the final hurdle in our happily-ever-after.

He learned his lesson this time. He got that old fantasy out of his head.

Maybe it was good that he'd found out that Princess was no princess, even if it came at the expense of a lot of heartache for me. At least now there would be no pining in the back of his mind for what could've been. There were no other big loves in his life that he'd ever told me about, so now we could close the book on the past and just be with each other.

More money in the sunken car.

I wish I could tell you that this was the last time, that I never caught him cheating and took him back again. But that would be dishonest. There was one more: a student at the school named Brittani. I walked in on them after hours in the private lesson room.

"I swear, nothing happened!" he said. It was true that they were both clothed when I walked in, but even so, it was 10:00 PM, and there was no explanation for why they were in there all alone with the lights out in the rest of the place.

Still, he swore he hadn't even kissed her. She was a skinny little married woman in her twenties who wore her hair in pigtails and had a couple of toddlers at home. I wondered what her husband thought about these "private lessons." Ridiculous.

Philippe cried that time. Big, heaving tears, telling me that he knew it looked bad and that he was so sorry he had ever cheated on me and it would never happen again. I threatened the girl within an inch of her life and told him to fuck off—but of course I didn't really mean it.

The very next morning I called him and said, "Is this what I can expect for the rest of my life?"

"No, sweetie. It'll never happen again. I promise." And then a few minutes later, in a bid to appease me, he suggested that I should go with him to meet his family in Paris.

It looks ridiculous in retrospect—the desperation that led me to accept this level of crap. I shake my head as I force myself to admit how hard I worked to keep up appearances, to pretend everything was okay so I could just keep living this fantasy that this handsome man really, really loved me and just had momentary lapses of judgment. We stayed together. I agreed to go to Paris.

He didn't find full-time work, so over time, I paid more of his bills: car insurance, cell phone, food. Friends raised their eyebrows about that, but I really wasn't worried; he was trying, I told them. He had even made a tai chi DVD that I tried selling at the studio. I think I sold five copies, but that wasn't the point. The point was that he was *trying*. And that I had my companion again.

In March 2006, we started house-hunting. It had been more than four years since we'd started dating, and we agreed that it was time to take the next step. It didn't escape me that living together would enable me to keep closer tabs on his comings and goings, but my main objective was just to be together more. Because as stupid as it was, and as pathetic and self-hating and whatever else you want to call it, I still loved this man. Deeply. As long as we weren't fighting about other women, we weren't fighting. Things were good. We were still having adventures around the world and quiet nights at home, and even after four years, his little quirks were still endearing.

He told me he would miss his "pet dove" when he moved.

"She follows me and waits for me," he explained proudly, as he scattered bread crumbs around the yard where he'd made a nice garden. "She's always waiting for me after work, and sometimes she even follows me in the car."

He tried to convince me that she had sometimes followed him all the way to my house, which sounded a bit unlikely, but I went along with it.

After months of searching—me with enthusiasm, him not so much—we found our future home. It was an amazing deal: a just-being-built 3,500-square-foot five-bedroom home in Allen, Texas, just north of Plano. It was only fifteen minutes from the school. We had based our selection on the model home. The one we selected was only about 30 percent finished when I made the deposit. We would be able to pick out stains, tile, granite countertops, carpet, bricks, and all the other amenities of putting a house together. I couldn't wait to get out there and start planting flowers in the backyard. Digging in the dirt was such great therapy for me.

This was going to be our fresh start, a new place for both of us to spend the rest of our lives together, without any bad memories or former attachments. No ghosts of relationships past.

And then came Stacy's wedding. The start of her new life; the end of mine. The realization that I'd wasted four and a half years on a man who didn't love anyone but himself—who'd been playing me for a fool all this time. He'd steadily scheduled his days around who he was going to have sex with literally every day, 365 days a year.

It was then that I realized that I was the dove. The woman always waiting for him, even after he was out and about with other women. The one he could satisfy with a couple of handfuls of crumbs. Always ready to follow him, to be there when he wanted me. How blind I had let myself become—had forced myself to become, really.

I only thought I knew what it meant to feel small, insecure, and alone before. Now, faced with the reality that the man who I thought I would be with for the rest of my life hadn't really loved me at all—and not because of me, but because he was incapable of really loving anyone but himself and was cheating on me with a multitude of women—I sunk into a despair worse than any I'd known before.

What meaning did my life have now? What purpose? Single again and now with an STD, I felt hopeless about ever having real love again, and I couldn't imagine a happy life without it.

The weeks after our breakup in June were useless. I spent most of them crying. Calling the other women and alerting them about my HPV was my first step toward feeling something other than just self-pity. I craved support; anger would've been more productive than depression, so I tried to move forward toward realizing what a jackass *he* was and not just how stupid *I* was. That's what I wanted to hear from these other women—"Fuck Philippe! What an asshole! He fooled me, too!"

He just kept amping up the proof of this assholery, too. We had met to exchange "stuff"—he gave me back the cell phone I'd bought for him and I handed back his piles of clothes and personal items, but there were big-ticket items he hadn't given back. Two weeks after our breakup, Philippe called me and announced he wanted a severance package of $500 or he wouldn't give me back my camera or laptop.

"Philippe, you know those are mine, and you need to give them back!" I couldn't believe it had come to this.

"If you don't give me the five hundred dollars, I'm going to tell the cops about the drugs that I planted in your house."

"You *WHAT?!*"

"I've hidden drugs on your property, and if you don't pay me five hundred dollars for the camera and laptop, I'm calling the cops and telling them where to go look for them." I could just see the smarmy smirk on his face. "Meet me in the parking lot with the cash and I'll give your stuff back."

"How am I going to know where the drugs are?"

"I'll tell you as soon as you give me the money."

I incredulously called Jane Logan to deal with yet another crazy Philippe incident. Even though I'd always suspected there were things going on between them, I respected her expertise as an attorney, so I bit the bullet and called for her help. I asked her to stay at my home with her cell phone so when Philippe told me the location, she could check to be sure the drugs were there. I wasn't about to trust him to give me the right information and stop blackmailing me.

When I arrived in the parking lot, he was waiting across the street from the karate school. I had the cash in hand and fanned it out for him to see—straight out of a movie scene. He hauled out the laptop and the camera and set them down. I had Jane on the phone at the time.

"They are buried under a rock in your backyard. The far right-hand corner of the flagstone under the cabana," he said. It just so happened that he was the one who had helped me put that flagstone together one summer afternoon a couple of years before. Those were better times.

"Jane, check the far right-hand corner of the flagstone under the cabana." After a few minutes of searching, Jane found the drugs.

"They're here, in a blue plastic container."

We finished the exchange and drove off. I wouldn't see him again for months.

On my camera? Naked pictures of him with Brittani.

The massive drug stash included a couple of small joints and a few prescription pain pills. Hardly something that would've meant much to the police, but he had gotten what he wanted. The $500 was ridiculous but worth it for me to disentangle from this jerk for the rest of my life.

If only.

CHAPTER 9

We Need to Talk

Somewhere during 2005, I had started scheduling in a nap every day; it was something Philippe had even teased me about after seeing it in my calendar.

"I see you have a nap scheduled for today," he'd say with a funny little smile.

"Yeah, so what?" It made me defensive.

"Oh, I just think it's funny how you take a nap every day. It must be nice."

Stupid aging process, I thought. *Is this what being fifty-four does to you?*

After our breakup, it only got worse—I was tired and weak most of the time. But come on; I was going through a horrendous breakup. Of course I was extra tired and weak.

But there were also these weird white patches in my mouth sometimes and blood in my urine that doctors couldn't explain; plus, I was anemic. It wasn't related to the cervical dysplasia, they said, and sent me to a hematologist for testing. That didn't turn up anything unusual, so they suggested maybe something was wrong with my spleen and sent me for more blood work and an abdominal ultrasound. I had the laser surgery to remove the precancerous cells, which was deemed successful pending follow-up. I still didn't feel well afterward, and because of my crappy insurance, I was paying out of pocket for all these additional tests that revealed no answers. It was hard to get out of bed and go to work each day when I felt so weak, but I pushed myself.

It took me the better part of a month to get through all the phone numbers in Philippe's phone records after I found out about the HPV. I started with the two who'd left voice mails on the day of Stacy's wedding. They were both thankful for the warning; the first said that she'd just met him recently, so it was easy for her to disentangle from him. The second thought they were in love and about to move in together.

The third was Maddie, a single mom in her forties who had already stopped seeing Philippe before my call. It didn't take long to find out that she was Philippe's neighbor, and that I'd heard of her before because Philippe had referred to her as "the crazy drunk lady with the kid problems."

"I think I saw a picture of you in his car one day," she told me. "I asked him who you were and he said you were just a friend and you were happily married."

Maddie was the friendliest of the women so far, and she told me that she was going to keep an eye on his house to see who else came and went. There were lots of different cars coming and going there, she said. True to her word, she'd call regularly after that with descriptions of the steady stream of women she saw walking in with Philippe. He hadn't slowed down at all.

It was good to have someone like Maddie to talk to. Even though I wasn't happy we were in the same boat, it turned out that she'd gotten HPV from him, too, and had been as fooled by him as I was. We compared notes and were able to lean on each other when either of us needed to talk.

I still had one more trip booked with Philippe—we were supposed to go to Las Vegas in July for a martial arts expo—and

Maddie helped me decide that it would be good for me to get away by myself rather than canceling. When I got there, though, all I felt was lonely. No one to go to lunch with, no one to see shows with . . . it hit home how different it felt to travel without a partner.

When the phone rang in the middle of the night with a hang-up, I assumed Philippe was playing games, checking up on me. But then it rang again the following morning and a girl's voice was on the other end.

"Who is this?"

"It's Brittani," she said.

Brittani. *Brittani?!* The little pigtailed bimbo who was taking "private lessons" after hours?

"Diane, do you know where Philippe is?" she asked, as if she were chitchatting with a friend.

"I have no idea, Brittani. Why would you think I know where he is?"

"We haven't seen him in over twenty-four hours and we're worried about him. He hasn't shown up for work."

Brittani had left my school when Philippe switched to teach at a gymnastics center in Plano, so I guessed she had been seeing him all this time.

"You're asking the wrong person," I said, and hung up the phone abruptly.

I called my friend and office manager, Debbie, to try to work out why Brittani would call me. Obviously, she knew Philippe and I had broken up. Debbie called the owner at Philippe's new job and was told that he had been hospitalized due to dehydration. It sounded fishy to me; he'd been athletic most of his life, so why would he let that happen now? Not to mention that "dehydration" is the excuse all the celebrities use when they're actually in rehab.

I remember thinking to myself that there was something else wrong, but I just didn't know how to figure out what it was. And I was doing my damnedest not to care.

⧙⧙

Some of the women I had alerted never spoke to me again, though some stayed in touch. One of them, yet another woman named Susan, had been very quiet on the phone and didn't say much of anything. A couple of weeks later, she had a friend of hers call me back to say that she appreciated the warning even if she hadn't said so, and that she was going to stop seeing Philippe.

Maddie suggested that at least a few of us should get together for "a meeting." The meeting, of course, should involve drinks. Philippe's assessment of her as the "crazy drunk neighbor" was entirely unfair but not altogether meritless; she did love to find reasons to party.

I thought it was a great idea, so we met up at a local Italian restaurant called Patrizio, at an outdoor table because the place was so crowded. It was hotter than blue blazes, but at least we found a shady spot. Maddie was the first to arrive. She was in her early to midforties; thin as a rail, with visible cheekbones. Short like me, with hair dyed red. I thought she looked a bit under the weather, but then I probably did too. Stress does that to you.

Next came Lupita, five feet two with long auburn hair streaked with errant grays. She was in good shape for her age, which looked to be about sixty. She was the first one I'd called about the HPV, and was the one who thought she was about to move in with Philippe.

Darja introduced herself with a thick Eastern European accent that was very difficult to understand. She was a quiet and reserved woman with short red hair and big, beautiful eyes. She was taller and more solidly built than the rest of us. In spite of the typical

Eastern European stoicism she exhibited, she clearly wanted to talk this out.

After we got settled, we all ordered a round of peach Bellinis, the house specialty. While we all had contracted HPV, it was definitely not a somber mood—it was more of a celebration than a wake.

The conversation came fast and furious, focused mainly on what a schmuck Philippe was and how he treated all of us. Although Lupita had only broken up with him in June, she already had a new fiancé named Roger, who had recently gotten into an altercation with Philippe.

"He told Philippe he looked like Bozo the Clown."

We got a good laugh out of that.

"Well, then we got into a car chase . . ."

Hmm. That sounded familiar.

"Roger called the police because Philippe was threatening him. He pulled into a parking lot and, just as the police showed up, Philippe was pulling a knife out of his glove box. So now he has to go to court for a weapons charge."

Oh, I can't even pretend that didn't make me happy. Whichever way revenge wanted to come, I was okay with it.

We talked a lot about how Philippe had managed to win over each of us and juggle all of us. For one thing, we realized that he almost never used our given names—he called all of us "sweetie." No wonder he'd never slipped up and used the wrong name.

Lupita had been convinced they were getting married soon, which made me wonder if Philippe had intentionally set me up to break up with him on the night of Stacy's wedding. How long could he keep up this charade of telling two women he was going to move in with them? And what was she smokin'? After our conversations, how could she trust anything he said?

Darja met him—no joke—at an actual meat market a few months earlier and hadn't discussed exclusivity with him yet. Of course, she had no idea just how "unexclusive" they were.

Maddie was juggling being a single mom of three kids and trying to take care of her house by herself, and she realized Philippe was watching her sometimes.

"I hated doing yardwork," she said. "And then my lawnmower broke, so the grass got way overgrown. Then one day I came home and found that someone had mowed the lawn for me. He was outside and smiling, so I figured it had to be him. I went over to say thank you."

What a perfect plan to win over a middle-aged damsel in distress. That's what we all had in common, though probably none of us wanted to admit it—we were all a little desperate, a little needy. He found women who were vulnerable, and he played the role we each wanted him to play.

"We had sex for the first time on my birthday in 2004. We didn't use a condom, and afterward, I was embarrassed and worried. I said, 'I can't believe we did that the other night.' He was very nice and said, 'Don't worry. I'm very careful. I get tested every year, and I'm clean.' He seemed to take a lot of pride in that."

Maddie worked as a caregiver and also had frequent drug and HIV tests due to her job. Philippe was the first person she'd slept with since her last test. They dated off and on for the next eighteen months, with him swearing that he wasn't seeing anyone else and that the women whose cars she saw in his driveway were just friends.

He was vain, we all agreed—spending more time in front of the mirror and using more hair products than many of us. His black Corvette was a classic "chick magnet." He didn't seem to have much of a physical type, though. The women I'd known about so far ran the gamut from their twenties to their sixties; some were in shape, some were not so in shape; they were different nationalities and coloring. He was borrowing money from some of us, but not all.

We got to the personal details, too. He had refused to wear condoms with all of us, and somehow we all let him get away with that. No one thought he was particularly good in bed, and he pushed us to do things we weren't necessarily comfortable with—some of the women mentioned taking pictures in the act, for instance—but he was really good at making all of us feel special.

"If he could see us now . . ." Maddie said.

"Well . . . maybe he can!" I said.

Oh, it was a stellar idea, and I'm not sure who had it first, but Lupita grabbed the camera and took a picture of Maddie, Darja, and me smiling widely and giving him the middle finger. We decided to print it and mail it to him.

A camaraderie was born on this day that filled a need I hadn't even realized I had. I think we all felt a bit better about ourselves, right until the moment when Lupita's new fiancé came to pick her up, with his grandbaby in his arms. He was well over six feet tall, broad-shouldered, with the look of a construction worker and the brains of a hammer. I disliked him immediately, and my jerk-meter was spot-on. He sauntered over to our table and announced himself like this: "You women are stupid. I mean, just crazy. How could you be so idiotic to all date the same guy at the same time." It was a statement and not a question—and it was shocking. He ranted and raved for a good three or four minutes in his high and mighty fashion while I was boiling in my chair until I couldn't take it anymore.

"Let me tell you something, moron: You have no clue what you're talking about. Plus, you are way out of line. So just go on back to whatever vile, dark place you crawled out of and leave us the hell alone."

But Roger stood his ground. "Oh yeah? I'm not worried about you."

I would've stood up on the chair if I'd really wanted to make a strong point. Instead, I closed the space between us—a classic power move.

"You need to leave. Now!" I said, staring him down. I couldn't believe that Lupita had just gone from one asshole to another. The other two women slunk down in their chairs, humiliated.

"Let's go, Lupita," he said, ordering her to leave as he walked out. She apologized to everyone and gathered her things and left. I shook my head in disgust and dismay.

Once the tension was broken, we had a good laugh about that SOB. Who was he to judge us? Little did I know that it would be just the first of many, many such instances. But even with that hiccup, the meeting was an overall success. The in-person bitch session had turned into something deeper than that; it was a couple of hours where we could each see that we weren't crazy—that we had all been taken in by the same master manipulator. It helped.

Later, I found out that Lupita had bailed Philippe out of jail, after the knife incident with her fiancé. It really was stunning how much power he had over some women, even after the truth had come out.

⁂

Maddie kept calling to tell me about the cars of the various people who arrived in Philippe's driveway. When she described a purple Chevy, I thought for sure it must be Brittani—and when I had a friend with access to DMV info run the plates, I found out I was right.

"Next time you see that car, let me know and we'll have a little fun," I said.

And so it was that I found myself in Philippe's driveway with a camera, capturing the car and plates in front of his house—though I didn't quite get the money shot. I wanted a picture of them together, so Maddie and I camped out behind a tree next to his house. She chain-smoked while we waited.

Finally, about two hours after Brittani had arrived, Philippe came out and loaded a bag into her car. I snapped a couple of shots and he spotted me.

"You're harassing me!" he screamed. He intended to sound threatening, I'm sure, but it came off as whining like a little boy who'd gotten pushed on the lunch line. I wish I could've seen his face when he'd opened the flip-off photo.

I didn't say a word, but I thought, *You think this is bad? I've just begun to harass you.*

He moved Brittani's car from the driveway to the street. I snapped more pictures.

"I'm calling the police!" he said.

"Go ahead. I'm just taking pictures."

Right afterward, I went to Walgreens and made two copies of each shot—nice, clean shots to show Brittani's husband that his sweet little wife with the stupid pigtails was cheating.

At 6:30 AM on Monday, I rolled onto the street that I was looking for and spotted her husband's car still in the driveway. Good—he hadn't gone to work yet. I sat there and waited calmly until after 8:00 AM. A lady approached the car and I rolled down the window.

"Can I ask what you are doing here?" she asked, polite but tense.

"Yes ma'am, I'm waiting to show the man that lives here pictures of his wife's car in my ex's driveway." Nothing like the cold, hard truth to catch someone off guard. She backed away, mumbling something about watching out for predators and wishing me luck.

Finally, after almost three hours, Brittani made an appearance in short shorts and a white top with her hair pulled back yet again in those ridiculous dog-ear pigtails. She took out the trash and went back in without spotting me.

Two minutes later, her husband, Eddie, came out the front door. I gunned the engine and parked in front of their driveway, shaking as I climbed out of the car with the envelope full of pictures.

"Excuse me, Eddie." I faltered a little. The excitement of revenge didn't feel as sweet when facing this decent man whose world I was about to crush. "I don't know if you remember me. I'm Diane Reeve. I met you when Brittani enrolled at Vision Martial Arts."

"Yesss?" He raised an eyebrow.

"I just thought you might like to know that I watched Brittani's car for over two hours last Friday afternoon at Philippe Padieu's house . . . and I thought you might want some pictures to prove it, just in case you decide to talk to her about it."

He stared at me dumbfounded as I handed him the envelope. It was obvious that he was in shock and not sure exactly what to do. He had no affect, no questions, no rage, and no other emotion. He just looked blankly at the pictures as I explained how I had obtained them.

"Do you think they're having an affair?" he finally asked sheepishly.

"Well . . ." I drew in a breath. "I don't know what else she'd be doing there for two hours. I guess I would give it about a 99 percent chance."

As I finished the last sentence, Brittani came out the door.

"Diane," she said softly and calmly, "There's really nothing going on." I couldn't believe she was totally trying to bullshit both of us. "Philippe and I were just talking."

"For two hours?"

"Yeah, we were talking about Jeff's ankle injury and how to use BOB." BOB is an acronym for "body opponent bag," a plastic dummy used to practice kicks and punches.

"What a pile of crap."

"It's true, Diane." Like she was talking to her three-year-old. I just wanted to slap her.

"You've really got to give this Philippe thing up. Here's my cell number—call me if you want to talk sometime."

You're the last person I would ever call, I thought. I dissolved into tears as I drove off—relief, shame, and satisfaction all rolled into one. I left with the image of Eddie in my rearview mirror, his arms folded in disgust. I wondered which one of us he was disgusted with. I wish I had remembered to mention the naked pictures of Brittani he'd left on my camera.

It was a couple of months later when Eddie called the school to set up an appointment with me. I didn't know if he planned to vent, threaten, kill, or sue me, but I was surprisingly okay with taking my chances.

I closed the door to the office in the school and he sat down with a thud into my chocolate brown wicker chair next to the door.

"I guess I have just one question for you," he started after he thanked me for meeting with him. "Do you still think they are having an affair?"

I wasn't quite sure how to respond. I knew in my heart of hearts they were. But he wouldn't have gone to all the trouble of asking me if he didn't have some hope, which made it hard to answer. At that point, I saw no point in adding to his hurt more than I had to.

"Yes, I do. I'm sorry," I said as gently as I could.

He let out a huge sigh of resignation and caught his breath. "But she says they are just friends. And I have an old friend in my life without anything going on."

"I would really like to give you some hope, and certainly you can make your own decision on this. But I just don't see much of a possibility that this is all innocent. I know Philippe too well. We were together for four and a half years."

"Yeah, I know," he mumbled. "Thank you for your time." He stood up.

"Good luck, Eddie," I said as he walked away, dejected.

⟡

Even though the original surgery was considered successful, at every follow-up visit, I was told that the cervical dysplasia had not cleared up. It hadn't gotten any worse or spread, but it was still there after five months, and that wasn't normal. The anemia was still there, too, and that wasn't normal, either. Both things should've cleared up within a couple of months.

I continued making doctor's appointments with some frustration, hoping there was an answer for my problems. In December, I got rid of my crappy health plan and switched to a better one. In my downtime, I continued trying to figure out how to make sure Philippe would wind up alone and babbling to himself in a fetal position on a street corner.

Which is not to say that this quest for vengeance wasn't intermingled with some very weak, sad moments. I was cleaning out my closet one day around Christmas and came across a pair of his shoes. In my loneliness, I had a moment of missing him, missing having someone who was a big enough part of my life to leave shoes in my closet. For a brief time, I felt bad about my ill will and thought that maybe I should call a truce in time for the holidays. I left those shoes on his front door with a note, expecting that he'd at least call to say thank you. He didn't.

Well, screw you, too.

I went back to owning my anger as soon as the Christmas spirit passed. When I wasn't busy plotting, I was just extremely depressed. For the past twenty years, I'd had a passion for martial arts. I loved training, teaching, and passing on the empowerment that I had gained. But since the breakup, I had started to lose that passion. I had no interest in going to work or training. There was no color in the world. Everything blended into shades of gray.

Without a lot of thought about it, I had kept Philippe's cell phone active and plugged in so I could warn any of his exes in case they happened to call. They didn't anymore.

Then, on January 25, 2007, at about two in the afternoon, his cell phone rang. I let it go to voice mail, then listened to the message.

"This is Keisha from Dallas County Health Department. This call is for Diane Reeve. Please call me at 214-555-1212, extension 315. It's important that you return this call as soon as possible."

So many questions ran through my mind. It was an incredibly strange call to get on his phone. Why would someone from the health department use that number to call me? I worked up my nerve and called right back.

"You have been named by a client of ours as having been exposed to an STD," Keisha explained. "We would like to have you come in for some tests."

I fully panicked. "*What* STD?"

"I can't really discuss that on the phone."

"Who gave you my name?"

"I can't really discuss that either."

My mouth went dry. A freight train roared through my head and I couldn't breathe. My heart went past my throat and outside my chest.

"I have an appointment with my doctor tomorrow. I'll get tested there."

"If you have any questions, please call."

Hell, what good would that do me? You wouldn't tell me anything. I hung up.

The freight train in my head morphed into the clanging of alarm bells. All the puzzle pieces of my health problems that had been swirling around in my head for the past six months started to fall together, forming one gigantic answer. All the pieces landed on the floor in front of me and they had just three letters: HIV.

Shaking, I picked up the phone and called my friend and office manager, Debbie.

"Oh, it's just a prank," she said, and when that didn't persuade me, she added, "I'm sure it's okay," trying to convince herself as much as me.

When my head cleared a bit, I scrolled through Philippe's phone to the last number that had been dialed. It was Susan, who I'd met with in October. Thank God she picked up on the first ring.

"This is Diane Reeve. We met a few months ago at Avanti. I just got a call from the health department. What can you tell me about that?"

As long as I live, I will never forget the chilling words I heard next—four words that would change my life forever: "We need to talk."

My knees hit the floor.

"Are you where you can talk privately?" she asked. I realized I wasn't breathing. I forced myself to.

"Sure," I said out loud. *Oh God, oh God*, I was saying to myself.

"About two months ago, I dumped Philippe," she started. "Because of everything you had told me about what he had done, for a month after we broke up, I struggled with anxiety about STDs. Finally, at the end of December, I just went to my doctor and got tested for everything." She paused, and I stopped breathing again.

"I got my test results on January 2. I am HIV-positive."

More "Oh Gods" filled my head until I almost couldn't focus. I tried my best to express my sympathy, and I'm sure it was dismally ineffective.

"Keep in touch; let me know," she said with 1 percent cheer and 99 percent melancholy.

I went to the bedroom and cried. I knew. I didn't have to see a doctor. I didn't have to get tested. I knew. I *knew*. It was the only thing that fit. And there was only one person who could have given it to me.

I tried to put it out of my mind, which was, of course, impossible. I went to the school that night and got a scintilla of relief from the extreme anxiety while I was on the mat teaching. It was excruciating. I smiled placidly while I was literally dying inside. I don't know how I slept that night. And the next day, facing my gynecologist, Lisa Umholtz, was a daunting task. I explained it to her the best way I could.

She was sympathetic but matter-of-fact and walked away as they did the blood draw.

"Try not to worry about it, Diane. The results probably won't be in until Monday."

I left the office in a fog. I moved through Thursday night's class in the same plastic-fake-smile manner as I had on Wednesday. I also talked to Debbie a couple of times. On Friday my cell phone rang. There was no preface.

"Diane, this is Lisa Umholtz. I'm sorry. It's positive."

"Thanks," I said, which I didn't in any way, shape, or form mean. Then I lay down on the floor and died.

CHAPTER 10

AIDS

Death was all I could think about—how I was going to leave my children without a mother and my grandchildren without their grandmother. I had HIV—had probably had it for a long time—and that meant my life was over.

First came the crying, hours of crying, balled up alone in my house. Then I called Debbie and told her. She was shaken but unwavering in her support. Then came the "whys": *Why me? What did I do to deserve this? Am I a bad person?*

I played back my whole relationship with Philippe in my mind, going over all the opportunities I had to wake up and get rid of him—starting with the very first time I found his profile still online after we'd had the "exclusivity talk." I should've known then. Or the first time he disappeared when we were out of town. Or the first time I caught him cheating.

I am so, so, so stupid.

I wondered when, exactly, I had contracted this disease—what was my cutoff date? If only I'd broken up with him six months sooner, or a year, would that have been enough? Or had I caught it from him the very first time? Was it in Cancun? Or Guadeloupe?

Guadeloupe . . . the sorest point of all. I could just sit there and poke at that particular wound all day and make myself feel like the biggest idiot who ever lived. Four thousand dollars, weeks of

99

my life, to keep my ex-con boyfriend in my country, so he could repay me like this. With a disease that would kill me.

I made an appointment with my counselor because I didn't want to tell her over the phone—I knew that once I got started, I wasn't going to be able to just hang up. Then I called my mom.

How do you tell your mother that you're HIV-positive?

She cried but was less upset than I had expected. I wasn't sure if it was because she understood too little or too much. Was she too old to have been aware of what HIV was all about? Or was she so with it that she knew about the newer medications? Or maybe she was just trying to be strong for me so I wouldn't be afraid. It didn't work. I knew I was going to die. I just didn't know how long I had.

My girls were next. Stacy was pretty philosophical when I told her. "Well, Ma," she said, "nowadays you pretty much just have to take a pill and you're okay." I didn't want to scare her by contradicting her, so I just agreed and pretended everything was okay.

The problem I didn't share with her was that I'd just changed my insurance policy—one with lower copayments and better overall coverage. There had been one little sentence in the terms that would be a disaster, though: *HIV treatment is not covered under this policy.*

I remembered reading it; it didn't bother me a bit. I said to myself, "Oh, I don't have HIV. I don't fit any of the risk factors for HIV—I'm a straight, middle-class woman. Besides, I'm too old for that crap."

And I didn't tell Stacy that I knew it would be next to impossible for me to find insurance now that I had been diagnosed. With a preexisting condition of HIV, no insurance company would touch me (this was before the 2014 changes in our nation's health care system). I had no idea what the medications were going to cost, but business at my school had slowed down ever since *I* had slowed down. There hadn't been much left over each month.

Of everyone I told initially, telling my daughter Megan was the hardest. She had just graduated with a teaching degree from the University of Texas and had moved back home while she looked for a teaching job at an elementary school. When she came in that evening, it was as dark outside as I felt inside. I tried to be casual, but she saw right through me.

"Mom, what's wrong?"

I tried to ease into it by starting with a review of all the health problems I'd been having. I danced around it and skirted the issue for as long as I could, postponing that inevitable instant that things between my daughter and I would never be the same.

But eventually there was nowhere else to go in the conversation.

"I got tested. I have HIV."

I'll never forget the look of horror that crossed her face. It drove a dagger into my heart.

"Oh, Mom, oh, Mom" was all she could say as she began to sob.

I tried to console her, to reassure her that things would be okay, but how could I do that when I couldn't even convince myself?

Just as she began to get control, a new burst of sobs sputtered out, and she clasped her hands over her mouth.

"Oh God, Mom, I used your razor."

I really didn't think things could get more horrible in my life until that statement landed with a thud. It was like I had been dog-paddling for days in the middle of the ocean and somebody had just thrown me a rope . . . and it landed around my neck with a boulder at the other end.

Now I really struggled to console her. "Honey, it will be okay. I don't think HIV lasts outside the body for long. And I don't even remember the last time I cut myself shaving. Just to be safe,

I think you should have Dr. Umholtz run a test. It'll be fine, I'm sure, but I don't want you to worry about it."

I gave her a long mama bear hug, and I cried myself to sleep again.

✎

One of the other things I worried about was the school. How would I be able to keep up now? Would I lose my business? What if people found out? Would they all run away from me as if I were the leper I now considered myself to be?

I Googled "sports transmission of HIV" and found that the Centers for Disease Control had never had one documented case of sports transmission of HIV. But I could already feel those judgmental eyes looking down at what a wicked, nasty person I was. I felt so dirty and ashamed and was sure I would be an outcast.

And then what? How would I earn a living? Go back to nursing? The only thing I could think of worse than being HIV-positive was being an HIV-positive *nurse*.

What the hell am I going to do?

In the midst of this paralysis, I called Susan back.

"I'm positive, too," I told her.

"Oh, God. I'm so sorry."

She cried.

I cried.

We talked.

We cried some more.

We talked some more.

And then the conversation went in a completely different direction.

"Did you ever talk to him about STDs?" she asked me.

"Very first night, he told me he was 'clean.'"

"That's what he told me, too. So he would never use condoms. Do you think . . ." she got quiet for a second. "Do you think he knew?"

I hadn't even considered that. Philippe was a jerk, but it would take straight-up evil to knowingly spread a deadly disease.

"It's just that he reacted really strangely when I told him," she said.

"You told him you're positive?"

"Yeah. I called and said, 'I'm afraid I have some bad news. I wanted to let you know I'm HIV-positive.' Then he was just silent for a long time. I said, 'Philippe, are you there?' He said yes and I said, 'I wanted to let you know because I gave your name to the health department . . .' That's when he got really angry."

He interrupted her, screaming, "You gave them my name? You gave them my *name*? You're trying to ruin my life!"

Susan was taken aback. He hadn't said, "I'm sorry" or "I need to get tested, too," or expressed any worry or regret—his only concern was that she had told someone his name. That just didn't add up to either of us. She said they had exchanged nasty e-mails afterward, and he threatened to expose her at work. She had an important position with a national banking company, and that really got to her.

"How many women have you infected? You're not going to get away with this," she wrote, acting on a hunch.

"THEY'LL NEVER FIND A COMMON DENOMINA-TOR!" he said.

My God, he *knew*.

He knew, and he was doing this on purpose. It was such a horrible thought that it took time to process; I had to keep repeating it to myself. *He did this on purpose.*

His words to Susan made that perfectly clear to Susan and me both, and steeled my resolve. All these years, I had worked so hard to get him back whenever he strayed. But now I was really going to get him back—in a totally different way.

The more Susan and I talked, the angrier we became. I thought about all the numbers on his phone, in his black book. How many women were there who, right at this moment, had been infected by him and didn't even know it? How long had this been happening? What if they had moved on to other partners and were now spreading it unknowingly? HPV was bad enough, but HIV was a whole different ball game.

"What he did to us was just criminal," I ranted, at first just thinking theoretically.

"Completely. We should do something!"

"No shit. You think we can keep him from doing this to anyone else?"

"I don't know. How?"

"It's got to be against the law. People die from AIDS. We should call the police."

We decided against our local police departments for privacy reasons and decided instead to call the Frisco Police Department, where he lived.

"You call," I said, feeling like I had about all I could handle at that point. She agreed to do it. As our conversation wound down, she told me that I needed to get some more testing done.

"It's not enough to know you're positive. You have to know how much virus you have and how many T cells you have."

"How do I do that?"

"You've got to go to the health department. They'll test you for free." I got scared all over again.

"Will you go with me?"

"Sure."

At the end of our call, she said, "See ya." I didn't know then that I would hear that signature good-bye of hers hundreds of times; that we would wind up as partners in the fight of our lives.

∞

My daughter's test was negative.

No matter how much I had assured her, I can't pretend that I wasn't terrified before that result came back. The "what ifs" were awful. But we cleared that hurdle, thank God. Now on to the next.

Susan called to say that she'd heard back from the police, and had some initial success, but the detective assigned to our case was out for the next week on vacation. I imagined her shrugging her shoulders with resignation.

"Bullshit," I said. "I'll call and try to get us assigned to someone else." I wasn't one to waste time. Ten minutes later, I called her back. "We're assigned to Detective Tom Presley. We have an appointment tomorrow afternoon."

First, though, I had to have my blood test done in the morning. I walked into the lobby of the Dallas Health Department, where the STD caseworker I'd spoken with, Keisha, was waiting to walk me over to the clinic. *Nice touch*, I thought. She was about five feet five, but her presence loomed large. She was very kind and concerned, though I could tell she had done this a million times before. The blood draw was straightforward, and they said my results would be back in a week. When I was done, as I came around the corner, I bumped into an old friend from my nursing days. Apparently she worked here now. She raised her eyebrows, as if to say, "What are you doing here?" without actually saying so. I took a big gulp of air.

"Hiiiiii," I drew out while my mind was racing through options of what to say before settling on simple honesty. I gave her a thumbnail sketch of what was going on. She was automatically and marvelously sympathetic and offered her assistance. "If there's anything I can ever do . . ." I filed that little statement away in the back corner of my mind. And boy, did it ever come in handy.

After talking some more with Keisha about Philippe, I gave her the list of all the women whose names and phone numbers I knew.

"I appreciate what you did with contacting the women about HPV, but it would be best if you left these notifications to me," she said. "They may be hostile to you because you're the ex and then not really hear what you have to say. I'll contact all of them this week and stress how important it is for them to get tested."

That was fine by me. I didn't need the additional stress. Then I left to meet with Tom Presley.

The long ride to the health department had worn me out, so I was glad that Tom agreed to meet me at home to take my initial statement. It felt as if I were getting sicker by the day, like a never-ending case of the flu. Imagine having the flu *every day*—the kind where you struggle to pick your head up off the pillow and plant your wobbly feet on the floor—and trying to work, run errands, and go about your normal life with the same expectations placed on you as on everyone else. Add to that the hopelessness of knowing that this was going to be the "new normal." If anything in the world could make me suicidal, it was the thought that I would never again be my old "Force of Nature" self. It was an exhausting struggle to even consider living like this for the rest of whatever time I had left on this earth.

I peeked out the window, waiting and watching until a man in an off-white collared shirt and dress slacks appeared with a young woman alongside him. They walked up the sidewalk to my house, and it struck me how odd they looked together. Tom was a big, cherub-faced bear of a man and Tonia was a cute little blonde.

Each was there to help in a different way. I invited them inside and we sat at my kitchen table.

Tonia Cunningham was the victim advocate for Frisco PD, and her role was to provide grief counseling and resources to help crime victims cope with their losses. She did everything right to make me feel more at ease when I became emotional while telling the story. As I finished my statement, Tonia took my information and told me that I might qualify for the crime victims' compensation fund—reimbursement from the state for expenses that are related to crimes. I wasn't ready yet to think through what that meant. Tom reminded me that I had a long and uncertain road ahead; there were no guarantees. I knew he was talking about the case, but it was profoundly accurate about my health as well, and just as ominous.

It took about an hour to take the statement, and I don't recall much, except that I knew it was the first step. I was hoping we could just tell the detective what happened and he'd go arrest Philippe, but he told me there would be a lot more to it than that.

The next week, I met Susan at Frisco PD headquarters. Frisco was the suburb north of Plano, where I live. Plano had been the "it" town in the seventies and eighties, but it had maxed out at about 260,000 over the last few years. So now the new "it" town was Frisco. There were streets and streets of homes worth half a million dollars or more, which always made me wonder, "What do these people do to afford that kind of house? And how do I get a job like that?"

On the "other side of the tracks," literally, were the $80,000 houses that were built in the sixties and seventies. That's where Philippe had moved, and where Maddie lived.

Since Frisco was now the new "it" town, the police department was in a brand-spanking-new building, paid for by the taxes of all those folks living in those very expensive houses. It was a huge, modern, three-story building that sat high up off the parking lot like a glistening white perfect hatbox. The three flags directly in front stood as a stark contrast to the white building behind them: the U.S., Texas, and City of Frisco flags waved proudly as I walked up the steps to the glass doors. A lot of Texans still consider that they reside in the "country" of Texas. It's a state that was based on strength, courage, and a willingness to fight to the death. I believed that I would need all those traits and then some to see this thing through.

The only problem, as we'd quickly found, was that it was also a state where intentional HIV transmission wasn't a crime. We'd have to find a different charge that would fit the crime.

Susan had notes from her conversations with Philippe all typed up and in a folder, along with a few threatening e-mails he had sent her. She had also copied some of the laws we thought might apply, which we presented to Tom in his office—though he was ahead of us in that regard.

One of the most fascinating aspects of this whole ordeal was that if Philippe had just kept his mouth shut, no one would've ever been the wiser. But if I were an Academy Award–winning screenwriter, I could never have come up with anything that crystallized Philippe's attitude quite like, "They'll never find a common denominator." I could just imagine the leer that slowly crept across his face as he uttered those words—the words that I hoped would eventually do him in.

"From what you ladies are telling me, we have at least a case for aggravated assault causing bodily injury," Tom said.

That's good, right? I thought to myself.

"But I have to warn you, this may not ever be prosecuted. We would have to have proof that he knew, and proof that it was him who infected both of you. And even then, if one or two victims file statements, there's a good chance the DA's office won't even take a look at it."

We slumped and hung our heads at the same time.

"But, if maybe three or four victims file statements, there would be a better chance. And if you can get five or more, so much the better." I could tell he was laying out our plan for us.

Neither Susan nor I were put off by the thought of finding five or more victims. In fact, it seemed very likely that he had infected far more than five women, and we were going to have to be resourceful enough to find them and convince them.

I called my nursing friend at the health department and explained what we were doing. "If anyone you contact on our list comes up positive, can you please pass along my name and number and tell them we're filing a criminal case? We need all the victims we can find."

She agreed but told me that it might be a challenge to find women willing to talk about it and file charges. I didn't want her to get in trouble, so I never told anyone her name. I started referring to her as my "insider." At least it was better than "deep throat."

It never occurred to me that there was a choice—that I was making a *decision* to take this on. For me, it was simply something that had to be done to get a predator off the streets. How could I sit back and let that slimy bastard continue infecting women night after night?

I taught courage for a living. Martial arts instruction is 50 percent self-defense and 50 percent character development, and I wasn't about to wimp out of my obligation to demonstrate good character. John Wayne defined courage as "being scared to death, and saddling up and riding anyway." I was already saddled up and Tom Presley had just told me which way to ride. I signed the typewritten statement before me and thought, *That's one.*

Susan signed hers the next day. *That's two,* I thought.

The rest wouldn't be that easy and would take some time. Tom had already warned us that it would probably take at least six months to get an arrest. And that was only *if* we could get multiple women to file statements. Six months felt like forever—and given my declining health, I wasn't altogether convinced I was going to be alive in six months.

Back to my phone records. Even though Keisha had suggested I leave the notifications to her, there were at least a few people I wanted to notify myself—mostly the ones who'd come up positive for HPV. The first person I called was Philippe's neighbor, Maddie, and it was a gut-wrenching conversation. She thanked me and promised to call the health department, since she didn't have health insurance.

On the world's most appropriate day for such things, Valentine's Day, Susan and I made a long trip to the health department again to get my more detailed blood test results. The parking lot was packed. Apparently lots of people were sharing a less-than-romantic holiday in a government office. I wondered if they'd have a candy dish.

Keisha again met us in the lobby and we exchanged pleasantries while waiting for the elevator that would take us to the STD clinic on the third floor. The building was very old, around six stories, with dirty tile floors. When we got off the elevator onto the third floor, there was a door immediately ahead with a big-lettered sign proclaiming "HIV/AIDS Clinic." Walking through that door changes you.

To me, at that moment, I was no longer first and foremost a martial artist, or a mom, daughter, friend, teacher, or nurse. I was an HIV victim. It consumed my whole identity. The psychological reality that was setting in was as bad as the physical reality that had wrecked me.

The doors opened to reveal an emotionally devastated woman on her way out. Her eyes were red and swollen, and her cheeks were stained with tears of agony. My heart broke when I recognized her: it was Maddie.

We all hugged in the hallway. She knew and we knew. And now we were three. I like to think God intended us to be there for her at that exact moment.

Susan and I were ushered in to a nicely decorated private office with a sofa, side chair, and a fish tank. I guess that was to help with relaxation because this was the room where people like Maddie got the news about their diagnosis and people like me found out just how bad it was. You could tell when people walked out of the door which way things had gone.

My hands fidgeted nervously in my lap and Susan tried to calm my nerves. It seemed like an eternity that we waited in that office and, as I may have mentioned, I'm not a patient person. Finally, in walked an older lady.

"Hello, I'm Karla Carter. First, I want you both to know that you should start planning for your retirement because you're going to live a long time."

Bullshit. She's just trying to let me down easy, I thought.

"I have a folder here with your test results," she said calmly and slowly. "Do you know how HIV works?"

I didn't tell her I was a nurse, which was always how I dealt with being a patient. I wanted things explained to me in very simple terms. Today in particular, I knew the details would be lost on me in my state of mind.

"It's like a seesaw." She began drawing a diagram. "The virus is on one end; that's the viral load. And T cells, known as CD4, your immune system function, are on the other. When the viral load is high, then the CD4 tends to be low—your immune system gets overworked by the virus. And vice versa: when your viral load is low, then your CD4 should be high.

"HIV-negative people have zero viral load and a T-cell count between five hundred and fifteen hundred. But when you have HIV, your body starts to multiply copies of the virus, and as they increase, they destroy your T cells."

And then the bombshell.

"Diane, your viral load is over 1.2 million copies per milliliter." She said it in the clinical way only medical personnel deliver. Millions. I tried doing the math about how much virus was in my entire body and what I mostly came up with was, "That is a crap-ton of virus and this is horrible. No wonder I feel like doo-doo!"

"The CDC has determined that when your CD4 count falls below two hundred, you have AIDS," she continued and drew it on the diagram.

Without hesitation and with absolutely no emotion in her voice whatsoever, she continued.

"Your T cell count is forty-five."

Did she just say . . . Oh my God. Oh my God. Oh my God. I have AIDS!

I was close to vomiting into the trash can but worked hard to keep myself in control. All I could muster in response was, "This is a sledgehammer." I especially didn't believe the part about retirement now.

My vision was blurred and I felt light-headed, but I could see tears welling up in Susan's eyes. I was too numb to cry. If I truly processed what I'd just heard, I'd just explode and evaporate right there before everyone's eyes.

I was thinking straight enough to tell Karla about the Aetna insurance plan that didn't cover HIV, so she arranged for me to come back to assess my status and get me some healthcare assistance.

When I went in for the additional evaluation, the nurse, a tall, thin, and very gentle woman, took a detailed history and physical. She was astonished by my relative lack of symptoms other than my fatigue and weakness. At my current T cell count and viral load, there should've been many more symptoms, and I should've been a whole lot sicker, she explained. I really couldn't imagine being a whole lot sicker than I was.

If anything can be lucky with AIDS, I guess that's one of them. It gave me some small measure of comfort that I was "strong" enough to have overcome the usual symptoms—though it may really have been that I was too unaware to pick up on them.

She found no balance difficulties and no swollen lymph nodes or vision problems, although she did mention that she could've looked at my original blood work and recognized immediately that I had AIDS. I wondered then why none of the three physicians I had seen multiple times during the last umpteen months had. No one even mentioned the possibility of HIV.

The nurse finished up the exam and told me about a possibility for my care. She knew from my records I had no insurance.

"There's a doctor I know," she explained, "a really good HIV doctor who is beginning a study on a new combination of HIV meds. I'll get you an appointment, and if you qualify, you'll get your meds, labs, and visits free for two years."

Tears of gratitude came to my eyes. Her recommendation was especially promising to me because if you want to know what doctor to see, you should ask a nurse.

"You'll just have to take a blood test to check your reaction to the medication first. It should be fine unless you're of Scottish descent. Some people of Scottish descent have a violent allergy to one of the medications."

My heart sank lower. My maiden name was Landrum, and I knew it was most likely derived from a little town in Scotland called Lendrum. Oh please, God, don't let me be allergic . . . just this one thing, pleeease.

"I'll be there," I promised.

The next day, I listened to the voice mail at the school, and there was a message from a voice I didn't recognize.

"Diane, I just wanted to let you know that Philippe is HIV-positive." That's all the message said, and the woman hung up. No name, no number. And she had no way of knowing that I already knew.

Caller ID showed me that she had called from a 1-800 number tracing to Drive Financial Services in Dallas. Of course, I tried calling back, but it was a switchboard, and I had no idea what to say or who to ask for.

The only thing that made sense to me was that this was someone else who'd been with him and was infected, trying to reach out and warn me like I was trying to warn others. I was desperate to know who she was, to connect with her and tell her about the case and offer her support. To this day, I don't know who she was, or even whether or not we were strangers or knew each other. But above all, I appreciated the kindness of the warning. I just wished it had come four and a half years sooner.

CHAPTER 11

Off the Record

Another day, another potential victim. Maddie had given me a new license plate that had been in Philippe's driveway overnight and I had it traced to a man named Vincent Marquesi. It was a Chevy pickup truck. Not a very feminine sort of car, but we figured Vincent's wife was driving it around. That is until Keisha gave me a different perspective.

"Women don't give HIV to men," she stated flatly—which was, of course, not entirely accurate. Women *can* give HIV to men, but it's much more difficult to transmit that way, except by needle -sharing. It's far more common for it to be sexually transmitted from man to woman or man to man. Men typically get it from being bisexual in jail.

"Nooooo . . . seriously, Keisha?" I drew in a breath. "If I lined up all the men on the face of the earth, he's the last one I'd pick to be bisexual."

Did he love sex? Sure. Would he do any woman, any size, any age, anywhere, anytime? Clearly, as I was painfully finding out. But to me, Philippe was the most macho SOB who ever lived.

I had to ask Maddie. I wanted to know if she might have more insight.

"Do you know what it means to be on the 'down low?'" I asked her.

"What?"

"It means men who have sex with other men without calling themselves gay or bi. You don't think Philippe could be . . . ?"

"Well, he called the house and my girls answered the phone one time. They told me he sounded effeminate."

"Naaaah," I said slowly, still disbelieving. This wasn't near enough to convince me.

But I just couldn't let it rest. Could it really, possibly be? How did I miss that? How fricking blind had I been?

I called Susan. She started out in agreement with me (whew!), but it wasn't totally out of the question. Lots of men in prison have sex with other men just because it's the only sex they can have. As we tossed the idea back and forth, I wondered out loud if Keisha had other info that led her to believe Philippe might be bi.

Then a thunderbolt hit me. "Hey, Susan, did Philippe ever tell you he used an alias?"

"I think so," she muttered.

"Like Philly White or Philippe White?" I asked. Something disturbing was rumbling around in the back of my head. I remembered that when he moved to Detroit, he had sometimes used a different last name.

"Yeah, yeah! I know he had two names because I remember him using two different social security numbers."

"What if . . ." I stopped.

"What?"

"What if Keisha already met Philippe?" I was thunderstruck. But Susan didn't get it.

"You mean he was with her, too?" She almost came unglued.

"No, silly! What if he'd been referred to the health department before, but she didn't immediately remember because he was using a fake name?"

"Ohhhhh. Ohhhhh! That makes sense! That's why he freaked out when I said I had given them his name!" (How many Philippes could there be at the STD clinic at Dallas County Health Department?)

"I've gotta go."

Rather than put Keisha on the spot, I called my friend at the health department. "Um, I know this is probably out of line, but can you check the records and see if there was ever anyone named Philippe White or Philly White who was referred?"

"Hang on." It was against protocol, but she didn't hesitate, and didn't even ask me why. The clicks of the computer keyboard were way too many and way too long. Seventeen years later (or at least a minute), she came back on the line.

"Yep, here we go." She read off some information. "Is this your guy?"

"Yes! He's in your records?"

Then she dropped the bomb. "Keisha was the one who talked with him. I remember because he refused to come down here. So she met him somewhere over by I-35 and 635. He had a black Corvette."

Holy shit.

"When?"

"It was in September 2005."

"This is it! That's the proof we need to show that he knew he was positive when he infected us!"

"But you know you can't use this because I never told you, right?"

"Aw, crap."

HIPAA (Health Insurance Portability and Accountability Act) laws prevented her from telling me anything on the record. It was a screamingly unfair setback—here was a government agency that had proof that this man had lied about his HIV status and knowingly had unprotected sex with dozens of women, and they couldn't provide that information to anyone, not even to another government agency like the police. His right to privacy was considered more important than our right not to die.

HIPAA laws can kill you.

We would have to find another way to prove to the court that he knew, but at least now *we* knew for sure that he had tested positive in 2005, and possibly sooner. No wonder he'd been so angry that Susan gave the health department his name—they had already warned him before and now they'd know that he wasn't transmitting unknowingly. You can't be held responsible for transmitting unknowingly.

Susan asked Tom if we could subpoena all the doctors and clinics that the health department recommends for HIV treatment, considering he almost certainly went to one of them. But they gave us a thumbs-down on that. A judge would want something more than a hunch before allowing subpoenas to go out.

Meanwhile, my friend told me that Keisha had continued working to get Philippe into her office, which she finally accomplished in mid-February 2007. She read him the riot act about the fact that he'd been called back a second time after being informed that he had to disclose. She told him that he had to write down a list of all the women he'd been with since she'd spoken to him in September 2005.

At first he tried to just give a couple of names, but my friend, the insider, told me Keisha wasn't the kind of woman you want to cross when she's angry. She forced him to sit there and fill out the whole sheet of paper, repeatedly asking, "Anyone else?" "Who else?"

"She practically had him on his knees crying at one point," she said.

When he was done, there were twenty-six names. These were just the ones he could remember and name, and this only covered the last eighteen months. I felt pretty good that our list had twenty-three women on it; if his list was accurate and matched up with ours, then we'd missed just three women so far.

Then she made him read the list aloud, for no real reason except to make him squirm. He choked a bit when he got to my name—so she made him repeat it.

"What was that name again?"

"Diane Reeve."

"Say that one more time?"

"Diane Reeve."

"Okay, just making sure I heard you."

I loved the scene my friend was painting—like Keisha was in total control and humiliating the hell out of him. After he had finished naming names, she told him that he couldn't ever again have unprotected sex without disclosing his HIV status.

He nodded.

"*Ever*," Keisha said. "Are we clear? Say 'yes.'"

"Yes."

"Because it seems like we were not clear last time. But this time, you're going to stop screwing around and infecting people, right?"

"Yes."

Like hell. Luckily, she didn't actually believe him.

She and Tom, along with a doctor from the Collin County Health Department, went to Philippe's house on February 22, 2007, with two official cease and desist orders, one from each county:

Dallas County Health and Human Services (DCHHS) has determined based upon reasonable cause that you . . . are infected with HIV/AIDS, a serious infection that is spread from person to person through contact with certain bodily fluids (blood, semen, vaginal secretions), and that you present a health threat to others by continuing to practice behaviors which are known to transmit HIV/AIDS.

Pursuant to the Texas Health and Safety Code 81.083, you are hereby ordered:

1. CEASE AND DESIST any activity which puts others at risk of infection, including (without limitation):

   a. The misrepresentation of your infectious status to future sexual and/or needle-sharing partners;

   b. The engagement of sexual intercourse (including oral, anal, or vaginal) or needle-sharing activity without first notifying the participating individual of your HIV/AIDS status; and/or;

   c. The donation of your blood, bodily fluids and/or tissue.

2. REPORT to DCHHS Early Intervention and Testing at 10:00 AM on FRIDAY, MARCH 2, 2007 to receive HIV/AIDS prevention, risk reduction and undergo the Accelerated HIV Intervention Program. . . .

Failure to comply with this Health Authority's Order may result in DCHHS referring this case to the Dallas County District Attorney's Office for petitioning the District Court of Dallas County for further actions as authorized under Tex. Health & Safety Code Chapter 81. Additionally, should you fail to comply with this Order you may be charged with a Class B misdemeanor, which may result in a maximum fine of $2,000 and/or confinement in jail for a maximum of 180 days.

Now it wasn't a request, or a moral obligation, or advice—it was a legal document that said he had no right to sleep with women without protection unless he disclosed his status, or he could go to jail. I wasn't all that impressed with the low fine or the "180 days" listed on the order—someone's life ought to be worth a lot more than $2,000—but that had nothing to do with our case already in progress. That was the standard language they had to include about the penalty for future violations.

It was Tom's first time seeing Philippe in person, and he wasn't impressed. They said that Philippe couldn't wait to get them out the door, so he just scribbled his name fast and grunted his good-bye. I was elated thinking about how Philippe must have felt in that moment, hearing that he was well and truly caught. Would it change anything? Would the fear of going back to jail be enough to make him stop now?

Maddie called me that night. There was another car in the driveway. Philippe had struck again.

∽

Despite all the leads and possibilities, finding additional women willing to file was proving problematic. My friend, the insider, said she'd heard about a lengthy conversation with a woman on the list who had tested positive and who now lived in Washington, DC. But the woman wasn't interested in outing herself or contacting me.

"There was this mean lady with a heavy accent who hung up on me when I told her about the HPV," I said to Susan. "You call her. Maybe she won't yell at you."

So Susan did, to better results. What she found out broke my heart.

Nena had been seeing Philippe for around a year, off and on, when she learned she was pregnant with Philippe's baby. When she told him that, he wanted her to have an abortion, telling her that he couldn't be a father now because he was in a "committed relationship" with someone else—presumably me—and that he couldn't afford child support. Then he took off for France . . . with me. He wouldn't even meet with her in person to talk about it. He blew her off by phone.

Nena was a religious woman from North Africa, who often traveled back and forth to visit her family, and being an unwed mother would mean being shunned by her community. That weighed heavily on her but turned out to be a nonissue because she had a miscarriage just a couple of days before I called, and she was still hospitalized. I had no way of knowing this at the time, but she had answered her cell phone in her hospital room.

But what was worse was that she had found out she was HIV-positive on that same day I'd called her about the HPV. She didn't have the energy to care about HPV; she had bigger worries. If anyone found out about her status, she could never go home again. Her country has a travel ban on people with HIV.

In fact, there are thirty-six countries, territories, and areas that put some kind of restriction on letting HIV-positive people enter and stay, and hers is one of the strictest. They require anyone applying for a work permit, student training, or residency to take an HIV test at their Health Ministry's central laboratory (no outside tests are accepted). They're also among the seventeen countries that will actively deport visitors whose HIV-positive status becomes known.

Nena's family was still there, in a place that makes the American AIDS stigma look like a welcoming committee with home-made pie. People lose their jobs and are thrown out of their homes because of HIV. Even though the antiretroviral drugs are free there, only a small minority (about 20 percent) of those who are infected actually take the medication. There's very little education about STDs and a whole lot of denial. "Good" women are not supposed to have premarital sex, so Nena was in an even more socially dangerous position than if she'd been infected by her husband.

I had to guess that all the fear about secrecy is what kept her from warning me on the phone that day. It bothered me to learn that one of Philippe's partners knew he was spreading HIV and didn't take the opportunity to warn me when given the chance. Maybe she was in shock, or maybe she figured it was far too late for it to make a difference with me. But I tried to push all that aside because Nena, who I later learned also had MS, obviously needed someone to talk to. She was opinionated and harsh sometimes, but she needed friendship. We all did. No one else could really understand what this kind of devastation and betrayal felt like. Our families supported us, and the friends we told sympathized, but nobody lived it, breathed it, obsessed about it, or cried about it like we all did. We *got* each other because we were sisters. Just like biological sisters have the same blood coursing through their veins, so we had a zillion of the same tiny, destructive monsters flowing through ours. It was a sisterhood that no one wanted to be a part of, but having each other was the thing that really saved us, one and all.

A few weeks after she told him she was pregnant, Philippe had e-mailed Nena to ask how she was doing.

"You're only calling to make sure you're off the hook," she wrote back. "Do you think I want you for the father? You couldn't be the father of an ant!"

His reply was, "Sorry, I didn't know you would be so angry at me."

She didn't tell him about her HIV test, and because of her background and her intense fear of being found out, she wouldn't file charges. It was a loss for us, but one we had no choice but to accept and try to understand.

And to keep looking for others.

Right after this, I got a furious phone call from one Jessica Mahler, a former black belt student of mine.

Jessica was a physical therapist who had come to me for training after a bad experience at another martial arts school. We had become fairly close, but during my relationship with Philippe, they developed an intense hatred for each other. I never understood it at the time, but I had passed it off as just a personality conflict.

I hadn't spoken with Jessica in quite some time when it came back to me that she was now spreading the news about my AIDS diagnosis. It had been less than a month since I'd found out and I was still very raw; I'd shared the news with very few people. But one of them had told her, and then she ran with it—including telling Jane Logan. It made me so angry that I had a lawyer draw up a letter telling them that I'd file a lawsuit if they continued breaching my privacy. Things had just quieted down when my phone rang late one night. I was half asleep when Jessica called, yelling into the phone.

"Why did you give my name to the health department?"

"What? I have no idea what you're talking about." I really didn't. "Why do you say that?"

It sounded like she was going to bite my head off through the phone. "I had a few friends over tonight and one of my neighbors who works at the Dallas County Health Department rang my doorbell in the middle of the party. He wanted to let me know that I needed to get tested. For HIV. In front of everyone at the party!"

It was all I could do to keep from bursting out laughing. *Serves you right for trash-talking me,* I thought. *Doesn't feel so good when you are the one being stigmatized!*

But of course I just listened.

"There was a huge debacle, my husband is questioning me, and my friends think I'm a slut. You know I detested that bastard Philippe . . . how else would the health department have gotten my name?" She was getting louder and terser.

"I have no clue, but I do know that Philippe had been asked for a list of all his contacts. Maybe he did it to spite you. Or did you really put yourself at risk with him?"

She hung up. I never found out what really happened—was she a jilted ex-lover and that was the explanation for all the animosity during our class? Had Philippe listed her just to mess with her? Or had Keisha scared the hell out of Philippe so effectively that by the end, he was just throwing extra names in there to appease her?—but the whole party thing didn't hurt my feelings one little bit. In fact, it gave me one of the few smiles that I'd had since Susan had uttered those fateful words in January. That seemed like two lifetimes ago.

◌◌

Tom's big idea was for Susan or me to get Philippe on the phone, play nice, and get him to admit that he knew he had HIV. "Playing nice" was going to be some of the finest acting I had ever done. I practiced faux concern.

At Tom's office, I was lucky enough to get Philippe on our first try. My heart was in my throat as he picked up on the second ring.

"Bonjour, mon ami," I said, in probably the worst Texan French accent the world has ever known. Then I asked, "Ça va, ça va?," which was an informal way of asking "How's it going?"

"Huh?" he responded.

So I repeated it.

"Ça va, mon ami?"

"Who is this?" he demanded.

"It's Diane. Are you okay?"

"*HOW THE FUCK DID YOU GET THIS NUMBER?*" he screamed into the phone at me. That was a question I was totally unprepared for, though I probably should've thought through a good excuse beforehand. I fumbled and stumbled around. "Oh, honey, I've called so many people looking for your number. I can't even think how I found you." Did it sound convincing?

"I heard you were sick," I said, trying to change the subject. "I'm just worried about you."

I tried to make him the focus of attention, which I was sure he would love. I kept going without giving him a chance to respond.

"I was just thinking maybe I could help you somehow. A job, maybe? We can work something out and I'm really—I'm okay. I'm negative."

Would it make him feel relieved? Had he worried about me at all?

"After what you did to me, do you think I would ever have anything to do with you again?" he asked.

I replied, "I just thought you might need some help. Maybe we can meet for drinks and discuss it. I didn't do anything to you. Maybe we can get together and talk." That was the end of my prepared script.

Click. And that was that. He hung up, and I had gotten two useless sentences out of him. I was shaking, disappointed, angry, and dejected. I felt like I had blown it.

Tom comforted me and said, "You did fine. At least we tried. Maybe we can try again."

But we didn't. It was pretty clear he wasn't going to reveal anything to me. I wouldn't hear Philippe's voice again for months.

The next day I got another call on Philippe's old cell phone. It was his mortgage company. The bastard was behind on his house payments.

When you're the victim of a crime, it's really hard not to get excited when anything bad starts happening to the perp. I took some satisfaction in knowing he was struggling to make ends meet financially, and that was just one of the many things that was closing in on him. His web was unraveling; his women were finding out about one another—and about his diagnosis—and leaving him behind.

I saved the number and called it periodically over the next few months to see if he caught up on his payments (he didn't). I had his social security number, and that's all it takes to get status information about most anything you want on someone. Susan did the same thing with his car payments. He was behind on them, too.

Maddie noticed an increase in luxury cars pulling into his driveway. Oh, how he was trying. I felt so foolish to have helped him with his bills for so long. Now I just hoped we would have him behind bars before many more victims appeared.

CHAPTER 12

Scarborough Renaissance Festival

Tom had warned us not to go up to Philippe's door or to confront anyone on his property, which was smart advice for lots of reasons, but it was also sad. It meant that we couldn't warn any new women in time, and it drove me crazy. We could warn them only *after* they'd left his house, after they'd probably slept with him already. It worried me that the case wasn't moving fast enough to save more women; by the time an arrest would be made, surely there would be more of us in this position.

And it was a hell of a position to be in. I was dying, actively dying, and I didn't have the $2,000 per month I'd need for medications, so I was unmedicated all this time and just kept getting weaker and weaker. I went crazy trying to get new insurance, but as I suspected, no insurer wanted to touch a new customer with AIDS. My only realistic hope was to get into that medical trial. Even then, getting my numbers up would be a long process. Once they drop into AIDS territory, it's harder to pull them up—and you always carry the AIDS diagnosis afterward, even if your CD4 number gets back into the normal range.

It took me almost two months to get an appointment to see Dr. Louis Sloan. Finally, at the beginning of April, I made my way to his huge downtown Dallas office. It had its own infusion therapy rooms, as well as a pharmacy just for his patients. This was definitely someone at the top of his field. He went over the test results from the DCHD and started the qualification process for the study.

He told me the same number for my viral load: greater than 1.2 million. *At least it's the same as last time*, I thought to myself, until he educated me. Once the load gets over 1.2 million, they just quit counting. *Crapola—I must be pushing a bazillion by now.*

My CD4 was at an all-time low of 31. It normally takes four to seven years after infection for that number to drop below 200, so the signs indicated that I had been infected early in the relationship.

I knew that I'd have to be in pretty good shape to qualify for the study—no researcher wants someone to die in the middle of a study or be too far gone for any medication to fix and mess up their results. So despite that I was struggling just to get out of bed every day and stay awake, I did my best Mary Poppins impression at each visit and pretended to feel better than I did. You can't fool the numbers, though—Dr. Sloan told me that my kidney function test showed that I wouldn't qualify for the study.

The test to measure kidney function is called a glomerular filtration rate, and it had to be above 51. Mine was 45. So not only was I out of the study but I found out I had kidney damage, too.

Dr. Sloan was a good man, though, and he wouldn't give up on me. He tried everything to get my kidneys up to par: getting me to drink fluids, take IVs, whatever. But my kidneys were too ravaged by the HIV and my numbers just wouldn't perk up. I was beyond panicked—but not ready to give up. There was still a spark in me that was impossible to extinguish. The doctor kept trying with me, and I kept making new appointments.

After delivering the news each time that my numbers still weren't good enough, he would always take my mind off my troubles by just shooting the breeze with me. We talked about cutting-edge studies for a cure and his many presentations to AIDS conferences all over the world, and he always wanted me to teach him a new self-defense technique. As much as I hated going to the doctor's office so often, it was always a pleasure to see Dr. Sloan's wide grin and starched white lab coat. It accentuated the lack of hair on the top of his head!

The day I ran out of options and was permanently ruled out of the study in May, I had to fight back the tears. Without saying a word, Dr. Sloan walked out of the exam room door and a few minutes later came back with two huge bottles of pills in his hands: thirty days' worth of lifesaving medicine; $2,000 worth of medicine that he gave to me because he cared.

This is a God thing, I thought as the tears fell.

One Epzicom and four Kaletra per day, he told me, brushing off my gratitude with just the hint of a smile. The pills were the size of the moon, and he told me they caused nausea and diarrhea. But I didn't care. He was my hero. Finally, *finally*, there might just be some hope.

Two weeks later, I got the news that I had qualified for a special high-risk pool insurance. It was $1,000 a month—triple what I had been paying for insurance—but it would cover everything.

"You're going to live," Dr. Sloan told me, which I didn't actually believe, but it was nice to hear. I was willing to do whatever it took to extend my life, and I knew this would give me a fighting shot.

The pills were even more awful than he had prepared me for. They were giant things that got stuck in my throat and caused hours of daily nausea and digestive problems for no immediate payoff. I didn't feel any better; the pills just added horrible new symptoms. I knew I needed to take these medications if I wanted to stay alive, and yet it was hard to convince myself to swallow another one. I cried every time I took a pill.

This is going to be my life forever. It's never going to go away, I thought. But then I had a second thought: *I'm a badass bitch. I will adapt.*

One of the key tenets of martial arts is to have an "indomitable spirit." To get to black belt, you need to prove that you have this indomitable spirit by never giving up. I still didn't know how long I had to live, or whether we would ever see any measure of justice, but if I was going out, I was going out fighting. I would not be broken.

෨

One of my favorite things to do in the springtime was to visit the Scarborough Renaissance Festival in Waxahachie, just south of Dallas. It usually ran from March through Memorial Day, and it was filled with artisans who brought all kinds of exotic products for sale. There were chair swings, jewelry, swords, stained glass, beer goblets, long skirts, and chain mail purses. Most items had a medieval theme.

There were also a number of activities. You could ride an elephant, get your hair braided, wind your way through the maze, or watch belly dancers with their flashy, colorful costumes and their almost naked hip writhing.

I was so miserable that I wasn't sure how long I'd be able to stay, but I was determined not to miss this year's festival. It didn't take much for me to convince Susan that we needed a break from all the stalking either. So in early May, we headed out one muggy Saturday morning for the forty-five-minute drive, coating ourselves with sunscreen and bug spray.

The festival was right off the highway, but it was essentially forty acres in the middle of nowhere. The front gate was mocked up to look like a medieval castle and was peppered with young guys in tight pants and white ruffled shirts with puffed sleeves spouting a comedy routine and joking with the festivalgoers who waited in line.

As we headed through the narrow pathways with all the little booths, we came across the first of a number of fortune-tellers. Susan and I looked at each other and knew we just couldn't pass it by. We put our name on a waiting list, and forty-five minutes later, we entered the darkened little room of a gypsy woman with rocket-fire hair. She sat behind a small table draped with a deep purple cloth. A single candle burned on the table. She introduced herself as Rose, took our money, and invited us to sit down.

I wasn't sure if she was going to read our palms or what, but I didn't have time to ask because she started in immediately.

"You two are good friends—almost sisters," she said. "But you haven't known each other for very long." Susan and I looked sideways at each other with raised eyebrows as she continued. "You have something in common: a deep, dark secret.

And you share knowledge of a very evil man."

Both of us audibly gasped. Before I knew it, Susan and I were pouring out some vague details of what had been happening to us in the past few months. It didn't take Rose very long to propose a plan. She was very strict and stern, almost like a mother admonishing her children.

"You must gather up everything that is related to that evil man, and you must be sure that it is all removed and discarded. This is very important, and it must be done immediately. You must rid your living space of all the evilness that surrounds this man. Do you have a picture of him?"

I nodded.

"Then you must burn his picture and light a Christian candle over the ashes before you dispose of them. This is important for your emotional well-being."

She went on about a few other things that seemed irrelevant to me at the time. My head was so filled with plans of how I was going to implement her suggestions that I really spaced out on the rest of the conversation.

Susan and I almost couldn't get out of there fast enough. All we could talk about for the rest of the day was what she had told us and how vulnerable we really were. The indication was that there was some amount of danger associated with Philippe and we needed to be very, very careful—like we needed more fuel for our already fever-pitched paranoia.

Within a few days I had gone by the Mardel Christian Store and picked up the required candle. It was a cream-colored, vanilla-scented candle in a glass jar with a beautiful silver braided cross on one side. I really didn't look at it that carefully when I bought it, but when I got it home I noticed that there were glistening glitter specks inside that sparkled when it was lit.

I couldn't quite bring myself to dispose of everything that was related to Philippe. Crap, it was practically half my house. There were T-shirts, a snorkel from a trip, a couple of bottles of Jamaican rum, numerous glasses I had "lifted" from just about every trip we had taken, and I don't know how much other stuff. There were coffee mugs, a couple of wire Eiffel Towers, a painted rooster, a wooden lion, just stuff and stuff and more stuff. And I couldn't begin to count the pictures from every trip that we had taken: Paris, Rome, Amsterdam, New York, Las Vegas, New Orleans, San Francisco, Jamaica, and Guadeloupe—pictures that reminded me of the good times. I couldn't bear to toss them out, but I couldn't have them around, either. I did feel the evilness that Rose had talked about.

So the next time I went to the school, I grabbed a big cardboard box from one of the orders that we had placed for martial arts supplies. I gathered up everything and threw it all in that box, taping it closed tight with duct tape so the evil couldn't escape. I called it "the box of evil."

Within a week Susan and I had set up a time for her to come over. I had grabbed my favorite picture of Philippe: the one I had taken in Guadeloupe when he was sitting at a table with a glass of wine in front of him and a cigarette dangling from the fingers of his left hand.

I had never seen Philippe go near a cigarette—at least not tobacco. But in Guadeloupe they sold a French brand called Gitanes, and he said it reminded him of his childhood, so he picked up a pack. I didn't think to ask him then if he smoked cigarettes as a child. He smoked with all the elegance and demeanor of a sophisticated royal, very king-like in his presentation—which, of course, dovetailed nicely with my fantasy of who he was at the time.

When Susan got there, I immediately took her upstairs to show her my handiwork. She was sufficiently impressed with the duct-taped box. I had stuffed it in the closet of the upstairs bedroom I had converted into an office. I almost never went up there, so it wasn't around to remind me of anything.

I had made a couple of copies of the picture. One for me and one for Susan—the original went into the box along with the other stuff. Somehow, I guess I knew I might need that stuff someday.

We lit the candle and held hands as Susan said a prayer. It was a surreal, semi-religious moment.

We sat on the bricks in front of the fireplace and I lit the corner of her picture, then mine. I held on to it for as long as I could before the flame grew too large and hot—just as I had held on too long to Philippe, and just as his flame of destruction had gotten too large and too hot.

And then I just let it go. It fell neatly into the logs left over from the last of the winter's fire. I heaved a huge sigh and watched as the corners curled and the paper turned to a gray-black ash.

"Done," I said flatly to Susan, as I raised my palm for a high-five.

"Done," she agreed as she tapped, then clasped my hand.

Done. Sort of.

CHAPTER 13

An Unlikely Team

The scales of justice move ridiculously slowly, if you ask me. Tom Presley had warned us that building a case would take months. He also told us that he was returning to the life of a beat cop in the summer because the stress of being a detective was taking its toll on him both physically and emotionally—which he proved by showing us a picture of his ID from four years ago; he had gained more than forty pounds, and his hair had grayed considerably. Like every good detective, though, he wanted to finish up the cases he was connected to before the transfer. So we knew he hoped that this arrest would occur on his watch— and we sure hoped that, too. Tom was a stand-up guy. He was soft-spoken and always polite and respectful, but somehow he maintained a warmth that was hugely comforting to all of us. I really liked him a lot.

We now had three people willing to file charges, and we wanted more as soon as possible. Brittani was my next likely candidate, but I just couldn't bring myself to be the one to call her—too much bad blood. So Susan made the call . . . and blew my mind when she reported back.

"She already knew she was positive."

Brittani explained to Susan that she and her husband were now divorced and that her husband was negative. I guess it took those test results for him to finally believe that his wife and Philippe weren't "just friends."

In fact, Brittani was the first of us who had learned about her status, in October 2006. I was furious. She hadn't given my name to the health department or warned me in any way. I don't care how angry you are or how much you hate someone; you don't condemn another human being to certain death.

After Susan explained about what we were doing with the criminal case, Brittani seemed noncommittal.

"But when I explained the part about the crime victims' compensation she became very interested," Susan added. "I think she's on board, but she's not sure yet."

I hated this girl so deeply for so many things, and yet I needed her on our side for this. It was a conflicting feeling. But still—we were on the road to four.

Susan was so bothered by her conversation with Brittani that she called Philippe about it. She and Philippe were still dating until December 5, and she learned that Brittani had informed him that she had tested positive for HIV in October of that year.

"That must be devastating news. I'd really like to come over and comfort you," Philippe had told Brittani at the time. By then, she knew she could truthfully substitute any word meaning a sex act for the word "comfort." She thought it was an odd response—he didn't seem at all worried about the possibility that he had it, too.

Susan confronted him about it, admitting that she'd spoken with Brittani. "What did I ever do to you?" Susan asked. "Why would you continue dating me and not tell me that you had a deadly disease?"

"I got tested and I was negative."

"I don't believe you."

"I don't care what you believe. It's true. I used to get tested all the time and I was always clean."

"Where did you get tested?"

"The place is out of business now."

How convenient.

"But you knew. At least in October, you knew."

"This conversation is ended. I want you to stop calling me and harassing me. I have nothing further to say to you."

⁂

Tom unofficially deputized us, giving us his blessing to seek out other victims and send them his way. Maddie had stayed in touch with Darja after our lunch together, so she reached out to her and found out that she was negative. So was Lupita. Beyond the ones whose numbers we already had, we used whatever means we had available. I requested Philippe's cell phone records for the past year, Maddie kept taking down license plates in his driveway, and we called in favors to do our sleuthing.

I had a friend with access to DMV records, which meant that we could find out the names and addresses of the car owners; no phone numbers, though—just addresses. Sometimes it was easy to find phone numbers connected with the addresses and sometimes it wasn't. This made things trickier because we'd have to visit people at their homes to tell them the horrible news. We never knew how people would react, if we'd be faced with husbands and kids, or if we'd get caught—and God forbid that Philippe was there!

Of all the women Susan and I followed, talked to, left notes for, or turned in to the health department, the one I wanted to see most was Princess (Patricia). Knowing that she'd been with Philippe off and on for seven or eight years, I feared there was a good chance she was positive. Plus, I was pretty curious about what she looked like. After all, he'd left me for her, and had called her the love of his life.

So when Maddie gave me the tags on a red Mercedes-Benz and it belonged to one Patricia Denton, I couldn't call Susan fast enough to plan a little visit. It was still pretty cold outside, so both of us had our jackets on as we climbed into Susan's gold SUV to head out on another mission.

I was always a little bit nervous when we went into our Cagney and Lacey mode, but this one just about pushed me over the edge.

Patricia's apartment building was only half a mile or so from where Philippe was now working. Susan and I were smart enough to verify that his car was parked at work before heading to Patricia's, figuring that since she was so close, Philippe might be over there before his overnight shift.

It was around 10:45 PM when we rolled up to the gates at her apartment. But since it was a gated complex, we couldn't just drive up to her place. It seemed like we had to wait forever until a car came by that we could follow in. Once we got inside, we trekked through the parking lot searching for the Mercedes or any sign of Patricia.

Then Susan's phone rang—and it was Philippe! It was just a stupid coincidence that he happened to call at that moment. Almost immediately, an argument ensued. He whined that she was harassing him. She shot back that he had tried to get her fired by sending e-mails about her HIV diagnosis to her workplace. Before long, it was a knock-down screaming match. He told her that he was recording the conversation and that "the knife cuts both ways . . . The next time I see you, it ain't gonna be pretty," he told her, adding that he knew some crazy Mexicans who could take care of her.

Now, let me tell you something I may not have mentioned about Susan: We were opposites in many ways, starting with the fact that she was a good ol' Bible-thumping Southern Baptist and I . . . was not. I was outwardly emotional, she was cool and reserved. The worst swear word I'd heard her use to that point was "crap," which I didn't understand at all, given what we were dealing with.

So you can imagine my surprise when polite Susan, the one who spoke softly and didn't like causing a scene, suddenly screamed, "You bastard! You evil, slimy son of a bitch!"

If Susan hadn't been so mad and I wasn't so intent on trying to hear what he was saying, I would've been rolling around in the grass laughing my ass off.

What he was screaming was unintelligible, but Susan surprised me even more. "So what are you going to do about it? Why don't you just go cry on one of your *boy*friends' shoulders? *And get the fuck out of my life!*"

I was stunned into reverent silence as she hung up the phone. We high-fived.

"Shit!" she said. "That really felt good."

I have to admit, since the whole thing started, one of the things I felt shortchanged on was not being able to scream at Philippe. I was relegated to talking calmly to my therapist about it and quietly fantasizing about slitting his throat, but hearing Susan haul off on behalf of both of us helped.

We walked around in the parking lot a few more minutes, but gave up and got back in the car. She wasn't home. We tried again a few nights later, creeping around slowly as we had done before. That night, though, we found the Mercedes! I walked alone toward the window of the nearest apartment—and I actually caught a glimpse of a tall blonde in her black underwear heading for the bedroom and slamming the door. Just before she slammed the door, I spotted a picture on the wall of the blonde with two teenage boys. I knew from Philippe's stories that Patricia had two boys.

"That has to be her!"

Susan and I banged on the door. "Patricia, we need to talk to you about a very important matter. It's about your health."

Silence.

More knocking and more shouting.

Silence.

As we stood thinking of what to do next, the gate at the back of the apartments opened, and a squad car slowly cruised in.

"Shit! It's the cops!" I said, as Susan grabbed the trash in front of Patricia's door. She thought we might find clues—pill bottles or test results, maybe. I giggled. "Man, we're desperate, huh?"

We hightailed it back to the SUV, slamming the doors and ducking so low that we couldn't be seen by the cops, who were still cruising. They drove right past us, but I'm surprised they didn't hear us, we were laughing so loud. That was the last time we tried to talk to Patricia at her home, but we continued calling. She never called back.

At the end of February, Susan got an e-mail from Philippe:

Well, I see you're back to your old tricks, harassing my friends and business contacts. You should be aware that I've filed criminal complaints against you for harassment, and however you obtained my phone records—misrepresentations, plates, or going through my mailbox—I'll take further actions on this as well. You should also know that mail tampering is a federal offense! Misrepresentation is fraud, and there's records of all of this! Contacting all these people is pure harassment, Susan. I had to turn in all my phone records or face criminal charges, and everyone will be contacted by Health and Services for tests. . . .

I was also tested twice, the first time was negative . . . I had two partners that were either negative or were in denial and lied about it! For these reasons, and no other, I didn't know or had no reason to believe I was positive and continued to have unprotected sex!

I did care about you at one time, and am the one that gave your name up to the Health Department several times. Last time we were already not seeing each other. It's not a support group that you're in, but some sort of hate group that you belong to, and probably the sad heart club, who can't move on with their lives, even though most of them will die of old age rather than AIDS unless they go off the deep end, mentally and emotionally, like you're doing!

Now, I realize no matter what you said, by your actions of contacting recruiters and trying to ruin me financially or going after my current relationships, that you feel I've no rights to go on with my life, unless it's with you? I would never have anything to do with you, in a million years; you're very vindictive, hateful, and cruel! Not trying to help either one of us, but seeking out vengeance and hateful acts. You're not doing this for anybody but yourself!

Vengeance is not a sweet dish, but a bitter one. In the end, we reap what we sow and what comes around will come back to haunt you in a very bad way!

We judge others as we live, and you're in a very dark place, Susan. Get help, counseling, therapy, prescriptions, you sick bitch! Up to now, the gloves were still on, but this will change very quickly. I'll make your life hell!

Maniacal ravings of a lunatic. What an ass he was! His e-mail and our ongoing stakeouts had some unforeseen consequences for each of our psyches. Both of us became concerned that Philippe would find out what we were up to and take some kind of revenge on us. Now that we were talking about criminal charges and possible prison time, the stakes were a lot higher than just taking pictures to show Brittani's husband.

I had deadbolts installed on all my doors, something I had never felt I needed because of my ability to defend myself. I also started leaving the porch light on in the evening. When Susan felt particularly spooked, she would leave her house altogether and spend the night with her daughter. It was a little different for each of us; I lived with a constant, low-lying paranoia, while her pathology took on mystical attributes. She'd be fine and then suddenly get "spooked" at random. I could never figure out any pattern, but once every week or two, she would call me in a panic. "I've got to get out of the house. I just have a feeling that something's going to happen," and the line would go dead.

We truly feared for our lives, which made waiting for something to happen all the more excruciating. In reality, just about every day some progress was being made in some way, but at the time, it seemed exactly the opposite. I cannot count the number of times I asked Tom, "When is it going to happen? When will he be arrested?"

He kept telling me to be patient and that the police and the DA's office were moving very carefully to be sure they had an ironclad case.

"We're just trying to do this right," he said. Then he offered a candid admission: "You know, a few years back I dealt with an HIV-positive man who filed a report. After he used my pen, I threw it away. I've learned a lot since then."

I nodded. I really appreciated his honesty and candor. It was like he was telling me that he accepted us because of what we were doing—where he wouldn't have before. Not everyone had learned so much. The stigma of HIV was what stopped several women from coming forward and filing charges, even though the victim advocate, Tonia, arranged for us to select fake names when we filed to lessen our chances of being outed in the community. I chose the name Barbara Sutherland for no reason other than that I thought it sounded good.

Tonia was my kind of woman. She had a no-nonsense, logical, and matter-of-fact approach, but with a strong helping of empathy and understanding. I would spend hours on the phone with her. She patiently listened to my sobs and wails, and meticulously outlined the process that was necessary to accomplish my mission —seeing justice done. Even though she wasn't HIV-positive, she came as close as anyone I knew to understanding the torture I was going through. She never failed to say exactly the right thing. Along with the support from Susan, it helped.

It struck me early on what unlikely partners we all were in this fight; we were all "the other woman" to one of us. In any other situation, we might've been bitter enemies, but in this one, we were a genuine team, particularly Susan and me. As my teammate, she was usually willing to do dirty work for me, like when I asked her to call Jane Logan.

I had already given the health department Jane's number based on my lingering suspicion that she and Philippe had been together, and my insider probably was by then breaking some important rules by whispering information to me that I had no right to know. It was clandestine and wonderful. She wouldn't tell us everything, or spill dirt on everyone, but there were several times when she revealed if she knew anyone at the department had spoken with someone. In this case, she told us that she had called Jane, who was very hostile about having been named at all. She refused to get tested at the health department but did say she would get tested on her own. That was the moment I officially hated Jane Logan.

It was the confirmation I had been waiting for. If she had never slept with him, that's what she would have said, not that she was going to get tested on her own. Here was a woman who had pretended to be my friend for years—who listened to me talk about how much I loved Philippe and who offered me advice about winning him back. I had rescued her troubled son with a number of private karate lessons. Once I spent several hours a day with him when he got suspended at school and she called me from her plane desperately begging for help—and it turned out she had been sleeping with Philippe throughout our relationship after all. I helped her son and in return she slept with my lover. What kind of backstabbing bitch *does* that? I hated Philippe for this, but against all reason, I hated her more. By then I had acknowledged that he was just a sociopath, but the betrayal by her didn't have a worthy excuse. She was just a garden-variety, A1 bitch. I still can't quite explain the hierarchy of anger in my mind—I hated Philippe more than Brittani but less than Jane.

Jane called the health department later to say that the test was negative. I wondered if that was true. And if it was true, I was kind of pissed. It didn't seem fair that she'd been with him often enough to have a key to his house and yet wasn't infected. Now I can tell you from a rational, decent perspective that wishing HIV on anyone is a horrible thing to do. I can also tell you that in my darker moments, I wished it on her anyway.

Because I didn't fully believe that Jane had tested negative, I had Susan call her while I was sitting nearby with my ear pressed to the receiver. I wanted to hear something—anything—that confirmed it one way or another. Plus, I wanted to hear what trash she would talk about me.

Despite that I was poised to take notes, Susan didn't get much out of Jane. She just reiterated that she was negative in a nonchalant way that left us both feeling very unsure about its veracity. At least I felt smug about the fact that Susan took an instant dislike to her.

Aside from Jane, every time a woman came up negative, it caused mixed feelings: I was happy for them, but sad for me. Why couldn't I have been one of them? Why did *they* get lucky and I didn't? I guess four and a half years with Philippe is why.

Jackie Ellings, another nurse in her late forties who was unhappily married with kids and had been seeing Philippe on the side (and whose plates Maddie had written down during one of her spy watches) was one of those women who dodged a bullet. I had tracked down her phone number and called her.

I didn't like revealing the HIV news over the phone when I did track down numbers—I felt there was less of a chance of them ratting us out to Philippe if we met with these women face-to-face rather than if we were just anonymous voices on the other end of the phone. But this one was different because she was married with a family. I knew that if I postponed telling her, she might put them at further risk in between. So I just spilled it. And so did she.

"We met on New Year's Eve at Arthur's," she said. "We've had sex maybe seven or eight times. I asked him about STDs and he said he was clean!"

"I know . . . that's what he tells everyone."

"You know what's weird, though? He said something about how he was dating a girl with diabetes who had to use needles."

"Huh. I don't know who that would be."

Then it occurred to me—he was already setting up a defense. He made that up as an excuse so that if she came out positive, he could pretend that it wasn't his fault but the fault of this imaginary, needle-sharing, diabetic woman. On the plus side, they did use condoms. Maybe he was learning something after all. Or, more likely, she insisted because she was married.

Jackie went for testing the next day. We were genuinely happy for her when she revealed that her test was negative, and Susan suggested going out to dinner to celebrate. We invited Maddie, too, since she'd been the one to alert us to the license plate. It was a risk because two weeks earlier, Maddie had gotten a bit out of control after drinking too much at the country club where I had a membership. Her behavior embarrassed both Susan and me, but we chalked it up to stress and decided to give her a mulligan.

Jackie was a trip! She had short, spiky red hair and an athletic build. The company was nice and the food was good. We were all having a pretty good time, but after only one glass of wine, Maddie became tipsy. I was nervous when she ordered another drink. But it didn't stop there—she quickly ordered a third, and she was gulping down drinks from our glasses, too!

The drunker she got, the louder she became; it was an instant replay of the country club incident. When she was so plastered that she slurred to Jackie, "Are you a man or woman?" Susan and I wanted to crawl under the table.

Jackie seemed unsure of how to react, but she didn't have time to think of anything anyway. Before she could respond, Maddie started pawing at her. I mean, actually groping her—feeling her up! Finally she climbed into Jackie's lap, declaring, "Oh, I don't care if you're a girl or a boy—you're just cute!"

Susan and I looked at each other with mouths agape. "I'll call Dan to come and pick her up," I said. Dan was renting a room from Maddie. I mumbled a quick apology to Jackie, who was wincing.

A few minutes later, the hostess, Susan, and I had to carry Maddie outside to Dan, who was waiting in his truck unfazed. Apparently, he had done this before.

We went back in to pay the bill and all of us felt a little bad, alongside the snickers and snorts. I proceeded to walk Jackie to her car in the parking garage. I continued to apologize, but she took it all in stride. Of course, she had other things to worry about. It was only her initial test that had come back negative. She still had several more tests before she was fully in the clear. A recent infection may not show up on antibody tests for up to three months. We wished her well, and stayed in touch from time to time. It was nice to find out that she remained negative.

Maddie was another story—just about everyone who encountered her really liked Sober Maddie, but Drunk Maddie would become a far-too-frequent guest in our lives. We began noticing how often she was hammered on the phone or when we'd visit.

Everyone handles their problems differently, I told myself. *Maybe it's just . . .*

No. It wasn't just a coping mechanism about the diagnosis. It was a real problem. And just like the HIV, it was something we couldn't fix for her. I hoped against hope that it wouldn't stand in her, or our, way.

I felt sad for Maddie because of the way she couldn't seem to get it together, I felt sad for Nena because of her multiple sclerosis (MS) and how she couldn't go home again, I felt sad for Susan because she was in so much conflict with her faith and family, and I felt sad for me because I still wasn't getting any better. But if you ask me, the worst part of this whole sordid affair, the one I felt the absolute saddest about, was Laura Sumner.

CHAPTER 14

Laura

Sometime in August or September 2006, Philippe had taken a job stocking shelves at Target on the midnight to 8:00 AM shift. It was a long way from his old job as a network security analyst, but I guess he hadn't found a wealthy benefactor yet and had to do something. It was at this job that he met Laura.

Laura said she was in her fifties, but she looked considerably older, with thinning gray-blond hair and a haggard appearance. She didn't have any family or friends that she ever mentioned, no ex-husband or kids. In fact, it didn't seem like she had any connections or community network at all. Lions seek out the weakest antelope in the herd when they're looking for a kill; that's what Philippe did here. They had been dating for just a few months when we found her.

Tracking Laura's license plate to a nearby address, Susan and I made a Saturday afternoon trip to her house. But when we got there, we realized it wasn't a house. It was an apartment in row after row of apartments, and no apartment number was listed in the DMV database. Undaunted, Susan and I drove up and down each aisle of cars in the parking lot, trying to spot her vehicle. It was the same vehicle that Maddie had seen a month earlier on, the night of the cease and desist order.

We canvassed car after car, tag after tag. But just about when we were thinking of giving up, there it was: a gold Honda parked right next to the curb under a carport, with the right plate number. Since we still had no way of knowing which apartment was hers, we took a giant risk and left her a note placed carefully and inconspicuously on the windshield under the wipers.

"Laura, there is a very important matter about your health." Then we left both Susan and my phone numbers with a directive to "Please call."

I sent out a silent prayer that this note wouldn't seal our fate. If she disclosed those phone numbers to Philippe, he would know that we were the ones behind all this—that it hadn't ended with Susan naming him to the health department, but that we were tracking down his new conquests and were indeed "ruining his life." Who knows what he would do? All kinds of vengeful ugliness rattled around in my head.

We drove away slowly, hoping to catch a glimpse of someone retrieving the note. But it remained steadfastly on the windshield, its ends flapping in the breeze, as if waving good-bye, telling us not to worry.

Laura did call that day, and she talked to Susan.

"I'm worried about this one," Susan told me afterward. "I think she has some serious psychological issues."

Laura had blurted out a number of strange things during the call that sounded delusional—things about being watched and followed. Mind you, *we* were pretty paranoid about being watched and followed, too, but we had good reason to be! She, on the other hand, had a bunch of nonspecific ideas in her head about all sorts of people who were out to get her. It was surprising that she had been willing to call a mystery phone number.

It took two hours on the phone with Laura to get her to agree to meet with us. And we couldn't come to her place; she came to mine.

When she came to my door, Susan and I had been at my house for an hour plotting our strategy. Based on the initial conversation, we knew she was at best psychologically fragile. As a former psych nurse, though, I suspected there might be a more worrisome diagnosis.

This mysterious woman arrived with a big floppy hat and sunglasses, looking over her shoulder. She kept the hat and glasses on the whole time she was there.

We spent a good hour doing all the talking while Laura took copious notes. As she got more comfortable, she started to explain all her cloak-and-dagger antics with the disguise.

"UC," she almost whispered. Undercover. "People are getting into my apartment all the time and moving things around. It's maintenance that has a key. And once someone left bloody towels all over my bathroom." She was more animated now.

Susan and I glanced at each other sideways. "But I fixed those guys. Every time I go out now, I put books and tables in front of the door so they can't get in."

If she was blocking the front door, then how was she getting back in herself? I imagined her passing through the walls like a ghost. For that matter, how could she open the door to get out once she put books in front of it? A lot of what she said just didn't add up, and to me it felt like paranoid schizophrenia. I really felt sorry for her.

How could Philippe prey on such a fragile person? It reinforced for me how little he cared about anyone but himself. She had two legs and a place to stick his dick. What happened above her neck was of no interest to him. It was unclear if Laura was still dating

Philippe. You couldn't really reason with her like you could with someone whose brain was healthy.

I don't know how we ever convinced her to get tested, but she took our advice. At our second meeting, again at my house, she took copious notes again without sharing much of her own story. At one point, though, she dropped her paperwork from the health department onto the floor. Susan and I both looked at it as we helped her pick it up. On the top of the page in the right-hand corner was a big number eight with a circle around it. Susan and I never said anything about it, but it left a big question mark in my head.

I called my friend the next day. I told her we'd seen Laura's health department papers and about the big number eight at the top. "What's up with that, angel? We only know about six: me, Susan, Maddie, Brittani, Nena, and the woman from DC. That leaves one person unaccounted for."

She just *mmm-hmmed* and didn't give a straight answer, telling me that she had spoken with a lot of women. She had totally jeopardized her job for us, so I couldn't push too hard. It left my mind reeling . . . was it the mysterious woman from Drive Financial who had left the voice mail? Was it Princess/Patricia? Or maybe Jane Logan had lied about being negative.

◈

I don't know how many one- and two-hour conversations Susan and I each had with Laura (some in person, others on the phone), all spent listening to a bizarre and pathological reasoning system—a brain gone rogue.

As far as we knew, we were the only friends Laura had in the world. And we tried our best to be just that. It wasn't easy. Her paranoia seemed to always get the better of her. She'd start a conversation seeming perfectly lucid, but most of the time, if the conversation was long enough, it deteriorated into the murky world of biochemical defect. And off she would go—on a rant about how someone was watching her, so she always wore a hat, a wig, and sunglasses when she was out (except she didn't always).

She swore to us on numerous occasions that she had seen Philippe with a red-haired woman in a lab coat, and that the woman was driving the black Corvette. She worked for the pharmaceutical industry, in Laura's mind. And then there was the one about duplicate Philippes—that one really creeped me out.

There was a good Philippe and an evil Philippe, and she fervently believed they both actually existed and were identical lookalikes. Evil Philippe was being set up by the "Pharms" to infect women and reap bundles of money off us for the medications. Good Philippe was just a poor sex addict and meant no harm. He was the fall guy for the whole thing. According to Laura, Good Philippe needed to go to a sex addict clinic to be cured. She was also pretty sure that AIDS was nothing but a big scam to get people to pay lots of money for medication so drug manufacturers could get rich.

She was so sure of the power of the Pharms and their intent to do away with anyone who stood in their way of making big profits that she made Susan hide in the bushes with her to talk. She didn't want to have any personal discussion in my house, where she was sure the Pharms had set up cameras to read our lips.

Of course, we had shared with her about filing charges and finding more victims. We agonized over getting her to understand that there was just one Philippe and that he'd done her very wrong. But even though she always seemed to carry the diagnosis form from the DCHD with the big number eight in the corner, sometimes she wouldn't even acknowledge that she was positive. Other times, she would admit to having been infected, but as long as I knew her, she never told us anything about her CD4 or viral load.

In the HIV-positive world, those numbers are everything. It's the measure of the amount of virus wreaking havoc on your system and the definitive test of how well your immune system is or isn't working.

People live and die by these numbers—literally. Technically, people don't die of AIDS; rather, they die of opportunistic infections or cancers that a normal immune system would just throw off.

Early on, about the first two or three weeks postinfection, you're in a latent phase, where the viral load goes down and the CD4 goes up. Then, slowly, the numbers get worse. Ideally, when an HIV-positive person takes antiretroviral therapy (ART), the medicine keeps the viral load at such a low count that it can't even be detected by current tests. That's what they call an "undetectable viral load." When I was first diagnosed, undetectable meant less than 50 copies per milliliter. Since then, tests have become more sensitive, measuring down to less than 20 copies per milliliter. Being undetectable is the holy grail of being HIV-positive. You are not cured, but the virus is kept at low enough levels to decrease inflammation and allow the immune system to rebuild. It's also just a hair's breadth short of impossible to pass the virus on to others when you're at undetectable levels.

CD4 is just the opposite: you want those numbers to be as damn detectable as possible. The CD4 cells are the warriors that do battle with bacterial or viral enemies. Normal is 500 to 1,500 T cells per milliliter. But HIV kills the soldiers, and more virus equals fewer soldiers.

In the early days of the epidemic, for governmental funding purposes, the CDC selected a CD4 of 200 as defining the difference

between HIV-positive and AIDS. You could also get that diagnosis with an AIDS-defining illness as well—certain life-threatening
illnesses and cancers that are particularly dangerous to people
with HIV. Things like *Pneumocystis pneumonia,* invasive cervical
cancer, and Kaposi's sarcoma are AIDS-defining illnesses. But
the 200 count wasn't a scientific measurement; it was just a cutoff
number to define who got government assistance and who didn't.
If your T cell count was 201, you weren't "sick enough" to require
assistance; if it was 200 or below, you were.

As our support group (Susan, Maddie, and I) grew to include
Laura, Nena, and later others, one of the hottest topics of conversation was always numbers.

"How are your numbers?"

"Up 25, from 250 to 275" or "Not good. Dropped to 310
from 370."

We got all wound up in the numbers game, almost like the
stock market—when the numbers were up it was all good; when
they were down, not so much. All of us were open about our
numbers, except for Laura.

We tried all along to figure out why she wouldn't talk about her
numbers. She wanted to know about ours, but she wouldn't give
up one hint about where she fell on the viral load/CD4 seesaw. I
wondered if it was because if she shared her numbers, she'd have
to admit she was positive—and sometimes she would, but not
always. I eventually chalked it up to her extreme paranoia. She
continued scribbling down notes every time we talked to her, but
even when the rest of us talked openly about our own lives and
backgrounds, she preferred to share only her delusions.

Three weeks after Laura's diagnosis, we sadly found out that
her car was parked overnight at Philippe's house again. It turned
out that she was still seeing him. By mid-April, though, Susan and

I had spent enough time on the phone and face-to-face with her to convince her that she really should file charges against Philippe. I'm not sure if it was because we convinced her it was the right thing to do, or because the Texas Crime Victims Compensation would cover her medical expenses (which she only sometimes acknowledged having), but finally, after many excruciating meetings with her, she made the decision to file. Getting her to the police station, however, was quite a struggle. What paranoid schizophrenic trusts the police?

We weren't sure it would really happen, but she let us meet her in the parking lot of Frisco PD. This time she *was* wearing a hat, a wig, and sunglasses. As the rest of us did, she was going to use an alias. She didn't want us going in with her to file the charges, but she did it, God bless her—and hallelujah! We now had *four* complaining witnesses.

Even so, we left the police department more anxious than ever. We had been on the job for almost two months, and the hours and the worrying were beginning to catch up with us. Plus, Susan and Maddie were still working with Brittani, who had not, up to this point, decided whether or not to file. We were so close and yet so far away.

Yes, we had four women who had come forward to accuse Philippe of infecting them with HIV, but we still had no usable proof about when he knew he was positive. For his part, Tom was trying. He had checked with the immigration center in Guaynabo where Philippe got snagged on the way back from Guadeloupe, but he had no luck—they didn't do HIV testing there.

He and Susan also set up a pretext e-mail from Susan to Philippe: another attempt to get Philippe to admit that he had known for a long time he was HIV-positive. That effort failed as well, but at least Tom was working on it; I couldn't always say the same for the rest of the department.

Susan gave it one last shot with Brittani eventually, at the end of April. And finally, reluctantly, she also agreed to file. By that time it was almost May, and then the day she was set up to go to Frisco PD, her kids came down with some sort of bug.

I just wanted to scream! We had worked with Brittani for six full weeks, and now that day was here, but things got postponed. We were right on the cusp of having five women file, but I was going to have to demonstrate my *phenomenal* patience once again. The whole thing was killing me.

She canceled again the next time she was supposed to file, which made me think that maybe she was just playing with us and was never going to do it. But finally, a week later, she actually did it.

And now we were *five*.

We had reached the number we set out to reach—five was enough to be taken seriously—and I pushed for Tom to take the case to the next level, assuring him that we would still find others.

By the beginning of May, I had gathered my thoughts enough to conclude that issuing and acting on a search warrant at Philippe's house would net us some great, damaging info for the case. First, since he was a convicted felon, the number of guns he had alone would have put him away. But what I really wanted them to snatch was his computer. It must've been chock-full of names, numbers, and addresses of countless women, plus maybe more incriminating evidence. Frisco PD, in its infinite wisdom, decided not to act, even after I told them about the weapons charge he had pending (due to that little incident with Lupita's fiancé and the "Bozo the Clown" comment). It didn't move them.

What they told me was that in order to execute a warrant, they had to have a witness who had recently seen the evidence in question. Since I hadn't been to his house in almost a year, my knowledge that the computer was still sitting on his kitchen table wasn't good enough. I found the whole thing a maddening bullshit story. We could potentially save hundreds more lives if they looked at all his smut. Maybe thousands, if you count all the partners and future partners-of-partners of all the women who had no idea that they were infected. He was like Typhoid Mary.

I mean, a *lot* like Typhoid Mary. Mary Mallon, an Irish cook, worked for seven different families in New York over seven years, and every one of them ended up with a typhoid fever outbreak. Finally, an engineer discovered that she was an asymptomatic carrier of the disease. Doctors discovered active typhoid bacteria in her gallbladder and recommended that she have it removed, but she refused. She was put into isolation for two years and had to promise never to work as a cook again; instead she could work as a laundress. She agreed—then promptly changed her name and went right back to work as a cook. She worked at hotels, restaurants, and, finally, Sloane Maternity Hospital, where she infected twenty-five staff members, two of whom died. Right after that, she took off again, but was caught when she brought food to a friend.

All throughout that time, all Mary cared about was her own freedom. She set out to deceive people about her name (frequently changed) and background, and wouldn't even wash her hands when preparing food. She knew that literally everywhere she went, she was causing typhoid outbreaks and that people were dying. She flat-out didn't care. Finally, authorities decided she needed to stay in isolation permanently. She died of pneumonia after twenty-three years in quarantine in a clinic on an island in New York City's East River.

It was just the sort of end I hoped would befall Philippe: alone, in custody, and unable to infect and kill anyone else. For now, though, we had nothing but a piece of paper to deter him from continuing to destroy people's lives, and that paper had proven useless many times over.

As time went on, my own fears about my safety grew. It had been my habit for years to be aware and keep an eye on my surroundings, but I became hypervigilant. I was always looking over my shoulder, thinking the worst. "Some dumbass is going to rat me out and that sorry sack of shit is going to hunt me down and shoot me." I'm a black belt, but I don't catch bullets in my teeth.

Nighttime was the worst. I didn't usually leave the school till 10:00 or 11:00 PM, and I always came home to an empty house. I would search the kitchen and living room for any signs of something amiss. I'd peer around the corner to check out the closet—and I'd always check the locks on the doors two or three times before going to bed, trying to stay in control of my safety. I think a lot of people who have been traumatized in some way by a criminal carry at least a part of the experience with them for the rest of their lives. Once your security and trust have been breached, life is really never the same.

Finally, I got so tired of the anxiety that I had a home security system installed in my house. It helped, but not totally. Doctors call it PTSD (post-traumatic stress disorder), and we were all diagnosed with it at one time or another.

As I tried to rationalize away my fear, I would think about a story my grandmother used to tell me. When she was a little girl in the early 1900s, her family got into a talk about snakes. Every adult had something bad to say about their experiences: a snake under the bed, or out in the garden, or a rattler on a rock in the sun. Maybe even a water moccasin down by the creek. My great-great-grandfather, Christopher Columbus Beckham, said,

"Aw, snakes won't hurt you," to which his youngest daughter, Hixie, retorted, "Maybe, but they'll sure make you hurt yourself!"

So much wisdom in so few words: what you fear might not do you harm, but if the fear overtakes you, you can wind up doing stupid things that put yourself in danger. So then I had an extra thing to get paranoid about: Maybe he wouldn't shoot me, but maybe instead I'd be watching my rearview mirror for just a second too long and *BOOM!* I'd die in a head-on collision. The mind does terrible things to us.

Maddie, however, didn't have long to worry about getting hurt. It happened to her for real. She called me one afternoon with her voice trembling.

"I just got into it with Philippe."

"Oh no. Are you okay? What happened?"

"Yeah . . . I'm okay . . . But I can't believe he did that!"

"What?"

"I was in my yard pulling weeds, and all of a sudden he was there, looming over me. It scared me, but it pissed me off, too. And then he started on me—'I know you're up to something— and I know you're harassing me' in that whiny five-year-old tone he gets. Ugh!" she sighed.

"Oh, I'm familiar with that tone."

"He told me that I shouldn't have gone to lunch with you girls. Well, I stood up to tell him to get the hell out of my yard, and he slapped me!"

"No way!"

"Yeah, right in the face. It left a pretty good-sized red mark, too!"

"What did you do?"

"I didn't know what to do. I was so shocked I just stood there with my mouth open, and I watched him disappear inside his house."

"You should call Tom."

"No, it's not worth the hassle."

"Maddie, I'm telling you, you need to get this documented in case there's more trouble."

"Nope. My renter has a sawed-off shotgun—I'll just keep it by the door."

Crap! I thought. *Wish I had a sawed-off!*

Her story just made my worries all the more realistic. If he had already hauled off and slapped her, what was going to happen when he found out the real extent of what we were up to?

I was watching too much *Law & Order: SVU*, but it's hard to tell if it was overall good or bad for my psyche. On the one hand, it gave me new nightmare scenarios to fixate upon—what if he planted a bomb in my car?—but on the other hand, the good guys always won in the end. God bless Mariska Hargitay. And I knew I was a good guy, so it made me daydream about the moment of justice that unfolded in every episode.

But I also had the very real threat of dying of AIDS. My numbers were slow to improve after I was medicated, and I was surrounded by kids at the school. Every time one of them sneezed on me, I saw the chain reaction in my mind—a cold, which would turn into a sinus infection, which would turn into pneumonia and kill me. I wish I could say that the fears were just silly, but they weren't so outlandish—I was in a vulnerable place with a near-useless immune system. At that point, it wouldn't have taken much to take me out.

So the double fears would play leapfrog with each other. Every night, I'd die a thousand times in a thousand ways in my imaginings. In addition to seeing a therapist, I went on antidepressants.

I threw myself into the case as a way of controlling what little I could control; I made it a point to be as educated as I could be on issues of the law and medical science. I also made sure to pass along everything I learned to the police and, starting in May, the district attorney.

Once we had five complainants filing, we'd been assigned to Lisa King of the Collin County District Attorney's Office, who called and asked to meet. It was hard for me to get out of the house at all by that point because the medications were not yet having any positive effect—only the negative side effects. I was nauseated and miserable, and I felt my energy level spiraling downward like water from a hole in a bucket. Because of that, Lisa was kind enough to offer to come to my house to meet with all of us. Susan, Maddie, and Laura were there. Of course, since she was still terrified of me, Brittani was MIA. She did stay in touch with Susan, though, and explained that Philippe had been e-mailing her, trying to get back together: "I think about you every day, always fantasizing about us, we were so great for each other," that kind of stuff. Couldn't you just hurl?

We waited eagerly for Lisa King's arrival, and she was as impeccably dressed as she was on time—expensive dark brown business suit, light-colored conservative blouse, and sharp as a tack. By her side was Samme Glasby, the investigator on the case. Samme was a classic Angie Harmon–type, with long, jet-black hair, and walked with a swagger—probably due to the small cannon she carried on her hip (I think it was a .45 caliber gun). They were both, in different ways, extremely sensitive and considerate of our circumstance. And they did their best to give us hope.

Often when I discovered something new online or thought of a possible angle we could use in prosecution, it would be in the middle of the night, and I was too distrustful of my memory to leave it for the next day, so I'd leave messages on her office voice mail at all hours. She took it in good stride.

"Every morning when I get in at 8:30 and see my message light blinking, I know it's you," she said with a grin.

I was glad she had a good sense of humor about it because I wasn't about to stop. We had lives to save—even if it might be too late to save my own.

Lisa quickly picked up on what was "different" about Laura, too. She brought it up gently: "Would you check on Laura, make sure she's okay every now and then?"

"We're doing our best," I told her. "She's one of us now."

CHAPTER 15

The Smoking Gun

It had been rumbling around in my brain ever since I learned that Keisha had met Philippe in September, the last time he was reported as HIV-positive. What had happened around that time? How would he have been outed then?

And then it hit me.

Jesus.

I time-lined the date and realized it was right around our Labor Day trip to Detroit to meet his family. When we got back from that trip, he was having pain in his lower back and sides.

"It's probably kidney stones," he told me. "I had them once before and it feels just the same."

"Well, what are you waiting for? You need to get to a doctor!"

"With what money? I'll just wait it out."

"Philippe, don't be silly. I'll write you a check."

Which I did—a blank check from the business so that he could fill in the doctor's name and amount.

He came back saying that they ran a bunch of tests. Soon after, the doctor called him to come back in for test results.

Crap. I knew from my nursing days that they don't call you in unless something is wrong. I ran down a list of diagnoses so bad they call you in to discuss them. It had to be something they could treat. Cancer? High blood pressure? Diabetes? Then I began to wonder about sexually transmitted diseases, and in particular, HIV. All of a sudden it was hard to breathe, but I had to keep calm until I knew more.

"I'll go with you," I offered, but he didn't want me with him.

"I'm a big boy. I don't need help."

"Well, if you won't let me come in with you, I'm at least going to wait in the parking lot so I can be there for you if you get any bad news."

"You don't need to. I'm sure it's fine."

But the truth was that I couldn't handle an extra minute of the unknown either. I kept my worries to myself but had to pop three Xanax the morning of the appointment. I wrote him another blank check, then we drove separately to the clinic and I sat out in the parking lot waiting for him. My mind raced with fear as I sat there; what could it be that they would tell him only in person?

But he came out of the doctor's office and walked to my car window with a smile on his face and a swagger in his step. There was absolutely no fear on his face—he looked like he'd just seen a good movie.

"How did it go?" I asked.

"Fine! All negative."

"All the tests were fine? Everything?"

"Yep!"

"Even HIV?

"Yeah, I'm HIV-negative."

"Well, that's a relief. Still doesn't explain why you're having kidney pain, though."

"It was probably just an infection. I'm starting to feel better already. See you later!"

He *knew.*

I couldn't dial the number fast enough. Thank God my office manager answered on the first ring.

"Debbie, you've got to help me!" I said.

"What?"

"Do we keep the canceled checks or bank records from a couple of years ago anywhere?"

"Sure. Don't you remember? They're in those boxes we moved to your garage when we ran out of storage space at the school."

Hell, no, I didn't remember! To be fair, I'd had kind of a lot on my mind since then.

All this time I'd been agonizing about how we could prove he knew he was HIV-positive—setting up phone calls and e-mails, and searching for people he knew. And all this time, what I needed could've been practically right under my nose!

"Oh God. You've got to help me. Remember when I sent Philippe to the doctor and gave him two checks to pay for those two visits for the kidney stones?"

"Sort of, I think."

"We've got to find those checks! We might be able to use them to prove he knew he was HIV-positive when he saw the doctor in September 2005."

"Everything before this year, we moved to your garage. I'll be there in ten minutes—we'll find 'em!" she exclaimed.

Everybody needs a best friend like Debbie. I seriously don't know what I'd do without her. By the time she got there, I'd already begun to dismantle several boxes. I thumbed through endless bank statements. We opened more boxes together, and there it was! My hands were trembling as I opened the folded-up bank statement for September 2005 and photocopies of the checks tumbled out.

There they were. The two checks that I had signed to pay for those visits with a man named Dr. Pedro Checo.

There was no definitive proof that he had been diagnosed at that particular visit, I knew, but the time line matched up perfectly, and the in-person follow-up made too much sense. I called Lisa King. "When can you get me those checks?" she asked.

Lisa was always rather matter-of-fact, but I definitely detected a note of excitement in her voice—excitement I had never heard before.

"I'll be there in thirty minutes," I promised. But I did take the time to run by the school and Xerox them just as a precautionary measure. ("Never trust anybody" was my new motto.) I tucked them into a large brown mailing envelope for safekeeping before heading to the brand-new Collin County Courthouse building.

As I headed up the escalator to the second floor, I clutched that precious brown mailing envelope like I was hanging on for dear life. At the time, it seemed like I was.

Lisa was waiting for me in the conference room. She was usually straight-faced, but I saw a heckuva smile. "I have to submit a subpoena for the grand jury to approve us getting his medical records. If this goes right, then we have our probable cause."

I crossed myself, crossed my fingers, prayed, knocked on wood, worried, bit my nails, and paced. At our next meeting in early June, Lisa told us that the subpoena had been approved and was on its way to Dr. Checo—as well as subpoenas to the Collin County Health Department and others.

A couple of days later, we were finally on the road to talking about an arrest warrant. Assuming they could get the records, the police were ready to file charges against "Philippe Padieu, AKA Philly White." Tom explained that there had been quite a discussion about exactly how to charge him. They tossed around the idea of attempted murder, but they decided it was too difficult to prove intent.

Since Texas has no laws against HIV transmission, they decided to go with aggravated assault—that is, assault with a deadly weapon. The deadly weapon, of course, being his bodily fluids. There would be five charges for the five of us who'd filed.

In Texas, assault with a deadly weapon—a knife, gun, or in this case, HIV-infected bodily fluids—was a second-degree felony. It carried a sentence of two to twenty years in prison. But Tom remembered that in part of my statement, I had mentioned that Philippe had already had a felony conviction: the robbery on the naval base in 1983. If there is a prior offense, the charges automatically upgrade to first degree, which is punishable by five to ninety-nine years in prison with no chance of probation.

That was more like it.

∽

There had been fewer and fewer cars in Philippe's driveway these days, but not because he had slowed down any. No, he had just wised up enough to pick up the women and bring them to his house so we couldn't track the license plates—usually.

But there was one more time when Maddie spotted Patricia's Mercedes leaving Philippe's house, and she followed her down the road. When they hit a red light, Maddie pulled up next to her, rolled down the window, and honked the horn. "I don't mean to scare you," she said. "I live near Philippe and I used to date him. There's something I need to talk to you about. Can you pull over?"

She did.

"I'm HIV-positive," Maddie said. "So are lots of other women who've dated Philippe. Have you been tested?"

Patricia was stunned. She had no idea about Philippe's diagnosis or all the other women. They wound up talking in depth, but Maddie kept quiet about the criminal case.

"I was supposed to move in with him tomorrow," she said sadly. "I have nowhere else to go. I'm broke."

"You can stay with me if you need to."

"That's sweet of you. You don't even know me."

"No, but you got taken in by him the same as I did, and I want you to be safe."

The puzzling thing was that she said they had always used condoms —even before the health department ordered him to. It was hard to believe. Maybe the "love of his life" was exempt from his hatred of women? Could he actually have cared about protecting her life but not any of ours?

Patricia promised not to say anything about speaking to Maddie, and asked Maddie to promise the same. She was worried that he would get violent if he knew they had talked.

"Don't worry—I never talk to him anyway," Maddie said. They exchanged phone numbers and Maddie told her to get tested and stay in touch.

"Thank you for telling me," Patricia said. "I have a lot to think about."

Her thinking stopped two weeks later when she did, in fact, move in to Philippe's place.

We were all disappointed. The quintessential con man had gotten away with it again.

Shortly after that, Maddie saw that the garage door was open at Philippe's house and only Patricia's car was parked inside. She went over and knocked on the door.

"There've been reports of a rapist with a knife around this area. You should really close the garage door," she said.

"I don't care," Patricia replied. She looked empty.

"Listen, if you need anything . . ."

"I'm not allowed to call you and you're not allowed to call me."

"Are you okay?"

"No."

"There are other people who would help you move out of here for free, give you a nicer place to stay than mine until you figure out what you wanted to do. You wouldn't have to be near Philippe."

She just stared blankly.

"Well, if you ever need anything, please call. There are others willing to help you, phone numbers Philippe wouldn't recognize. We could meet and try to help each other."

All was quiet for a few days, and then Maddie thought she spotted Patricia carrying boxes out to her car. Could she be moving out? But no such luck—her car was back that night.

The next time Philippe was out in his yard, he yelled something indecipherable to Maddie. She walked toward him so she could hear what he was saying and he yelled, "You'd better stay off my property!"

"This is a public street and I'm not on your property! You're the one who called out to me."

"Don't try to get Princess into your little girls' hate club! You're invading my privacy. I'm going to call the cops right now."

"Go ahead. Do you want me to sit right here or just have them come to my house?"

He acted as if he was dialing his cell phone and then went back into his house. Maddie went home to wait, but, of course, nothing happened.

Just because Patricia had moved in didn't mean that Philippe was going to stop sleeping with other women, either. Susan had visited Ernie's, one of his two main pickup joints, in March and had come face-to-face with him. They ignored each other, but when the woman he was flirting with went to the bathroom, Susan followed her.

"I don't mean to be nosy, but the guy you're talking with . . . have you been dating him?"

"I went out with him once," Sara said.

"Okay. Well, you should know that he's HIV-positive."

"Oh no! I was just with him once, but I know someone who's been seeing him for, like, eight months."

"Can you warn her?"

"I definitely will. And I know other women who've dated him in the last year or two, too."

Now it was six weeks later and that woman, Sara, contacted Susan to let her know that Philippe was back in action at Arthur's with yet another new conquest—and a threat. He had found out that she was warning the other women about his status and he came up to her on a Friday night to lean in and say, "I hear you've been spreading rumors about me."

"They're not rumors if they're true. I needed to contact a couple of friends of mine, so that's what I did. I got pulled into this at the bathroom at Ernie's when someone told me about it. This is just women protecting women!"

"Who pulled you into the bathroom?"

"I don't have her name or number with me, but it was one of your girlfriends who said she went out with you for a year and a half."

"I have a lot of girlfriends."

"Well, there you go. One of the girls had already been contacted by the health department and when the doctor called, he gave out your name."

Philippe seemed really surprised and agitated by this. He went down to the end of the bar to talk and dance with another lady. Then that woman came up to Sara and told her, "Philippe is saying he is going to sue you for slander and libel and is going to have you beat up."

Sara was terrified and left two messages for Susan that weekend, wanting to know if he was violent and capable of doing anything like that.

"I told her that, of course, there *is* reason to worry and to be careful, but that he usually just likes to threaten and bully people," Susan told us. "Besides, he has no male buddies to beat her up—he spends all his spare time messing around with women. And he doesn't have any money for lawyers or to pay someone to beat her up. She is still very concerned and is only going to go places where she can valet park. I told her she could call the police and let them know, but she doesn't want to do that."

He was never going to stop. The health department order didn't work, the multiple women telling them he had infected them didn't work, and the "love of his life" moving in didn't work. Until we could get this asshole behind bars, he was going to keep on infecting as many women as he possibly could, just because he was a sick jerk who enjoyed his power to kill. It was damn depressing.

∽∾

Since my diagnosis, I had cried about something pretty much two or three times a week. Sometimes it was because I was lonely. Sometimes I felt I'd never have another man in my life. I cried over my own stupidity and the thought of how sad my girls would be when I died. I cried watching commercials.

My counselor, Carol, kept telling me to get a dog. There are cat people and there are dog people; I'm a dog person. I knew it was a good idea—who wouldn't find comfort in a furry creature who was glad to see you no matter what, who gave you sloppy, wet kisses and a waggly tail for just coming into the room? But I didn't have the time or energy to look for a dog, or a clue about what kind I would want.

That's when Stacy came to the rescue. She'd just gotten a dog for her family a month earlier and they were all in love with her. Her husband had allergies, but the kids wanted a dog, so she'd searched online for a rescued Lhasa Apso—the cute little dogs that look like well-groomed mops. They don't shed and have low allergen potential. When I told her that Carol had suggested a dog for me, my beautiful daughter went to work.

Two days before my birthday in April, she called to say that the Lhasa rescue center had just gotten seven male puppies, about six months old. It was incredible to think that there were seven little brothers out there together that needed help. They had been rescued from a dumpster when a landscaper nearby heard their little yelps.

It was Friday, and I was exhausted from my work week. I promised her I'd go with her on Monday. Fortunately, she knew better.

On Sunday, I went to her house so we could go shopping for puppy stuff. A crate, a bed, toys, towels, puppy shampoo, food, and, of course, pet stain remover. We got everything unloaded at her house, and I was just about to go back home when she said, "Can you sit for a while, Ma?"

"Sure, honey." I wondered if she needed to talk. But she went to the kitchen instead, and when she came back, she had in her arms one terrified, shaking, shaved, and skinny little six-month-old Lhasa pup. He weighed a whopping nine pounds.

This time I cried out of joy. I was so grateful and excited and in love with that puppy all at once. My seven-year-old granddaughter sat down beside me to pet him.

"I couldn't wait till Monday, Ma. By Friday afternoon, there was only one left. I hope you don't mind that he's the runt of the litter. His name is Marlo. When they found him and his brothers, they were so matted they had to completely shave him except for his head and ears."

"Oh my gosh, you are so sweet—and so is he!" I said through more tears.

"You can change his name if you want. Here are his papers." She handed them to me.

"What should we name him, honey?" I asked my granddaughter, who was sitting quietly next to me. She continued to pet the terrified pup in my lap.

"I guess he must've been through a lot of bad stuff," I said. "He seems so timid."

"Yeah, he's really scared. He's spent almost the whole two days in the bathroom behind the toilet," Stacy said.

"Well then, we must give him a strong name to help him overcome his fright and become tough and powerful. How about Tiger?"

They smiled and nodded.

"Okay, Tiger, let's go home!" And that little nine-pound pup became one of the few things in life that made me smile.

By the time I got home I was exhausted. Since it was Sunday afternoon—the end of the weekend—I had missed my opportunity to work in the yard. During most of the spring and summer, I was out in the backyard every chance I got, planting flowers and tending to them. Being outside in the sunshine was as much a part of my healing process as Tiger was.

Everyone needs an outlet to relieve stress. Gardening was mine. I called it "diggin' in the dirt" because that's a big part of it—getting your hands caked with mud up to your elbows as you create a peaceful and beautifully colorful and scenic environment.

I come from a long line of gardeners—mainly, my grandmother, who farmed an acre of land every summer and sold fresh fruits and vegetables at her roadside stand when I was a little girl. She also sold fresh eggs, and she called her business Aline's Hen House. The little store was always packed with tomatoes, cabbage, okra, squash, cantaloupe, watermelon, and my favorite: black-eyed peas. What she couldn't sell, she would can to sell in the winter. It was a real sight to see all those different fresh foods growing in neat little rows. When I was five, it seemed that her garden stretched to the ends of the earth.

The vegetable garden was just half of it. She lived in a huge old Victorian-style house that was surrounded on three sides by a twenty-foot radius of flower gardens. And every square inch was covered with flowers. It wasn't like those landscaped areas in front of professional buildings where everything looks neatly placed in a precise and predictable pattern. It was just a huge, random blizzard of flowers—all kinds of wonderful-smelling flowers in every color imaginable. Some of my earliest childhood memories were of picking flowers in the garden.

When I became an adult and had a house of my own, I started with houseplants everywhere. And when I moved to the country, there was plenty of space for me to expand my horizons to the outdoors as well as inside. But with a full-time job and two girls to raise, I didn't get into the full swing of things gardening-wise until I moved to the house where I lived after the divorce.

It was at the end of a cul-de-sac, with a pie-shaped yard. It fanned out to easily four times the size of the average (tiny) backyard in Plano. I was thrilled with the possibilities. I transplanted some cannas from the old house and started with a few pots of flowers here and there. As I worked through my grief, it became a routine—there would be a summer project and a winter project. By midspring of that year, I had redone about half of the back-yard. But I felt better—a lot better.

Maybe it was just time that helped me heal, or perhaps it was something else altogether. But to me, digging in the dirt and watching the flowers grow was great therapy. And the flowers gave me peace, something I was desperately searching for.

So it was natural for me that when I was faced with death, that's where I'd go. All night long I'd worry about going broke, my kids, the business, the other women, the case, Philippe's revenge, being alone forever . . .

I worried about the subpoena that was taking far too long to get a response to (okay, it was probably just a few days—or forever —one or the other), and whether or not he'd ever be arrested. We only had a little over one month until we lost Tom Presley as "our" detective. I knew we were driving him a little crazy by then, but I also knew he cared and was doing his best. Who knew whether the next guy assigned to the case would even give a rat's ass about us? Would the whole thing be in jeopardy when he left? None of us were really sure exactly how all that worked, and we all fretted about it. For me, the worst part was that now there was nothing much I could do. These were the things keeping me up at night.

But then I'd wake up the next day and look forward to getting out into the yard. I might have felt nauseated most of the day, and exhausted and weak, but somehow I would scrounge up the energy to tend to those flowers, to prune the roses that are now almost as tall as I am, and to remember that there was still beauty and life left in the world.

CHAPTER 16

The Big Day

"I have news." It was Lisa King, the assistant DA. And that could only mean one thing.

"You got the medical records?"

"I did."

"And?"

"They're hard to read." Typical doctor's writing. "We have to send the records to an independent agency for verification before we can be sure and make an arrest. But it appears that he was diagnosed with HIV on September 12, 2005."

Son of a bitch! I thought, and then I said out loud, "We got him. We got him!!!!"

"I believe so, Diane," she said, and in my head, the angels were dancing.

Oh my gosh, we might actually make this thing happen before Tom leaves, I thought. But then a week went by with no news about the review. I bit my lip. I told myself they were working on it, and they would surely call soon. I funked my way into a huge downward spiral on June 17, the anniversary of the day Philippe and I had broken up—what I considered the beginning of this whole hellish nightmare. I really didn't feel like talking to anyone. But after a few more days, I couldn't take it anymore. We were three weeks away from Tom's exodus. I called him.

"Tom, it's Diane. I hate to bother you but I'm just wondering if the health official has finished checking Philippe's medical record."

"Well," he hesitated. "It didn't get delivered till this Monday, and she's on vacation now."

"What? OMFG!" I said, almost yelling. "We're finally within spittin' distance of nailing the bastard, and it took more than a *week* to get the records to her? Why the hell didn't you call me? I would've driven over and taken them myself!"

"Don't worry. We'll probably have them by the end of next week."

Before I could yell anymore, I quickly hung up.

A week—ANOTHER WEEK? Lord Almighty, why can't they just MOVE on this?

Poor Tiger had retreated to his hiding place under the bed. I collapsed on top of it and curled up in a ball to cry another bucket of tears. I was so tired of living my life in fear and worrying about if Philippe was still out there infecting new women.

The other women weren't pleased, either. Tom got his reassignment and was officially off the case at the beginning of July, we were given a new investigator named Leah Apple on July 7, and we'd all about hit our boiling point on July 10 when there was still no news. By that time, we'd found out that the subpoena was blocked. I thought it was ridiculous—who protects a predator? Assholes, that's who! In my mind, that doctor was the queen of the assholes. And now she was the one sitting on the other records. Why were we giving them to *her* to decipher? She was an enemy!

We said so—in slightly more polite words in an e-mail—to Lisa King.

"I know you're concerned because she 'blocked' the subpoena for the records," Lisa wrote back. "Their hands were tied because of the stupid law enacted by our legislature. Believe me, she's on our side and wished she could've complied with the subpoena. We were all trying to figure out a way around the law but could find no out for them to give us the records we requested. Unfortunately, the penalty for disclosing such records is as harsh as suspending a health professional's license. Everyone I talked to from McKinney to Austin about this hates this law. . . . My boss, is very eager to get this law in front of the next legislature to get it changed."

It was a little reassuring, but it was *July*, and Philippe was still trolling nightclubs and infecting unsuspecting women nearly two years after his confirmed diagnosis. And even though Lisa said she knew the doctor would comply with interpreting the records from Dr. Checo, she still didn't know if the doctor actually *had* those records in hand yet.

I called our advocate, Tonia, who decided it was time to go over Tom and Leah's heads. She made a phone call to their boss, Lieutenant Gregory Ward, who then called me for details. I tried to remember to use words that wouldn't have to be bleeped out on television. I explained that Tom had left the case and that Leah, who was in training, wasn't yet responding to our calls. He said that he'd look into it and find out whether or not any doctor had the records yet.

That did not please Tom.

"In my opinion, calling the Criminal Investigation Division lieutenant wasn't a good idea at all; in fact, it really is mud on my face and Leah's. When you've had questions, I've always answered them."

Well, actually, the CID called me, but it was true he had answered my questions, though sometimes the answers were not good enough or soon enough. And although I didn't enjoy the idea of getting Tom in trouble, I have to say, we got results.

"Not only did the doctor confirm that the diagnosis was made on September 12, but there's one other thing: Philippe also acknowledged that he had a male sex partner in 1999."

"Son of a gun."

Even though we had already thought through this possibility, hearing it confirmed was still shocking. He didn't even have the excuse of prison—he'd been out of prison for a decade by that time. It was right around the time he moved from Michigan to Texas, probably right before he met Princess and three years before he'd met me.

And who knows if there had been other men before and after that (like the pickup truck owner who was parked at his house overnight)? It was too much to think about all at once, so I just decided to focus on the great part: we had what we needed.

The date of the crime was established. Anyone who had been infected after that September was infected knowingly. It was time to get an arrest warrant.

⚭

We didn't know exactly when the arrest would happen, of course. I talked to Susan and Maddie daily. I whined to Lisa King. I queried Leah Apple. But nobody was talking.

Leah was nice enough despite our slow start and seemed to be very serious about our case. She was athletic and freckle-faced, with long, blond hair. I tried to restrain myself from becoming glued to her hip, but it took all my willpower.

Once, in a burst of comic relief, Susan, Maddie, Nena, and I crafted a sort of "Philippe's arrest" football pool. There were quite a few categories: date of arrest, amount of bail set, guilty or not guilty, and the length of sentence if he was found guilty. None of us actually put any money down, but we set up rules just the same. Whoever came the closest without going over got $20 per category. I bet July 20 for the arrest, $50,000 for bail, guilty, and life in prison. The last one wasn't so much what I *thought* he would get but more what I *hoped* he would get. And what I knew he deserved. It was a bit of fun, but it didn't touch the tension we were all feeling. And, inevitably, tension can often lead to personality clashes. In this case, it was between Susan and me.

In mid-July, we really started watching Philippe's house in earnest, waiting for those cops to show up with their shiniest handcuffs. Sometimes it was just Maddie, other times Maddie and me or Maddie and Susan. The anticipation was agonizing. Some mornings I could barely make it to the coffeepot, because I was slogging through a cloud of anxiety. "Will today be the day?" Susan was just as bad. She wasn't getting much done at work because she was either worried about what might be happening, or talking to Maddie or me about *when* something would be happening. Every one of us jumped a mile when the phone rang. It was excruciating, and the anticipation was eating away at all of us. And so during one of our watches, we really got into it.

Susan and I were particularly edgy because we were not only working our regular jobs full-time, but we were also still putting in twenty to twenty-five hours per week on the case. We were stalking, researching, plotting, interviewing, and tracking down people—because as much as we knew the people who were working on our case were competent, no one was going to care about this outcome quite as much as we were.

Patricia finally did move out, which meant there were new women showing up at Philippe's again. He couldn't seem to manage to be alone for even one night. Maddie tried to talk to a youngish brunette who showed up at his house, but Philippe shooed her away quickly.

During the course of their evening watch, they noted that Philippe's garage door was half-open. When Susan saw that, a mischievous idea took hold, and she just couldn't resist the urge to poke at Philippe a little bit. So she called him up and said, "Hey, Philippe, your garage door is open," and then hung up and called me, giggling, at the wonderful prank she had just pulled. To her, it was the sweetest comic relief to the ongoing tension. But it made my anxiety go through the roof.

Not only was I not impressed, I was appalled. What a stupid-ass, kindergarten stunt to pull, risking *everything* we had worked so hard to achieve. I could just visualize him putting two and two together, figuring out that Susan and Maddie were in cahoots, and then hightailing it out of there to forever disappear into a scot-free continued life of crime.

Some of the other women had already said that he had talked about maybe moving to Paris. I was terrified that what she had done was going to tip him off to the fact we were watching him for a reason, and with no arrest warrant, there was nothing stopping him from taking off permanently and becoming untrackable. I had even talked about it with Tom, and he acknowledged that the case would effectively be over if Philippe left the country—there would be little hope of him being extradited.

The thought of him sitting on a flight to Paris with a smug "fuck you" grin on his face and a drink in his hand flashed through my mind. It was at that crystallized moment that everything in my head exploded—and it all got vomited on Susan.

"You did what?! *You did freaking what? Oh my God,* how could you be so stupid? You risked all our hard work, our lives, and the lives of countless potential victims for a foolish minute of 'gotcha'? What kind of idiot are you?"

I was just getting warmed up. For a good four or five minutes more, I ranted and raved, kicked and screamed, and cussed and acted like a fool. I'm sure I don't remember all the hurtful things that I spewed out, but it must've been vicious and vile.

Then it was Susan's turn. We took turns screaming at each other for what seemed like an eternity, finally slamming the phone down in each other's ears at the same time. She wasn't done with me, though. An angry e-mail arrived the next day, and it was a small novel. She must've spent the entire night writing and rewriting because it got more and more hateful as she continued.

In it, she told me that I was a privileged, bullying child who thought she was always right.

"I have lost my taste to be involved in this case any further," she wrote. "*Screw it*. Do it on your own."

Within an hour, I received a phone call from Maddie, begging me to make up with Susan. I had to rant and rave some more—I was extremely wounded by her hurtful words. But I have to admit, Maddie was a good peacemaker. After she calmed me down, she did the same with Susan.

She followed up with an e-mail to the two of us saying that if we didn't stick together, we'd have nothing. "We have been there too much for one another, and for everything to be wasted on something so stupid makes no sense," she wrote, ending her letter with a simple plea: "I love you both, and I'm asking you to make up. This has been difficult on all of us—but never so much as now. Let's not give up our strength in the final lap of the race."

Well, hell. She was right. I'd let the stress take the driver's seat and had no business talking to my friend the way I had. I can look back now and realize that a lot of what she said was right about me at the time. I *was* prone to outbursts, and to pushing hard to get my way. Nothing in my life was okay, and I didn't react perfectly. Of course, neither did she. We were all a hair away from our boiling points, and it took very little to get any of us to bubble over.

I don't think I talked to Susan much about it; we both just mumbled "sorry" to each other and moved on. God bless Maddie for stepping in and putting it all into perspective. We couldn't afford to stay mad at each other for long; we had vitally important work to do. Leah called and told us to watch the house, but we didn't know exactly what was happening.

On the night of July 19, Susan called with some news: "My daughter just found a warrant for Philippe's arrest online. They're going to get him!"

"What? You mean they put all that stuff online? Shit! He could see it!"

Remembering what Lisa King had told me, I knew that once there was a warrant, they had to make the arrest within forty-eight hours.

"Holy crap!" That was Susan's exclamation phrase for everything. "Now we really need to watch the house!"

"You're right! Let's go to Maddie's first thing tomorrow."

"Cool! Tomorrow's Friday and I'm off. I can spend the whole day over there." I hung up the phone and looked up. *Thank you, God*, I whispered. I could barely sleep all that night, but when I finally did, I crashed hard and didn't wake up until almost 11:00 AM. I threw on a pair of running shorts, a karate T-shirt, and my flip flops, and I was out the door in a heartbeat. Evidently, Susan had the same situation. She was just getting dressed when I called.

By the time Susan and I got there, the stress had gotten to be too much for Maddie, and she was already half blasted. When she got tipsy, she became a blanket that just draped all over you. It was hard to shake her off. I tried to be as nice as I could, but right now our priority was something different. We sat on the couch talking, taking turns going to the bedroom and peeking through the blinds at Philippe's driveway—where his slick black chick magnet leered at us, as if to say, "You'll never get me, stupid bitches!"

All afternoon, we would talk and peek, peek and talk. We wore a path in the carpet traipsing back and forth to the bedroom where we could best see his house. I was the shortest, so I had to strain on my tiptoes to see over the hedges in front of the window. Maddie fixed us something wonderful to eat—she was a great cook—but still no movement at the house of doom. The whole neighborhood was eerily quiet. The heat of the strong Texas sun baked the concrete like a giant pan of brownies. We were all getting tired of going back and forth to the bedroom, and by 6:00 PM my fatigue and compromised state of health had taken over.

"I'm feeling awful," I told my friends. "I've got to work in the morning and I need some rest. It's probably too late in the day anyway, but you guys call me the minute anything happens."

Truth be known, I had started to give up hope. It had already been almost thirty hours since the warrant was issued. Maybe they just weren't going to do it—maybe something had happened. Maddie was a bit past too tipsy to care, so the stakeout was left in Susan's capable hands. Tiring of the back and forth traipsing, she put a chair in front of the window, but then she couldn't see over the hedge. After casing the house, she located enough books to elevate the chair to an acceptable height, and there she sat—perched on a chair on a pile of books while Maddie slept on her couch, and I on mine.

At 10:15, the phone roused me. Susan was on the other end of the line.

"He's on the move," she said. "He pulled out of his driveway at exactly 10:00. He had on his long-sleeve white dress shirt and a pair of jeans, and I know where he's going."

I knew I was done for the night, but I could barely contain myself. "Where?"

"Ernie's! Maddie and I are on the toll road heading south right now. I'll call you when we get there."

"Okay." I was about to pee my pants I was so excited. I just sat and watched the clock on the mantle tick away, silently measuring each second as an eternity.

෬

Ernie's was Philippe's Friday night pickup spot. It was a bar and restaurant that catered to an older crowd—perfect for him to pick up women who were lonely after a divorce.

At 10:30, I got another breathless call. "He's here! I knew it!"

"What are y'all going to do?"

"We are sitting tight and waiting."

"Okay. Man, I wish I could be there."

I learned later that Susan had quite a time containing Maddie as they waited in the car in Ernie's parking lot. Maddie kept telling Susan she was going to go inside just to see what Philippe was up to. Susan practically had to restrain her, until Maddie switched gears and just had to have a cigarette. Finally, at around 10:50, they headed to the Walmart across the street, where not only did Maddie score the smokes but insisted on finding a pair of slacks and a blouse. She was bound and determined to check on Philippe, and she knew it would attract too much attention if she went in wearing the shorts and halter top that she had on when Susan scooped her up for the chase.

They didn't get back to the parking lot until around 11:30 PM Philippe's slick, black death chamber was in the same spot, in front of the pancake house—which was now closed. At 11:31, Susan called me. I had never heard her so animated.

"THEY GOT HIM!" she announced, as if he had just been given a lethal injection.

"Oh my God. Oh my God. They got him! What happened?"

"Holy crap! We missed it when Maddie and I went to Walmart to get her some cigarettes!"

"How'd you find out?"

"The whole crowd was standing in the parking lot and I saw my friend Danielle. Everybody was buzzing, so I asked her what was going on. She said Philippe was at a corner table when two Addison PDs walked in. They asked if the black Corvette was his and he said yes. They told him someone had run into it and they needed him to file a report. So when he got out the door they pushed him to the ground, cuffed him, and threw him into the squad car."

"Whoa! Too cool!"

"You've got to get down here. You've gotta. You just gotta come celebrate with us."

"Oh man, Susan, I'm so wiped out . . . But you're right, I *gotta* come celebrate! Don't start without me." I already had my jeans on by the time I hung up the phone. We'd left our stupid fight far behind and were a team once more.

On the way down the Dallas North Tollway, all I could think was: *Finally, finally, finally, this awful anxiety has come to an end.* Then all of a sudden, it occurred to me that July 20 was the date I had picked in the pool for Philippe's arrest. Damn! I should've bet a hundred dollars. But really, that was a minuscule disappointment compared to what had happened. Nothing could dampen my spirits. Nothing.

Susan and Maddie were waiting for me at the bar. The place was still buzzing as I ordered three glasses of champagne. "To making things right," I proclaimed, as we clinked glasses and chugged. Just for good measure, we ordered another round, and this one I sipped ever so slowly, enjoying the moment until the bar crowd thinned out and it was time to call it a night. The three of us would've been jumping up and down had we not had the glasses in our hand. And in my final act of petty larceny, I slipped the champagne glass into my purse. "This one is *not* going into the box of evil!" I proclaimed proudly to myself. I haven't stolen a glass or anything else since then.

July 20. It was a very good day indeed.

⟨∞⟩

The next morning I was back at work, with a long-absent spring in my step. As I was taking a breather at 10:45, my cell rang, from an unknown caller. An operator came on the line and asked for a credit card number to pay for a collect call—from Philippe.

I . . . what? *What?!*

There really are not enough interrobangs in the world for the absurdity of that moment.

He was calling me—*ME*—from jail! He was using his one call to reach . . . *me*. It was the craziest thing I'd never imagined.

After the operator got my info (I was far too tempted to hear what this was all about), there was a brief click and I held my breath. This is how it went, just about word for word, as I wrote it all down right afterward:

"Hello," Philippe said.

"Hello," I said.

"It's Philippe. You're behind all this, aren't you?"

"What do you think? That's not the point. The point is that you knew and you lied to me."

"But I can't believe you're conspiring against me."

"I don't know what you're talking about."

"You know, with my neighbor. You know you still love me. They are after me for attempted murder. Somebody is going to make a career out of this. Why did this take so long?"

"I guess it takes a while to put things together. Where are you?"

"In Addison. I don't have an attorney. I don't understand the charge. What does it carry?"

"I think it's aggravated assault with a deadly weapon and it's two to twenty on each count and a ten-thousand-dollar fine."

"I thought you were negative."

"I almost died and you knew."

"You know I could've been negative, depending on the blood work."

"Are you on meds?"

"The doctor said I don't need to be on medicine, and I may not be on meds for a long time. This is not my fault. I didn't do anything wrong."

"Bullshit. The point is you knew and didn't tell me, and I could've very easily died. You didn't even report my name anonymously to the health department."

"Yes, I did."

"Only when they forced you to."

"You were breaking down. I thought you would freak out. And I didn't trust the test results with the other positives."

"I *was* freaking out! But better to freak out and know than to not know and almost die . . . which positives?"

"The HPV and herpes. I didn't have hepatitis, but I did have chlamydia one time."

"So they told you that you had *two* other STDs and you *still* didn't believe the HIV? *Bullshit!* So what happened with Patricia—is she positive?"

"I don't think so."

"Why did she leave?"

"She wanted to kill herself and she was tired of the harassment [from your group]."

"Well, Maddie only talked to her once."

"No, it was three times."

"Where is she now?"

"I don't know. You told me you got tested for everything."

"Don't try to blame this on me! I never told you I got tested for HIV. I didn't think I was at risk. If you hadn't cheated on me, we'd still be together. We'd have a beautiful thirty-five-hundred square-foot house, be working together, and making lots of money. We'd have everything. But you blew it."

"You knew I was cheating. Do you think I would still cheat if we got back together?"

"In a heartbeat. You were out looking for pussy last night."

"I only go there to talk to people."

"Yeah, that's why you spend half your nights away from home."

"Just get me out and we can be together."

"I don't have twenty grand."

"You can have the house. I'll sign it over to you. I had it appraised at one hundred thirty-seven thousand dollars, and I only owe about one hundred seventeen. I'll pay you back. I have a job now making five thousand per month."

"Oh yeah? Working for whom?"

"GMAC."

"For how long?"

"A couple of weeks."

"Oh, so is that who called me at the school from Drive Financial a while ago and said you were HIV positive?"

"I don't know."

"And you're still working at Encouragym?"

"Not for long, I guess."

"So I guess there's no hope for you then."

"Yes there is. You're the only one who can stop this. Why don't you just drop the charges? You know I always cared about you."

"Ha! You rarely even told me you loved me."

"Yes, I told you in French all the time. Look, you're not going to let me down. This will eat at you and tear you apart. We were in this together. I was never really sure I was positive. I wasn't sure the test was accurate at the time. I had no symptoms."

"So do you have an attorney?"

"I can't pay an attorney. I'll have to get a public attorney and then I'll be guilty. I only have a thousand dollars in the bank now and I'll get a thousand dollars next week. And what's this immigration hold?"

"Don't have a clue."

"Who else is it besides you and Maddie and Susan?"

"Who do you think?"

"Brittani?"

"I warned you to stay away from her."

"She came on to me. She was flirting with me. Look, I'll marry you and I'll do anything you want. We can still make it work."

"Philippe, I'm not interested in marriage to you."

I'm really not sure how I kept a straight face for that one. After all this—after all the women, the car chase, the HPV, the AIDS, the years of deception—he thought he still had that kind of hold on me, that marrying him was a prize I wanted to win. He made it sound like a benevolent sacrifice on his behalf. A jailhouse phone proposal. I would rather have set my own face on fire with a propane torch.

"You know you won't be able to live with yourself if you do this to me. We may still have a chance."

"Philippe, I won't be able to live with myself if I don't do it."

He had to go then, in order to appear before the judge. I sat there in stunned silence for a good ten minutes, just replaying the surrealism of what had just happened. The man I had just had arrested for intentionally infecting multiple women with a fatal disease had proposed marriage to me and offered me his house. The English language has a wonderful array of millions of words and expressions, and yet the only thing that fit this situation was, "Bwuuah?" Imagine a dog with its head cocked so far to the side in confusion that it falls right over. This was followed by hysterical gales of laughter.

After Philippe saw the judge, he was allowed to call me back. He informed me that they were keeping him on an immigration hold, which I didn't understand because I had stupidly proved his U.S. citizenship. But I sure didn't mind anything that was going to ensure his lengthy and uncomfortable stay behind bars. I would've preferred it if they'd just dug a hole and placed him *under* the jail, but I'd take what I could get.

"I need an attorney to get me off immigration hold," he told me. "And even if I do make bail, I'll have to be on a monitor. Come on, you know you'll be miserable."

Riiiight . . . if walking on air, smiling so wide the corners of my mouth touched my ears, and nonstop fist pumps is your definition of miserable. Oh yeah, and laughter—lots and lots of laughter.

"I won't even consider it." I didn't even try to say this with a straight face.

"I really didn't mean to hurt anyone. You're the only one who can help me. The only one with enough money and connections and power."

"Why don't you try Jane Logan or Kristen Alder?"

"I'm not involved with them anymore."

"Well, you're not involved with me either."

"Kristen and I were just friends."

"Oh, really? Then why did she get tested?"

"Well, we did have a relationship at one time. . . . You knew I lived a risky lifestyle. I thought I would never get anything. I've been in the lifestyle for a long time and I never got anything but chlamydia before. I don't want to spend the rest of my life in jail."

"I can understand that." Too bad, so sad.

"I want you to know I'll do whatever you want. I'm telling the truth. There is no reason for me to lie. You're not going to like hearing this, but all those women still care about me. They hate me but they still care about me."

"Philippe, that makes no sense whatsoever."

"Maddie was just as promiscuous as I am. Susan had another boyfriend but said they were using condoms. She was at the club as much as I was. Brittani had boyfriends other than screwing her husband. I'm guilty. But nobody is without issues."

"Oh yeah? I never cheated on you."

"You went out. You were on Match.com."

"I went on Match when you dumped me for Patricia the night before we were supposed to leave for Hawaii. I had exactly two dates, and I never had sex with anyone."

"Well, I'm not gay, no matter what Susan says."

And with that non sequitur, his time was up.

The second conversation had been just about as mind-blowing as the first for me. I tried unpacking all the psychological fuckery. He called me because I was the one with "the power" to fix it for him—a compliment of sorts. As if I could just call the whole thing off after months of investigation and government resources on a case by the State of Texas involving multiple women. I wondered if he really thought he had a chance of convincing me, or whether it was just a wild shot he figured he had to try. After all, I'd been dumb enough to take him back after he'd cheated more than once. Guess he thought this was just like that.

I think he knew he would be found guilty—there was no bravado about how he was going to beat this. There was also no apology or remorse.

After our call, he was transferred to the Collin County jail. Bail was set at $200,000, plus another $50,000 on the weapons charge. That was more than enough to keep him firmly planted until trial—which would likely not be for eighteen to twenty-four months. We were all going to have to practice patience, which was hard—but a lot easier now that he was unable to infect any more unsuspecting women or cause harm to us.

Soon after he got to Collin County, he chose a "friends list"— people who were allowed to visit him in prison. It was posted online. Top of the list? Me! How stunningly embarrassing. I got my name taken off quickly.

Jane Logan was on there, too, as well as Kristen Alder, another woman he'd dated named Deirdre Yates, and a historical romance author named Nikki Brewer. I don't know if any of them went to visit him, though I know some of them stayed in touch with him. Later, he substituted Greg Hyde, a friend and mentor from his teens and twenties in Detroit. And then there was Candace Wilkins, the tall blond I found in his little black book when he was detained in Guaynabo. *The fact that he still has women willing to talk to him is really quite a thing*, I thought. I had no idea yet just how intentionally obtuse some women could be, though I'd soon learn.

In the end, I couldn't help but feel a strange satisfaction knowing that I was the person he called with his one phone call from jail. Whaddya know? He finally chose me over all the rest.

CHAPTER 17

Telling Secrets

Philippe's arrest was big news around town. Before the media got wind of it, I knew I would have to disclose my status to more than just my family and closest friends. My main concern was my school and the black belts who were teaching for me. The first thing I wanted to handle was fear of transmission, so I had to get my facts straight.

I had already checked the CDC website full of stats on HIV/AIDS, which included a statement that they had no documented cases of sports-related HIV transmission. None. Yay! That was one hurdle I cleared. But I also considered whether I would need to "hang up my gloves" and not do sparring anymore. At that time I just wasn't ready to make that decision, so I decided to not spar for a while but to leave the possibility open for later on—somewhat depending on the reaction I got from instructors and students.

Heavy conversations with the women in our support group indicated that almost all of us shared a common fear of telling others about our status. Most of us, at times, wanted to go curl up in a ball in a dark closet and just die. We were all worried about shame and stigma. The aliases we used when we filed would screen us only so much. It was difficult to know who to trust. Once you tell someone, you're at risk of having the whole world know; as I mentioned earlier, you can't unring a bell. Plus, all of us had already had our trust betrayed by someone we loved.

I was pretty sure I didn't want to be vulnerable to that ever again. I had my "sisters," my counselor, my family, and a couple of friends, and I was initially quite fine with that support group. That's a relatively large support group compared with most people who are recently diagnosed with HIV/AIDS. One woman in our group put it best: "I'd rather have cancer. At least you can tell someone you have cancer." We all felt like lepers. A lot.

But after grappling with the idea, I decided I really needed help navigating through the muddy waters of what to say to students, family, and instructors. After all, Philippe had been a part of the school for four years, and a lot of people knew we were in a relationship.

So I invited my top two black belts, Barrett and Bob, plus their wives, for a small get-together at my house. Debbie and her husband Denny came along for moral support, since they already knew. We grilled some burgers and made small talk in the backyard abloom with the flowers of summer, but there was a sense of impending doom in the air. Even though the guys didn't know what it was, they knew something was up. They had both been around me for more than ten years, too long not to know. Karate instructors and their longtime students have a special relationship.

At the end of the evening, we were all sitting on the back porch as I disclosed the horrible news. I was relieved to see only sympathy and concern on their faces and tears in their eyes. I swore them to secrecy, and they solemnly pledged to uphold my wishes. Both couples gave me huge hugs and promised to take good care of me with whatever I needed and whenever I needed it.

One of my other black belts had known all along because I confided in her during the investigation. I wasn't ready to disclose to the other black belts yet, but I had to say something because I was sure they were about to hear rumors if they hadn't already. I called them to the office one by one, notified them of Philippe's arrest, and assured them that "I'm too mean to be sick," which wasn't a total lie . . . nor was it the total truth.

I braced myself for some media coverage but didn't expect the craziness that was about to happen. When the news hit, it *hit*!

On July 21, his mug shot was on every newscast on all the major stations. One of the local stations even sent a reporter to the school to get a statement from me, since Philippe had worked there. That was terrifying! I didn't want to go on camera; I was way too afraid that my face would somehow give away that I was one of the victims.

Luckily, my friend's boss was an attorney who volunteered to speak to the press. He did a great job at turning the spotlight off me, but he also recommended due diligence. This meant that we needed to notify every student of the past four and a half years of Philippe's status and urge them to get tested if they were at risk. We sent out more than seven hundred letters and I was very nervous about what the fallout would be.

Amazingly, only one student discontinued training. The parents of one of my twelve-year-old black belts just "didn't want to take the risk." I tried not to take it personally. I was honored that all the families except one took it in stride.

The odd thing about the first few days was that while the attorney was representing me to the media, his partner, who had represented Philippe on the weapons charge, was considering representing him on our case. I also learned that Philippe wanted to give Tara McIntosh his power of attorney.

Tara was one of the women I had called when I found his little black book in 2003. She had gone off on me at the time, claiming that he was in "hot pursuit" of her and trying to get her to marry him. I chalked it up as a bullshit story and didn't talk to her again until the HIV thing came up. When I talked to her that time, she went off on another crazy rant. I had to hang up—it just wasn't worth it. She even acted like a lunatic at the attorney's office—they finally had to ban her from coming in. He really had an endless supply of odd women willing to go to bat for him, even now.

The initial burst of intense media scrutiny died down after a week or so, but I knew that every time there was a hearing or whatever, it would be back on the airwaves again. My daughters were nervous for me.

Of course, it was also in the paper, and on a few radio talk shows. Mostly, the commentary was running in our favor (I had done an informal poll), but there were a few right-wing radicals that insisted that we "deserved" HIV because we were "sleeping around." And that's the nicest way they put it. I called this group the lunatic fringe. I largely ignored them because: (a) You can't fix stupid; (b) I knew it was a fear-based response; and, most important, (c) I really didn't give a shit what those judgmental, holier-than-thou jerks thought of me. I knew who I was and that the only thing I had done was love a man who couldn't be trusted.

But I did get a big kick out of a column written for the *Dallas Morning News* by Jacqueline Floyd. She came out strongly supporting us in the controversy over whether we were "innocent victims" or, as Sean Hannity suggested, "deserving whores." It's the South, and even though we expected that sort of mentality to a certain degree, we weren't fully prepared for a lot of the vitriol that was spewed our way. Driving home from the studio, I'd look at the houses I passed and wonder how many homes listened to—and agreed with—Sean Hannity and his camp. There was a pronounced segment of the population that bought into the "blame the victim" mentality. *"You should've known better." "You were stupid for falling for him." "You shouldn't have been having sex until you were married—so it's your own fault."* Even victims buy into the victim-blaming. Despite our sisterhood support, it was difficult to weather the criticism, to remember that no, we were not "deserving whores." That women have just as much right as men to be sexual beings. And I'm here to tell you, we will never evolve as a society until women and men are allowed the same freedoms and the victim-blaming stops!

Another phrase we heard often was "it takes two to tango," meaning obviously, we should've protected ourselves. I liked Jacqueline's response best: "It may take two to tango, but it only takes one to pull the trigger."

⌘

One afternoon in early August, Susan called out of the blue to ask me, "Hey, did you see on the news where that woman in Prosper killed her family and committed suicide?"

"Uh, I think so, why?"

"I just heard a report that a suicide note was found, and she warned the police to wear gloves because all the blood was 'contaminated.'"

"What are you thinking?" I was afraid to start thinking what I was already thinking.

"I'm thinking that this woman is married, she goes out with friends or something one night, and she ends up hooking up with Philippe. She cheated on her husband, but puts the incident aside in her mind until his picture pops up all over the news. She runs out to get tested, finds out that she's positive, and spirals into a suicidal depression. There's a husband and two kids—she's busted and she's doomed."

"Seriously?" I couldn't really totally take in what she was saying.

"Well, she fits the profile. Vulnerable, unhappy, attractive woman looking for a bit of escape from the housewife doldrums."

"Yeah, but isn't that a bit of a stretch?"

"Well, it would be, but the story broke two or three days ago—right after the news stories came out about Philippe. And the first reports of her suicide mentioned that comment in the note . . . and then there was no more mention made of it in any more of the reports."

"Let me call my insider at the health department."

When I mentioned it all to her, she was really guarded for the first time since I've known her. "It is *believed* . . ." she started, hesitated, then went on, "that she was involved with Philippe. I'll tell you more in person—got to go." And she hung up.

Stunned doesn't even begin to come close to my reaction. I wanted to vomit. Philippe Padieu was an evil monster for knowingly infecting even one of us. But now two children and a husband may have been his "collateral damage."

Susan and I considered all kinds of options: an anonymous tip to the police, a call to a sister who was listed as a survivor, even digging into it ourselves. But in the long run, we just couldn't bear to stir things up. That family had been struck with quite enough tragedy, and we weren't going to add to their despair by even hinting of an affair with Philippe as a possible explanation. So despite our best Cagney and Lacey instincts, we dropped it cold—though we never stopped thinking about it. I never did get to speak to my trusted insider in person again.

Right after that, the source dried up. The last thing I learned from her was that a couple of Philippe's supporters were trolling around trying to get information from her. First it was the romance author, Nikki, who showed up at the STD clinic early one morning pretending that she was a member of our support group. She claimed to be an irate ex-lover and was looking for Keisha—luckily, Keisha wasn't there that day and had time to look into her claim. The person who did speak with her said it seemed she was "playing a game." Then came Jane Logan. Keisha asked if Jane was still in contact with Philippe. When she said yes, Keisha said she couldn't speak to her, given the court case in progress.

The fact that Philippe still had women willing to sleep with him and do his bidding stunned me. What was wrong with these women? How desperate do you have to be to want to help someone like Philippe?

Once, the tips dried up, there was no more exchange of information, just perfunctory answers. It was heartbreaking to lose someone who had stuck her neck out for us so far. It became apparent that the department heads thought they were spending too much time and resources on Philippe's case—which I thought was a disaster, because it meant that there were more women out there who might never get tested and find out that they were carrying and potentially spreading a deadly disease. We did learn that at least ten more people—not just women, but also men— had come in to the department to get tested as a result of seeing Philippe's mug shot on the news.

⚭

In August, Maddie told me that there was a woman removing things from Philippe's house and one of the things was his computer. Shit! Why hadn't the police confiscated that thing? There's no telling how many women's names and contact info were on that computer. I ran the plates and found that the car belonged to the romance author, Nikki. I called the information in to Tonia, our victim advocate.

A week later, Nikki returned the computer to the house, telling Tonia she got it just to remove *her* information. According to Tonia, Nikki had hooked up with Philippe but tested negative. I wondered if there was a real reason the police still refused to confiscate the computer. The story was that there would be no "fresh" information on it, which was a different excuse from the last time they didn't confiscate it, but my hunch was that the police didn't want the computer because then they would be obligated to comb through hundreds, if not thousands, of potential victims' names and contact information. Due diligence would require that they track them all down, and that could take the better part of a century!

Then I learned that Nikki was writing a story about Philippe. This created no small amount of concern for me and for the other women as well. It was sickening to imagine that Philippe might be able to actually profit from his heinous acts. Soon after she returned the computer, she came back and was in the process of removing everything from the house in boxes. Not only was she removing plenty of potential evidence, but I had paid for about half the stuff in his house! It just pushed me right over the edge, so I scooped up Tiger and zoomed over to the house, top down, top speed.

Tiger was in heaven, the wind blowing his ears back as he lapped up the sunshine. But I was in hell. *How dare she! Who the hell does she think she is? It's MY stuff that she's taking out of there. Piss on her!*

Maddie joined me as I pulled in behind the beige sedan in Philippe's driveway. We knocked on the door. No response. We knocked louder—still nothing. Finally, I spoke loudly through the door. "Nikki, we just want to speak with you for a few minutes."

"No! Go away!" Now this was really pissing me off.

"Fine, but my car is behind yours, and you're not going anywhere until you talk to us."

So then she told me she was calling the police.

"Great! They can help me get my stuff from out of there."

I thought she was bluffing, but ten minutes later, sure enough, two youngish-looking cops appeared.

"What's going on?" Officer One asked.

"I'm waiting to talk with someone."

"She said you were pounding on the door."

"No, officer, I just knocked."

"That's right!" Maddie chimed in.

"I just want the stuff in the house that was stolen from me," I explained in my most conjured-up, matter-of-fact voice.

"Well, you'll have to take that up with the constable. When did you live here?"

Without thinking, I told the truth. "I never actually lived here . . ." Except for all intents and purposes, I *did* live there three days per week.

"Well then, you'll have to tell the investigating officer."

At that point, Nikki came out. "I just want her to know what kind of monster she was with," I explained.

"Where is the owner?"

"In jail," Nikki and I said together. But I was the only one smiling.

"When's he getting out?"

"Never. He's in on five counts of aggravated assault." I smiled again.

"She'll make sure he never gets out," Nikki said.

Was that supposed to make me feel bad? Because it actually made me feel dandy.

"I just want my property back," I said, which was mostly true. A little false. I also wanted to shake her and smack her cheeks and scream, *Wake up, woman! You're helping a predator! What is wrong with you?* I just kept thinking that if I could reason with her, I could get her to see the error of her ways. Of course, my temper was approaching the flaming red zone, leaving less chance of me reasoning in a reasonable way.

"I'm sure you have it all," she said.

"I know where you live." I didn't add the "you bitch" that went through my head.

"I'm sure you do." And she disappeared behind the large brown front door.

At that point another squad car arrived. The officers told me to leave, pointing out what had become rather obvious: "She doesn't want to talk."

"Have I done anything wrong? I go to someone's door with a puppy in my arms and knock on the door. Tell me how that's against the law," I challenged.

"Look, I'm not going to sit here in the yard and dance around the issue with you—you need to leave."

"Fine," I said with a shrug. "No law against parking in the street."

"Don't follow her."

"I won't," I tossed over my shoulder. Maddie and I parked down the street and watched and waited. The police remained at Philippe's house to "protect" Nikki from us, not leaving until she had finally packed up everything and driven away.

My brilliant idea after that was to turn in an anonymous tip that she was stealing evidence. But our victim advocate, Tonia, put the kibosh on that when she called up and let it fly that she was pissed at me. Evidently, she had spent the better part of the afternoon convincing the officers to keep my name out of the report so the media wouldn't get hold of it. God bless her!

Looking back, I know my anger issues were really getting out of control. I had been so busy working the case, I hadn't really had enough time to process all the things that I had felt—the sadness, grief, and especially the rage. They're all a part of the grieving process.

At the time it was hard for me to recognize that the whole ordeal had taken a huge emotional toll. My feelings roller-coastered from high highs to low lows. I was given to angry outbursts, wails of self-pity, thoughts of suicide and homicide. I couldn't get to sleep. I took a sleeping pill every night, finally falling asleep at 2:00 or 3:00 AM and then fighting to get out of bed the next morning. It was making me crazy, but not being so active in the case would've made me crazier. At least it gave me a focal point aside from my own failing health.

My therapist had me write hate letters to Philippe that I'd obviously never mail. I filled them with pages of vitriol and lists of all the things he'd stolen from me, from my sense of trust and security to my sexuality. One would've thought it would've been hugely cathartic. It wasn't. It was an impotent rage. No matter how many years he was imprisoned, or even if he died in jail, nothing could ever change the fact that I was a "marked woman" for the rest of my life. The combination of shame and hatred was unbearable.

In mid-September, Bennie House, Esq., was selected through lawyer lottery to be Philippe's court-appointed attorney. On September 18, the grand jury indicted Philippe. The case would go to trial.

Meanwhile, I went for another sonogram and Pap smear because my precancerous cells from the HPV still hadn't cleared. As I headed to the exam room, my doctor called out, "Hey, I've been looking for you."

"Oh yeah?" I bantered. "I love you, too."

"No, seriously. My business partner, Dr. Holt, has a patient who recognized your ex on TV. And she's HIV-positive, too." My jaw dropped. "Would you be willing to talk to her? She doesn't have much of a support system."

"Sure." I whipped out my business card and wrote down my cell number. "I'd be happy to help."

My mind was electrified during the exam and all the way home. Could there really be another victim—someone we hadn't talked to? And what were the odds of two women seeing doctors in the same practice in Plano being infected with HIV by the same man?

I called Susan on the way home.

"Oh my God!" she exclaimed. "Think she'll call you?"

"Don't know. We'll just have to wait and see."

It was a couple of weeks, but one afternoon before I headed to the school, I got a call from a number I didn't recognize. "Hello, Diane?" a woman with a Hispanic accent started tentatively.

"Yes," I said, holding my breath.

"This is Sophia Brissan. I'm Dr. Holt's patient."

In short order, Sophia poured out her story. She had met Philippe at Avanti, the jazz bar where I first met Susan, in January 2006, and they had dated until around April or May. (Of course, all the while he was "exclusive" with me, and seeing at least nine other women.)

She knew they weren't exclusive, and she finally dumped him when it became clear to her that he was using her—but not before he gave her his trademark "gift." She had been diagnosed with HIV a few months afterward but didn't know that he was the source until seeing the television reports.

I suggested she meet Susan and me for brunch on Sunday and she readily agreed. It was sad that we had yet another member in our "club," but I can't pretend that I wasn't also excited about the possibility of adding another woman to our case.

We met Sophia at the Malachite Room at the Dallas Hotel InterContinental, my favorite place for Sunday brunch. It was opulently decked out with what appeared to be green marble columns, and you have never such seen such a buffet in your life—it was practically an all-day affair with every breakfast and lunch food you could dream up, plus miles of desserts that were not on any Weight Watchers points list. In the middle of a table of seafood and cheese and crackers stood a huge ice sculpture. Every time I went there, it was a different one.

Sophia was fiftyish, very attractive, and well put together. She had on a nice business suit and looked very formal—and very sad. As all of us got to know one another, we felt a huge amount of sympathy for Sophia. Like Nena, Sophia's cultural background did not work in her favor. She didn't feel like she could tell anyone in her Latino family because of the stigma attached. She confided in her ex-husband because she believed she was dying and she would need him to take care of their child full-time when she was gone. He was remarried, though, so she couldn't talk to him very much either. She had been alone and isolated for more than a year, and I don't know how that woman was vertical. I couldn't have been.

By the time we finished with our over-the-top meal and more mimosas than I wanted to count, she was ready to file charges as well. The next week, we went with her to Frisco PD and she made her statement, making her the sixth woman to file charges.

Being with Sophia was particularly tough. She was more emotionally wrecked than I was—if that was possible. It broke my
heart to see her with silent tears rolling down her cheeks the entire
time she wrote out her statement. When she finished, we walked
her to the parking lot and gave her a hug before she drove away.
Then Susan and I hugged each other and burst into tears, loud
and long. I guess Sophia's more open grieving opened up some
of our wounds, too. As we walked to the parking lot and said our
good-byes, we had a second hug, desperately needed by both of
us. I hadn't felt that accepted since my diagnosis, and it gave me
an enormous sense of peace.

⚬⚬⚬

Not long after we met Sophia, a remarkably similar thing happened to Susan: her physician's assistant mentioned that she had
another patient who had also been infected by Philippe. Within
a couple of weeks, we were visiting this woman, Rhonda, at her
apartment.

Two cats sat curled up into sweet little balls on the beautiful
brocade couch. Everything was sunshine and roses in Rhonda's
apartment, and that suited her personality—she was this sweet,
grandmotherly type, about the last person you'd suspect would
have HIV.

Rhonda had been with Philippe only twice. She saw his mug
shot on the news and went right out to get tested at the health
department. The woman doing her test assured her that she probably had nothing to worry about, and that she'd never seen someone
test positive after such a short affair. Rhonda had left there thinking that she had learned a valuable lesson about protection but
would probably be okay. Instead, she was in exactly the same boat
I was: she had AIDS. Her T cells were even lower than mine: 30.

By that time, Rhonda was in a relationship with a man she thought was very special. She called him immediately to warn him, and his words were, "I guess we're over."

"That was the end of my life," she told us.

Now she was determined to find something good in this awful situation, and she immediately wanted to help protect other women. Because both times she had been with Philippe were in Dallas, that's where she had to file—but they couldn't add her to our case because she'd been with him in June 2005, just over two months before we could prove that he knew he had HIV.

Not that anyone believed that September 2005 was the first time he'd been told. His nonchalant denial in the parking lot of the clinic at the time told me that there was *no way* this man had just received a shocking diagnosis for the first time. But we didn't have access to records before that, no matter how we tried to find them. So Rhonda's report was filed and put on "hold." The detectives completed the paperwork and said they'd hang on to it in case any new information came to light—though I had a sinking feeling that what they really meant was, "We're going to store this in a dark filing cabinet forever." But at least she would be allowed to speak during the sentencing phase of the trial, assuming we got a conviction.

Nena, our North African "sister," also decided to file a report in Dallas after all, surprising us. She, too, couldn't be added to our case, but we liked knowing that there was a backup option in case we didn't get a conviction. He could be tried again in Dallas if we could dig up the right records.

Of course, not everyone approved of what we were doing: the ghouls of Padieu kept coming. I got a letter in the mail from Philippe's old lover Margaret Thomas—the one who, way back when, had advised me not to lend him any money. Appropriately enough, she had written it on Halloween. Her request was simple: the "reasonable thing to do" was for me to drop all the charges against Philippe—because the whole thing was my fault for not protecting myself.

Of course, he had put her up to it. They were his words. He was standing behind the curtains and pulling all the strings.

After I shared the letter with Susan, we decided to pull the curtain back for Margaret. We called and talked to her for more than an hour in what was, to say the least, a bizarre conversation. She revealed quite a bit of information to us: she wasn't giving him money, she said, but she was searching for expert witnesses to prove that he didn't transmit HIV to us . . . even though he gave her herpes and he told her that we were all swingers!

He told her I was behind the whole thing and that I could cancel it as easy as falling off a log. She said both she and Nikki were HIV-negative, and in May of that year, his CD4 had been 450 (again, normal range is 500–1500). The rat bastard; mine was less than one-tenth of that.

By the end of our conversation, she had agreed to rethink things. I'm not sure how much rethinking she did, but she was back in his corner in no time. At least we tried.

⁂

Now that we didn't have to work on getting Philippe arrested anymore, it freed up our time a little to work on other aspects of our case. Susan was the computer whiz, and she did a lot of searching to pass along information to our team, prosecutor Lisa and investigator Samme. They put up with us very well. It must've been a huge pain in the ass to have so many victims on one case. Only once did Lisa reach the point of exasperation and tell us that she had been prosecuting cases for more than twenty years and we needed to just trust them. Yeah, right—that's so easy for me.

We were extremely fortunate to be assigned someone who was open to input and who gave us the leeway to participate in the case. Not all prosecutors would be, I learned. We all formed an attachment to Lisa because she was so patient with us and always answered our questions. She also knew the right things to say. At a conference, our discussion came around to how all this occurred. How was it that this man was able to do this to all these women? Emotionally, it got to the core issue that I have been struggling with since my diagnosis: the "why." Why would he do this to me? Why didn't I see the red flags? Why did it have to be me?

I asked the question through tears. "But why, Lisa, why?" Her response was direct, and it cut off my whining like the swift and precise amputation of a gangrenous limb by a skilled surgeon.

"Diane, there is no 'why,'" she said flatly. And that's probably one of the most comforting things that anyone in the whole shootin' match has ever said to me. It was the first time I remember starting to feel like I was on a journey toward resolution of being stuck in the muck and mire of "why?" "Why" was a quicksand with no way out. Lisa's statement jump-started my healing process.

By far the best thing that came out of our Internet searches was the information about a similar case in Louisiana. The DA's office used a process called phylogenetic analysis to determine not only the strain of HIV but also who gave it to whom. Both Susan and my daughter Stacy found this case online on exactly the same day. Stacy is extremely resourceful and even found some of the court records.

"This is another God thing, isn't it?" I asked her. "This could be the key to proving our case beyond all reasonable doubt." I immediately contacted Lisa and was amazed by how quickly she moved to contact the bioscientist responsible for the procedure and get him on board with our case.

Dr. Michael Metzker was a well-published associate professor of genetics at Baylor University School of Medicine in Houston, senior manager at the Human Genome Sequencing Center at Baylor, and owned his own biotech company called LaserGen. Lisa characterized him as "scary smart."

Dr. Metzker conducted independent research in his laboratory to understand the role of genetic variation in disease and HIV transmission cases. He had about twenty patents awarded or pending with the U.S. Patent and Trademark Office relating to DNA sequencing. In his lab, they had developed cutting-edge technology that would be a tremendous help in scientifically verifying that Philippe was indeed the source of our HIV infection.

It was amazing news, and we were elated, but still a bit cautious. We knew that there were no safe bets in the criminal justice system. Dr. Metzker got a blood sample from Philippe in early fall, and then there seemed to be an eternity between his blood draw and all the rest of ours. Dr. Metzker and his staff were never informed of the name on any of the samples—they were listed by number only. That would then prevent the defense from saying that the lab skewed the analysis because they knew which sample belonged to Philippe. I thought it was a brilliant approach.

Along the way as we waited for results, I developed a brand-new fear, and once it took hold, it gripped me hard:

What if I was the one responsible for all this?

CHAPTER 18

1997

What if I had infected Philippe, and not the other way around, and then he spread it to all these other women? It was an idea that took hold because I was sicker than he was; his numbers were much better than mine, which made me worry that I'd had it longer. I thought about it and thought about it until I just couldn't hold it in anymore and brought it up at one of our support group meetings.

Now that there were more of us needing support, we met more often, both at my house and out at restaurants, at least once a month. We got something wonderful from one another that we couldn't get anywhere else: understanding. As much as other people in our lives wanted to be supportive, they just couldn't fathom what it was like getting this diagnosis and finding out that we were all infected on purpose. In that safe space, we seemed to take turns falling apart. Now it was my turn.

The ladies all assured me that they wouldn't hold it against me even if I was the one who transmitted it first, which was kind of them. But I wasn't sure if I could live with myself, which is why it was extremely lucky that Lauren came into the picture.

✎

As I scooted down Central Expressway on my way to get another of what already seemed like an infinite number of visits to Dr. Sloan, my cell phone rang.

"I saw you zipping down Central, you little speed demon."

"Samme! Hi! Where are you? And I am not speeding!"

"Hey, I've got someone I'd like you to talk to."

"Okay, what's up?"

"Her name is Lauren, and she lives in Ohio, but she used to live in Michigan. She gave me permission to give you her number."

This woman had known Philippe. But how did she find the Collin County DA's office and us? And why? In my wildest imagination I couldn't have dreamed what was about to happen. I pulled to the side of the road and dialed with sweaty palms and nervous fingers. I asked her how I could help her, but the help was coming my way.

"I knew Philippe a long time ago—1997, to be exact. We didn't date for very long, only a few months before I met my husband."

"Yeah?"

"My husband and I moved to Ohio in 2002, and in 2004, we decided to take out life insurance policies."

I had no idea where this was going.

"And we had to get HIV tests. We got rejected for the life insurance policy by mail with a note explaining that my husband's test was negative—but mine wasn't."

What a crazy way to find out.

She continued, "A few weeks ago, I was cleaning out my desk at home because we're moving. I ran across Philippe's business card, and out of curiosity, I Googled him and found out what he had done. I'm so sorry for you and the other women."

"Thanks." I still wasn't getting it. "Did you know who infected you?"

"No, not at the time. I gave the health department the names of my partners, but since I only dated Philippe for a few months, I wasn't sure how to spell his name. But when I saw what he had done, I knew it had to be him. It *had* to be him, Diane. It was Philippe who infected me—in 1997!"

It took a split-second before the tremendousness of that statement hit me.

"Oh my gosh, Lauren. I'm so sorry. Are you okay? How are your numbers?"

"I'm fine now. I'm fine. T cells are 450 and I'm undetectable. But I just wanted to tell you how brave you are, and I'm so glad you nailed the bastard!"

"Lauren, this means he's been infecting women for at least . . ."

"I know. At least ten years. Think of all—"

"—the women who could be out there not knowing," I finished.

"Riiight," she drew out the word, as if she couldn't quite imagine it herself. I was a bucket of emotions. I was appalled at the enormity of it, angry with him for now maybe hundreds of victims who he'd infected. And, quite honestly, relieved: I could finally stop worrying about where the HIV came from. There wasn't a shadow of a doubt in my mind: Philippe Padieu.

It's not my fault. It's not my fault!

It was the only sentence going through my head. *Thank you so much, Lord.*

Lauren described her relationship with Philippe. The beginning was hundreds of miles and years away from where I was when I heard the story.

"When I was twenty-four, I went out with some friends celebrating a birthday, and it was the perfect time in my life. I had a great job and a wonderful group of friends, but my marriage clock was ticking. I had dated in high school and college, even got engaged once, but that night I wasn't interested in finding a relationship. I was out to have a good time with my friends. But, as in a lot of cases, a relationship found me.

"As I was crossing the parking lot of the cute little Italian place we had gone to celebrate, we were approached by a tall, handsome, and well-built guy who walked with an unmistakable confidence. I really loved his dark, curly hair and was instantly attracted to him. He approached all of us and said, 'Are you ladies looking for your car?' in the most genteel manner.

"You know, I was no fool, and I certainly knew better than to talk to strangers. But he seemed so nice. He was soft-spoken and polite. And with the alcohol I'd had that night, he convinced me to give him a chance. After all, I thought, he's too nice to be a predator. And besides, I'm with four other women—what could possibly happen?"

"Sure!" I said.

"We told him we were walking to our car, and he said, 'Please let me drive you. It could be dangerous out here.' And he gave me that convincing smile of his. And that's what started it. Before I was out of his car, he had my phone number. And he didn't waste any time. He called me the very next day and asked me out. We had a lovely time at that little bistro that first night we went out. I really assessed him quickly, sizing him up for red flags, and I came up empty. I asked how old he was and he said 'midthirties.' I had no clue he was actually forty-two, since he could easily pass for thirty-five or thirty-six. All night long it was charm, charm, charm, until he charmed the pants right off of me!"

"Yeah, I know a thing or two about that," I agreed ruefully.

"I made him use a condom that night, and he grumbled but grudgingly agreed. But it didn't take long until he had me convinced that condoms weren't at all necessary. 'After all,' he said, 'I'm clean!'"

Gee, where had I heard that before?

"Red flags started to pile up quickly after that. At first it was just little things, like when he said he would call and didn't. But then there were missed dates as well as missed calls. Philippe was starting to lose this charm, and I was beginning to lose my enthusiasm. The final straw came on New Year's Eve, when we had a date for a 'very special' dance club—those were his words. I was going to turn him down, but my mom reminded me that I hadn't gone dancing in a while and I needed to get some adventure in my life. I have to admit, when he came to the door, I really was glad I had agreed to go. He looked amazing. We chatted all the way to the club. He even apologized for his sometimes erratic behavior. So, you know, I got my hopes up.

"Only then my heart was crushed when we walked into that club. The minute I crossed inside, I saw that his 'special club' was for swingers! Can you believe it?"

She didn't give me a chance to answer.

"'You tricked me!' I screamed. 'I did not!' he said. 'I just thought it would be fun!' 'Fun? *Fun?* It's disgusting and dirty! It's wrong—how could you?' He apologized, but by that time I was home and it was too late. Too late for him, and too late for me, too."

She let out a long sigh.

"I never saw him again. But I always wondered if he was the one who did this to me. And now, four years after my diagnosis, I know."

Because of her HIV, she and her husband had decided not to take the risk of having kids. Women with HIV can have successful pregnancies and avoid transmitting the disease to their babies as long as they're on antiretroviral drugs, their viral load is at undetectable levels, and they don't breast-feed. But there are no guarantees. It hurt to hear about another important thing Philippe had stolen from someone.

Lauren was infected much too early to join our case; we couldn't prove that he knew he had HIV back then. So the DA's office couldn't pay to have her blood sample tested to find out if he was the source of her infection. I hoped we'd find another way.

I was the fourth victim whose blood was sampled, and there were several weeks in between each test. Part of the delay, I later learned, was because the lab had to be wiped down and disinfected from top to bottom after each test to prove there was no possibility of sample contamination.

Once the test was done, there was more waiting. Lots of waiting for analysis and results, which is what the case—and a lot of my sanity—hinged on. We'd occasionally get a juicy tidbit in the meanwhile.

The first was that Philippe was kept isolated from the general population. This was for his "protection" because of his compromised immune system. Essentially, he was in solitary confinement, otherwise known as "the hole" in the state prison system. Some think of it as cruel and unusual punishment, but I thought of it as a good step. During his rare journeys outside the cell, he was forced to wear a mask—supposedly to protect him from communicable diseases in the population. This had, however, an unpleasant side effect for him: It made him easily identifiable, and no doubt he was none too popular. There had been enough publicity that he was very well recognized.

For a man who was so intent on never being alone, he sure had plenty of time to think now. There were no overnight guests. No clubs or bars. No "pet dove" waiting for him and following him around. Just a sick man alone in a barren cell.

The second tidbit was more important. Leah Apple and Frisco PD spokesperson Greg Ward conducted a videotaped jail interview with Philippe in which he gave details about his relationships. And then he confessed. Never did I expect that. Never did I even dare to hope for it. But he did indeed tell them that he knew he was HIV-positive and had lied about it. Still, he showed no remorse.

I think most of us were still wishing for it, even though we all knew deep down that he had no remorse. It's nearly an impossible thing to accept that someone who acted like he loved you was in fact playing a game all along and was intentionally trying to kill you. You want to believe that there's been a mistake—that he didn't really know. That he didn't understand. That he feels terrible knowing that you—you, of all people—got a deadly disease from him. There was always just a little bit of hope in each of us that he would break down and apologize and say he wished he could take it back.

Even though we had our own support group, and I had a licensed counselor personally, I believed that we could all benefit from professional intervention. After all, the diagnosis was relatively new to all of us, and someone who specialized in counseling for women newly diagnosed with HIV might be very helpful. I located an AIDS assistance organization, Legacy Counseling, and found out that they had just formed a women's-only group. When I called to register, the receptionist who answered was very friendly. I mentioned that a few other ladies would also be calling, and that we were all friends because we had the same transmitter in common.

"Oh," she exclaimed. "So there will be more of you joining the other lady that was infected by that guy in Frisco?"

I nearly dropped the phone! I knew she wasn't referring to anyone in our group because they had all asked me to scope things out before they signed up. "Uh . . . yeah," I stammered. "How long has the group been meeting?"

"It's scheduled every two weeks, but they've only met once."

I knew better than to overstep my bounds by asking for more info. We knew of ten Philippe victims so far who'd been diagnosed—this would make eleven. Several of us went to the next session, but there was only one other person there aside from the counselor: a tall, nice-looking black woman. Susan and I glanced at each other with raised eyebrows. Could this be number eleven? But soon enough we found out that this woman had been diagnosed more than fifteen years before in a state Philippe had never lived in. Damn! I wanted to meet this mystery woman.

I attended regularly for three or four more sessions. But the majority of the time, the rest of the group consisted only of various combinations of our own support group. After the next couple of sessions, I inquired about the mystery woman. But the counselor said she had only seen her the one time—the one before I started.

Double damn! I thought. *Another unknown, just like the woman who committed suicide. Hope this one is okay.* I gave the counselor my information to pass along, with a message to the woman that I'd love to hear from her, but that didn't bring her forward. We were sure she was out there, somewhere. It was frustrating. I wanted to help, but she didn't want my help.

I wished she had known what we were finding out: that the sisterhood changed everything.

It did for Rhonda, who had felt so alone before she met us.

"You women saved my life," she said one day, in tears. "I don't know what I would do without you."

It was a sentiment echoed by all of us. We were all growing closer and more thankful for this life-affirming group. Many of us were finding ways to move forward, and we all celebrated that. Rhonda, in fact, was about to get married and move to Las Vegas.

My first romantic "move forward" was a total surprise. After a seminar one night at my school, the presenter and I went out for a drink to share karate war stories. I thought we were just hanging out, but he evidently read things differently. When we got to my car, he planted a kiss on me that made the angels light a cigarette.

Immediately I went into panic mode. *What do I do? Where is this going? What if he wants to take it a step further . . . and what do I do if he does? How do I tell him? When do I tell him? What do I say? Abort mission—abort mission!*

As the leader of the group, not only was I the main interface between the other ladies and anyone we needed to trade info with (like the police, investigator, DA, counselor, and so on), but I also took responsibility for setting up our monthly group meetings. When it hit me that all of us would need some help with who, what, when, where, and how to disclose, I found a great resource. At UT Southwestern, there was a division specifically devoted to educating newly diagnosed people living with HIV about disclosure. It was a five-week course, four hours per week, and it was held at their location in Dallas. But after I spoke with the educator, she kindly agreed to do a class just for us. She and her assistant would come to my house for group meetings.

The program was called Healthy Relationships and it was a very thorough and enlightening program. We talked about the necessity for disclosure with friends, family, and intimate partners. I learned that there was a choice about when and how to disclose, but in my mind there was no choice about how I was going to handle my diagnosis with the new guy. I couldn't bear the thought of transmitting this vile disease to anyone, ever!

So on our second date, after dinner and on the way to the car, I blurted out the circumstances of my status. Fortunately, he didn't run away screaming or say it didn't matter and then disappear. I was prepared for either one. What he did was take me in his arms and hold me and tell me it was okay and he wasn't afraid. He had someone close to him who had died of AIDS, so he was very savvy about transmission. It was such a huge relief to be accepted like that. And it went a long way toward helping begin the healing process. Eventually I found that he wasn't right for me, but it was a great step to learn that not everyone would disappear. Maybe I wouldn't be alone forever after all.

Susan, on the other hand, had gone on a dating website meant specifically for people with HIV/AIDS, and she had started seriously dating someone. She was so happy, and I was so happy for her—until August.

August was when Susan told us she was moving to Utah.

CHAPTER 19

20/20

I know Susan didn't have to stick around Texas for my sake. People have lives. They move on. They follow their hearts. But I was sure going to miss her.

We had a support group filled with women who really loved and leaned on one another, but Susan was extra special to me. She was my steadfast partner in all this—the one I confided in the most, and the one who was literally by my side for some of the most nail-biting, crazy moments. We'd rifled through garbage together! And yeah, we'd had a fight, but she was my sister.

This just sucked.

We had a big going-away party for her, which was nice, but sad. Her boyfriend was from Utah, and they had an Internet romance followed by a visit, and then he swooped in to take her home with him. It was really fast, and I wondered if she was in over her head. But just like that, her house was on the market and she was packed up and leaving.

I've been abandoned again, I thought as I trudged around miserably. *Utah. Where the hell is Utah, even? What good things happen in Utah? Might as well be in another country.* Suddenly, I was irrationally angry with the entire state.

It's not like we wouldn't see Susan again. Of course, we still had the trial coming up. The original date was in September, but having a bit of experience with the court system, I knew darn well it wasn't actually going to start in September. Dates get pushed back over and over—that's the norm. I warned the ladies that we were in for a wait again, and that I wouldn't be at all surprised if it got pushed back until after the December holidays.

August did bring one redeeming bit of news, though. The DNA results came back, and it was official: Philippe was the source of all of our infections, with nearly 100 percent certainty. I was emotionally off the hook, and he was legally on it.

∽∾

Our victim advocate, Tonia, attended a conference where Andy Kahan spoke. Andy worked for the city of Houston running the crime victims' assistance office, where he was somewhat of a legend. Scores of crime victims sung his praises, saying that he was there for them at all hours, that he helped them navigate the legal system, and that he got personally invested in their cases. In addition, he was an expert on murderabilia: the sale of collectibles associated with a murder—when murderers in well-known cases sell their artwork or other odd items for money (like hair or fingernail clippings . . . I know, right? Ugh!)—literally profiting from their heinous crimes. Because of that, he had appeared on numerous television shows.

Andy and his attorney friend suggested that we should try to get more media attention on this case, particularly because Philippe had lived in multiple cities and there were so many potential victims out there who didn't know yet. We'd already had a lot of media coverage, but the only in-depth reports were local. Andy was talking much bigger—he had friends in high places. It was a lot to process, but Susan and I thought it was a great idea.

Andy and friend also offered to be our guides through the whole legal and media process, a wonderfully generous offer. We spent lots of time in our support group talking about problems with the victims' compensation fund, and Andy offered to take over on that front. He also spoke with the health department and told them to expect an influx of new cases because of our upcoming media—but he was met with a lukewarm reception. The director said that they felt the public had been adequately informed and they didn't need to do anything else.

I still don't know why they resisted us; the case seemed to fit exactly what the department was all about!

The week after Susan left for Utah, I met with *20/20* producer Shana Druckerman, an unstoppable woman in her late twenties. Andy had advised me that she came very highly recommended, but I was still a bit cautious—I wasn't sure of the angle they would use on the story, so I was looking for some guarantees from the beginning. And the first thing out of Shana's mouth after we exchanged greetings was, "I want to assure you, Diane, that on our program we will do everything we can to ensure your anonymity. We can use disguises and pseudonyms to keep your name out of the report."

Brilliant! We had been seated for all of three minutes and she had already won my trust. I found her very easy to talk to. She was straightforward, but she also knew how to empathize without sounding syrupy. Her plan was to film a group meeting, get our individual stories, and have most of the show "in the can" before trial—which had already been rescheduled for November. They would then get the trial and do a final interview with Philippe.

Shana asked me to contact all the group members to see which ones would be willing to go on the show. The only one I knew for sure that would do it was Susan. Laura wouldn't, but she really didn't belong on television anyway. We were having enough trouble with her in the group; she still showed up in disguise and took notes while everyone else talked, which made some of the women very edgy. When we told her so, she stopped coming.

To my surprise, most of the women were willing to be filmed as long as they could be disguised. Including Lauren, the woman who was infected by Philippe in 1997—which meant it would be my first time meeting her in person. Laura, on the other hand, was convinced the show was a conspiracy to help Philippe.

My next two months were filled with considerable angst. The school was beginning to be affected by the economic downturn. I had to have a hysterectomy because my body still wouldn't clear the cervical dysplasia. And I was in a serious wrestling match with myself about whether or not to disclose on camera.

As I had learned in the Healthy Relationships class, disclosure is a very complicated issue. We even drew a chart listing pros and cons of disclosure versus nondisclosure in various scenarios. But the class was focused primarily on friends, family, and romantic relationships. They weren't talking about disclosing on national television! I had my girls to consider, my school, and how I might handle backlash from the general public.

Courage is doing what's right even though you might be afraid, I remembered. And I was certainly afraid. I feared losing my business and being thought a laughingstock and a fool—or a slut or a desperate old woman. I feared a whole lot of other things that were so scary I couldn't even identify them.

I talked to my counselor. I wrote in a journal. I talked to Debbie and my top black belts. I talked to the girls and my mom (who were very nervous about the idea). And by the time Shana pulled up in front of my house with a huge black camera on her shoulder, I had made my decision and there was no turning back:

I was going to do it. Real name, no disguise, just me—in front of God and everybody. Why? Because it was the right thing to do. I was going to stand proud and I was going to stand strong. I felt it was more important to be transparent for the public good than to hide for my own comfort and safety.

I believed the show would be more powerful that way, and that I could make a small dent in the stigma wall. I thought it would bring attention to women who could potentially be victims or were already victims of Philippe or other knowingly HIV-positive men. I wanted women, especially those over fifty, to know that it could just as easily happen to them. And I wanted people to be reminded that it *can* kill you if you don't know you have it. I was resolute. I squared my shoulders and I looked right into that camera. We filmed at my home and the school, and spent a lot of time just talking, too. And you know what? It made me feel better. I still had to go through the trial as Barbara Sutherland because that's how it was filed, but once this show aired, there would be no more hiding. In the Texas legal system Barbara Sutherland was the victim, but I was Diane Reeve—survivor!

Before she left, Shana met with Philippe to try to convince him to be interviewed. I couldn't wait to hear what she had to say! On her way to the airport, she dished. He was pale and thin, she said, but she could tell how handsome he must've been before all this had happened. He wouldn't speak, though. She'd try again once the trial was over.

◌◍

We had a Christmas party at my house for all the women. Sophia suggested that we make tamales, and we were all really looking forward to having a group project. We did it just like Sophia's mother and grandmother had done in Mexico City years ago. She explained that it was an all-day deal, and I had to work that night, so we started around noon. She had already cooked three different meats for filling: chicken, beef, and pork. When she walked in the door and I caught a whiff of the delicious aromas, I knew it would be a great afternoon.

We patted out the masa in the cornhusks, and after filling them with one of the delicious meats, we would roll them up, fold them over, and stack them in a big pan for baking. We talked, laughed, tasted, and cooked. And before I knew it, it was almost 5:00 PM and we weren't even half done! Boy, Sophia wasn't kidding when she said it was an all-day project. I left them all at the kitchen table after we took a few pictures, and when I got home from work at 9:00, they were just finishing up. There were tamales everywhere! Sophia had brought a bazillion plastic bags, so we filled each one with a half dozen tamales, and I think we all ended up with about three dozen tamales apiece. Another reminder of how special this sisterhood was.

The trial had been rescheduled for the end of February, so the *20/20* shoot was planned for February 20 and 21 in New York City with the six of us women who agreed to appear. But then the trial date was pushed back again—this time until May 19. The more I thought about it, the worse it got. I was angry and depressed that they'd added yet another three months to the longest wait of my life. The trip to New York would be a good diversion.

The morning of the shoot, I got up at 5:00 AM to get ready so I could pick up Maddie and get us to the airport. I had barely slept three hours. When we arrived, a car picked us up and took Sophia and Maddie straight to ABC headquarters. Because we were shooting that evening, they needed to get their disguises done. Since I was going "au naturel," I got to go straight to the hotel and take a brief nap before I had to get my makeup done and then head to the W Hotel on Park Avenue. Our driver regaled us with stories about how he drove Barbara Walters all the time. It felt surreal.

We had a forty-five-minute wait before the shoot, and Shana started by ordering us all drinks. While the cameramen were getting set up, Maddie downed four drinks. *This isn't going to be easy*, I worried. But it really was. Today was a "B-roll" day, which meant that there were no interviews and no pressure—basically, our job that night was just to have a good meal and enjoy one another's company while cameras rolled for a while. Eventually, the cameramen went home and we got to just stay and chat as long as we wanted (well—as long as we wanted considering we had to be up and ready for our interviews early the next morning!).

Lauren fit right in with the rest of us, and we all had quite a wonderful time—laughing and talking like old friends, which, by now, we were. We had already lived a lifetime together.

Andy and a friend came in as we were winding down to give us a rallying pep talk. "Just be yourselves," he told us. "You're going to do great tomorrow! What you're doing is monumental. It's going to make a difference for so many people. This is very brave, and people are going to love you."

He was like our own personal cheerleader, which was just what we needed. Despite the fact that we were all having a good time, I'm sure I'm not the only one who was worried about what they would ask us and how this would all play out on television. It wasn't easy to fall asleep that night.

The ABC building was somewhat plain-looking and obscure, but inside it was swarming with activity, a big crew of people rushing around madly. Cameramen, soundmen, makeup artists, producers, consultants. We headed out to a nearby college to do the interviews.

At about 1:00 PM, Elizabeth Vargas arrived with her makeup artist. She met everyone personally, and I liked her immediately—she was warm and genuine, and took a real interest in each of us.

We started shooting at 1:30. The women sat in a semicircle, and everyone laughed when they made me sit on a pillow to even out the height difference between Susan and me. The questions came fast and furious: "How aggressively did he pursue a sexual relationship?" "Did any of you ask him to wear a condom?" "Did he admit to being unfaithful?" The questions were on target and professional, and the sympathy was evident in her reactions. Each of us got to tell our own stories, and it was very emotional for most of us. We talked about the heartbreaking situations that led us to Philippe and the aftermath of what it's like living with HIV.

"The worries pile one on top of another until there's no room left," said Maddie, echoing what we all felt.

Elizabeth was very well prepared—she knew our story to pinpoint accuracy, and when we finished, she and everyone else had at least a tear or two on their cheeks. It felt good to get it out. Someone had the presence of mind to get a group shot of us with Elizabeth—it's autographed and hanging in my office.

Now it was out of our hands. In short order, I was going to be exposed in a way I'd never previously imagined. As we said our good-byes, I gave Elizabeth a copy of my new favorite book, which perfectly expressed how I was feeling: *Well-Behaved Women Seldom Make History*, by Laurel Thatcher Ulrich.

CHAPTER 20

Almost There

As exciting as the trip was, I was just about flat the first day back. The hectic pace and travel knocked me right out. It was so frustrating to not be *me* anymore. Normal me could've picked right up and said, "Where next?" Me with AIDS was a totally different person. It made me feel so disabled. I clung to two hopes: that the medication would really start to work soon and that things would feel much better after the stress of the trial was over.

As of the end of March, the prosecution had submitted six pages of witnesses. Defense: zero. One of the reasons the trial kept being postponed was because the defense kept claiming they couldn't find an expert witness—which wasn't exactly true; it was more likely they couldn't find an expert witness who would go up against Dr. Metzker. But this time was different. At the last postponement, Judge Henderson mandated that the defense must have their expert witness in place by May 1 or we would go to trial anyway. So they were down to one last-ditch effort.

Shana from 20/20 called to touch base in April, telling me that she was going in to talk to the judge about allowing cameras in the courtroom. That might not seem like a big deal elsewhere, but in Collin County, Texas, it was a very big deal. Not even in the infamous 1980 case—where Candace Montgomery was accused of murdering her best friend, Betty Gore, with an ax—was there such a big deal about cameras in the courtroom. Books were written and a movie was produced on that case, but no cameras were allowed in court. When Shana told me what she planned to do, I was rooting for her, but I didn't get my hopes up. Imagine how stunned I was to find out that she got her way. I swear to God, that woman worked magic!

A week later, assistant district attorney Lisa King sent out requests for individual meetings with all of us—and that's when I really knew it was real. We were really going to trial this time. It sent me into a tailspin. I was happy that this long journey was finally coming to an end after more than two years. But I was as nervous as a cat in a roomful of rocking chairs. The what-ifs surrounded me day and night, like a heavy fog that just wouldn't lift. It weighed me down so much. Logically, I knew that the case was out of my hands and in the hands of a couple of extremely well-prepared and expert DAs. But having been so heavily involved from the start—or really before the start, if you consider the HPV phone calls a dry run—I felt that the outcome of the trial rested on my shoulders. It didn't; it was just my brain overacting, trying to center all the turmoil.

All of us were stressed out. Sophia had to take a week off from work because she was so frantic. Maddie, while in Michigan visiting her elderly father, fell and broke her wrist in two places. It took a good while to get it set, so she was double-stressed. She was sure her mental state had contributed to the fall.

When I went in for my three-month checkup with Dr. Sloan, my T cell count was higher but, of course, not as high as I would've liked. I was really insulted that my body wasn't cooperating in the way I thought it should. I wanted it to magically heal itself because that's what I do. I'm a warrior, and I go to war and fight and win. It's that black belt mantra of having an indomitable spirit.

But my body had a mind of its own. I talked to Dr. Sloan about the stress of the trial and how I was afraid it would contribute to my low T cell count. In his usual calm manner, he reassured me that I would be okay. I think it took me about a million times to hear him say that before I started believing it. If they found Philippe not guilty, I was sure I wouldn't be able to handle it.

And then my own stress got the better of me. A year before, at one of the infinite number of visits to the gynecologist, a routine bone density scan revealed that I had osteopenia. Osteopenia is a precursor to osteoporosis, or severe bone loss, and for me, it was a side effect of my HIV medications, so I had to start taking calcium supplements. Ugh—one more thing to swallow. It might've helped, but it didn't keep me from doing stupid stuff.

At the end of April I was rehanging a few pictures in my bedroom. Since they were hanging on either side of the dresser, I just climbed up on the dresser top so I could lean over and easily hang them. It was way too much trouble to go to the garage, get a ladder, set it up on one side, hang one picture, move to the other side, and so on. I didn't have the time for all that. I wasn't worried about hoisting myself up three and a half feet off the ground onto the top of the dresser. I'd been climbing all my life. (When you're five feet tall, you do that.) Plus, I had great balance and strength because I'd done karate for the past twenty years. But this time I overestimated my abilities.

When I reached down to pick up the second painting, it was heavier than I'd anticipated. The weight pulled me off balance and down I went. Despite falling headfirst, I was still able to get my feet underneath me. Not only did I save the painting, I landed the dismount just like a gymnast after a final vault off the balance beam! The one slight problem was the osteopenia and my landing slightly heavier on my right foot than on my left. It shattered the egg-shaped bone in my right heel. In fact, it almost smooshed it flat.

I set the painting down as I was rolling around on the floor, hollering like a wild banshee in pain. I mean real, *serious* pain. I've broken a bunch of bones in my life: my ankle, my nose (twice), my arm, and my big toe. But that heel fracture was the worst pain from a break by at least five times.

After thirty minutes of my screaming, poor Tiger had cowered under the bed and I finally got myself together. I got a broom and a mop and used them as makeshift crutches until my daughter Stacy showed up with a brand-new pair of real crutches. What an amazing child, God love her. Even though she was wrestling with my decision to disclose nationally, and exhausted from working two jobs, she still went to the trouble of bringing me those crutches at 11:30 at night.

The next day, my orthopedist slapped the x-ray up on the box and shook his head.

"Well, you really broke that bad boy," he said, with all the sympathy of a casual passerby. "We'll take another x-ray in six weeks." He was so matter-of-fact. I was totally unimpressed with his reaction.

I went home to take a Vicodin and lick my wounds. The crutch deal was a bitch, and it made me really irritable. I mean, more so than usual. It's no piece of cake to walk on your hands. And we were so close to the start of the trial.

◈

By that time, the defense had hired a private investigator named Theresa. I looked her up online, and it looked like she was one-half of a two-woman agency. She hit Maddie first.

"She's not so bad," Maddie told me. "She admitted that she was 'torn' about investigating for the defense. Then she gave me some books and materials about women in abusive relationships."

"Seriously?"

I liked knowing that they'd accidentally hired someone with half a conscience. Still, I knew not to trust anyone working for the defense. Maddie told me the woman drove a yellow Jeep, so I told my staff at the school to be on the lookout. Several days later in the late afternoon, there was a knock at my door. I looked out the front window and there it sat, leering at me with its big headlight eyes on its yellow Jeep face. I knew it was the PI. Tiger barked once and then the doorbell rang.

"Diane, it's Theresa Jackson, and I wonder if I could speak with you for just a few minutes?"

"I know who you are and I have nothing to say," I said through the closed door. I couldn't believe it, but she actually left without further attempts at conversation. She was even sent to Rusty's house—which I thought was a really low blow. Why would my ex-husband have any relevance to this case? He wouldn't have anything bad to say about me, but I sure didn't want him to have to endure a witness testimony. Luckily, he wasn't home.

Whether she gave up or the state quit paying, I'm not sure, but none of us ever heard from Theresa again. I wondered what she really thought of us.

I was afraid to get my hopes up as I headed to the courthouse for my trial preparation meeting. We'd been dealing with post-ponements for eight months, and I couldn't bear the thought of putting my sanity on hold any longer.

Lisa and her cocounsel Curtis Howard were seated at a large conference table, in a room with all glass walls. They grilled me endlessly. We started with my witness statement, all about how the relationship began, what we did in the bedroom, the visits to Dr. Checo, and the incident with Brittani. Imagine the highlights reel of your most embarrassing life moments playing in the background as you have to explain exactly what sexual quirks your boyfriend had and how that all played out—and then how you acted when you found out that you weren't the only one fulfilling his desires. I felt like I'd been run over by a train, but I knew that it was a piece of cake compared to what I would face on the witness stand, so I was grateful for the trial run.

I learned that they planned on flying Lauren in for the trial, so that if there was a punishment phase, she would testify. They explained a bit about the district court judge, Curt Henderson. He was a no-nonsense, push-things-through kind of guy. Lisa also let me know in no uncertain terms that she wasn't happy about the ABC thing. She strictly forbade me to have any contact with Shana until the trial was over. She just didn't want anyone blowing her case. I really couldn't blame her—I didn't want anything blowing it either.

Then she warned me that I couldn't mention Philippe's prison record at trial because it would prejudice the jury and cause a mistrial. If it came to a punishment phase, then I could let loose. I vowed to be guarded, though it seemed so unfair that the jury wasn't allowed to know that Philippe had a criminal history.

And then I got the pep talk. "Just answer truthfully," Lisa said. "Don't worry—you're strong and you'll do fine." I hoped so. I had been praying for that night and day.

Before we ended, they also told me that they were issuing a subpoena for Nena's testimony in punishment as well. And that sounded fine as frogs' hair to me. Who wouldn't have sympathy for a beautiful yet somewhat crippled woman who had MS and now, to make matters worse, HIV?

At Lisa's request, I was the one who prepared Nena to receive the subpoena. I called Susan first for advice about how to present it because Susan had a way of smoothing over ruffled feathers—and there was usually feather-ruffling when Nena and I were in the same room. We liked and appreciated each other, but our chemistry was just off most times. Nena wasn't a native English speaker, and at a time like this, I wondered just how fluent her English was. The complexities of the trial, and how the court process worked in the United States, were also a big barrier. At first she didn't understand what it meant to do a punishment phase deposition. She was not only furious but had a major meltdown at the thought of appearing in public as someone living with HIV. The conversation went like this:

"Nena, Lisa King really needs you to do a deposition so we can capture your statement and impact as part of the punishment phase of the trial."

"Absolutely not. I want nothing to do with this."

"Listen, this will be your one opportunity to get back at that sorry sack of shit."

Nena had a very strong personality, an in-your-face, tell-you-what-to-do battle-ax. Probably a little like me, if I'm being completely honest. She expressed her anger toward Philippe more openly than anyone else in the group (I was a close second), and she was extremely convincing. So I appealed to her sense of vengeance, but I knew it was also healthy for us—the best way for a victim to get closure is to be able to speak out about it and have a hand in the justice system. After some more back-and-forth, and with Susan weighing in with her support, Nena finally capitulated. Gradually, we helped her see the value in testifying—to add just one more nail in his coffin.

Her faith was a hiccup, though. She refused to be seen in open court because she didn't want to ruin her chance of ever going back to her native country, so Lisa and Curtis agreed to video-tape her testimony before the trial. Lisa reasoned it would help the case but also keep Nena's stress level down and hopefully not make her MS symptoms worse. She wouldn't have to face the jury, but she would have to face Philippe.

The huge elephant in the room was the prosecution's plan to air all our dirty laundry before the defense could. The more we all talked about it, the madder we got. Tonia, Andy, and friend had all told us previously that our past sexcapades were not relevant.

So one last time, we banded together to fight for our honor. We knew the prosecutors were in our corner, we just didn't agree with part of their strategy. Tonia walked beside me up the ramp to the courthouse and we talked about it. As I hobbled on my crutches, I was struggling physically, but the potential embarrass-ment and humiliation was really what bothered me. Having my sex life laid out in front of everybody seemed like a punishment to me. And then Tonia said something that really struck a chord: she told me that she knew that it felt like we were being victimized all over again.

"That's why I could never do what you're doing," she told me. "I've already made up my mind that if any assault ever happens to me, I would never report it. I just don't want to risk having to go through what you're about to go through—it's just not worth it."

Well, I was right there with her, but at this point I was already on the train halfway down the track. I just didn't want my drawers hanging out the window.

The conference lasted an hour or so—Susan and I stating our position, Lisa and Curtis explaining that they had to get the jump on bringing up our past. Their thought was that if we tried to hide it and the defense brought it out first, it could turn the jury against us for hiding stuff. I understood it all, and I knew it was really out of my control. I also appreciated them taking the time to explain the strategy. They really didn't have to tell us squat. But I left feeling like in order for things to go right at trial, I had to make a sacrifice. Of course, so did all the other women. None of us were happy about it. I was particularly angry because of the outrageous double standard women fight every day. A man fires orders and he's a leader—a woman fires orders and she's a demanding bitch. And in the realm of sexuality it gets infinitely worse. Men who are Lotharios are sexy, desirable, cool, and admired. A woman who acts on the same sexual desires as a man is dirty, a slut, a whore, or worse. Women have no acceptable outlet for their sexuality. So accepting the prosecution's strategy and agreeing to let them grill us on our sex lives was like climbing miles of barbed-wire fence to get free from hell. Which was worse?

I thought it through. Either I could stay in hell, or I could get ripped open and torn up but at the end of the day be free from fear and injustice for the first time in a very long while. *So, okay, I'll climb the damn barbed-wire fence.* I was tired of living in hell.

But the meeting wasn't a total loss. Lisa said Philippe had tried to get Jane Logan to testify for him, but she was having no part of it. House had filed a perfunctory motion for a change of venue— fat chance! And speaking of fat chance, Philippe had written his emissary, Margaret Thomas, the most shockingly chauvinistic letter: he told her that she needed to "lose weight, trim down," and send him a picture of herself in a bikini. And the slime just kept on oozing. But the tidbit I liked the best was that he said, "I'm a fighter, and I'll fight this to the death."

Oh yeah, dickwad, I hope so. I really, really hope so.

Nena's MS symptoms caused her to be hospitalized for a week, so her deposition had to be postponed. On May 13, less than one week from trial, I drove to Nena's apartment to get her to the McKinney courthouse. As I headed down the tollway toward her town, my anxiety level began to stealthily creep into my brain. Would Nena back out? Would she break down? Would her health hold out? Would her testimony be damaging, and would he be found guilty? All these thoughts tumbled through my head like clothes on the spin cycle of the wash.

Nena was ready when I got there, and I was again struck by how beautiful her apartment looked, filled with exotic artifacts that reminded her of her home.

Just getting her into the car was a challenge because of her MS and my broken heel. By the time I left my house in Plano, fought southbound traffic to get to Addison, then headed north to McKinney, it took two and a half hours just to get there. The victim advocate for Collin County met us at the ramp with a wheelchair for Nena. She offered me one, too, but I declined. *I don't need no stinkin' wheelchair*, I said to myself.

I was placed in a small conference room just outside the glass double doors to the courtroom, and as I walked there, I caught a glimpse of what was happening inside. Nena was sworn in on the witness stand. Old, stately judge Curt Henderson sat straight ahead in the judge's chair. To my eye, he looked conservative, but kind. Nena was immediately to the left in the witness stand. Only five feet away was the defense table where Philippe and Public Defender House would sit to watch. House, in his late sixties, was a bit stooped over. He was heavyset but moved fluidly. He had dark gray hair with some silver highlights and was a little bald on top—a typical grandfather type. Even from a distance, he gave the impression of being easy to get along with.

Because a defendant has the right to face his accusers, Philippe was in the room. He would not have an opportunity to speak though, only listen. When I volunteered to get Nena to McKinney, this was something that had never occurred to me—that I might have to see Philippe. Not yet, though. In this brief glimpse, I didn't spot him.

It was a real zoo that day. Halfway through Nena's testimony, Jane Logan came storming past me and into the courtroom. She was wearing a bright blue suit that looked almost neon—or maybe it was the sparks that were flying off her head. She interrupted the testimony. There was a heated discussion with Curtis and maybe House, too. I found out later that she had been subpoenaed as a defense witness and wanted a pseudonym. Plus, she was trying to call in a lawyer favor so she wouldn't have to testify. Guess she was scared her husband would find out—damn straight!

She got shut down on the pseudonym deal. Witnesses don't get anonymity—only victims. Unfortunately, she did manage to duck the witness gig. At least I got a little satisfaction that her world had blown up, if only for a short while.

Halfway through her testimony, Nena had a major meltdown and broke into tears, so everyone took a break. I didn't envy her. I knew that would soon be me. During the break, I gathered the nerve to stand just outside the conference room. I could see what had to be Philippe through the glass doors, though I wasn't sure at first. Before I could duck back into the room, he stood up and glanced over at me. We had a good ten-second stare down—and he was the one who blinked.

I was aghast. If I hadn't seen the jumpsuit and the cuffs on his scrawny wrists and ankles, there's no way I would've ever believed it was him. Philippe was a good six feet one and about 200 pounds when we were together. But the guy staring at me was stooped over by two or three inches, couldn't have weighed more than 145 pounds, and the bones in his cheeks stuck out like a skeleton. His hair was frizzy and long enough to cover his ears, but the frizziness made it stand away from his head, giving him a triangle-head look. He looked worse than horrible—sick and tired and old, but above all that, he looked like the Grim Reaper. To me, it was as if the veneer had been melted away, like the shell on an M&M. And once it was gone, the true monster in all his ugliness was revealed. He looked like pure evil. It was sickening. *This was the man I had loved?*

Nena came out soon afterward and she was exuberant. She knew she had done the right thing and could talk of nothing else all the way back to her apartment. She felt free, and vindicated. I longed to join her in those feelings. But first, I had a barbed-wire fence to climb. I was to be in court by midmorning on Wednesday the 20th, after the jury had been selected on Tuesday.

Right before the trial, I learned that the defense had subpoenaed my ex-husband Rusty as a witness. What assholes! He was in London on business, so they didn't get him, but I almost wished they had. They were banking on animosity, but I knew Rusty would tell them I was a good person. I also learned that Samme had just had knee surgery for an ACL tear, so she would be in a boot for the trial. *Great!* I thought. *We'll win the sympathy vote!* Maddie in a sling with a cast on her arm, me on crutches with a cast on my leg, and Samme in a walking boot, all in addition to the video of Nena in a wheelchair: we would look like the walking wounded. I just hoped that that would only be the appearance and not the reality.

Philippe turned down the plea deal prosecutors offered him: thirty years. "I'll be dead by then!" he told his attorney.

One could only hope.

CHAPTER 21

Trials and Tribulations

We weren't allowed to be at the courthouse the day the jury was selected. I tried to make things business as usual that day, but I couldn't think of anything except what was going on in that courtroom. Anxiety and sheer terror had permeated me so deeply that I was taking Xanax like Tic Tacs all day, and at bedtime as well. I wasn't eating or sleeping.

Wednesday morning, May 20, we were asked to be at the courthouse by 10:00 AM. My girls came to see me off, and Debbie came to the courthouse to be my official hand-holder. I put my crutches up against the wall next to the comfy couch where I awaited Philippe's fate (and mine) in the victim advocate room.

I had been to that room before, during trial prep, but today, with a lot more people, it seemed smaller. There was a little waiting room outside the door of the victim advocate room where I could see two victim advocates sitting at desks behind the windows.

One was the woman, who I had met when she brought out the wheelchair the day Nena had videotaped her deposition. We all liked her a lot because she was always checking to make sure we had everything we needed. She even brought in homemade chocolate chip cookies, the quintessential comfort food—what a blessing! I wished we could've asked her for an instantaneous guilty verdict.

The rest of the room was comfy and cozy; someone had really tried to make it as warm as possible. There was a couch and two chairs with a coffee table and a flat-screen TV. A bookcase acted as a room divider, and there was a large kitchen in an adjacent room with a small dining table, fridge, and microwave.

There were lots of snacks available, but none of us could stomach anything. Brittani and her new fiancé would only come as far as the little anteroom. She was polite as I passed through, but I could tell she was still afraid of me. I guess she was smarter than she looked.

I wondered if Lisa had been forced to subpoena Brittani's ex-husband Eddie as a witness. Lisa had mentioned that Eddie had been so furious he had threatened Brittani. He told her he would be there for every minute of her testimony so he could "get the scoop" on her sexcapades with Philippe. A subpoena was the only way to keep him out of the courtroom, since no witness can be present while another witness testifies. As angry as I had been all along, I couldn't imagine how pissed Eddie must have been.

Laura Sumner was sitting at the little conference table when I hobbled in. I had not seen Laura in quite a while because she had stopped going to our meetings when we questioned her for taking notes. Seeing her now was heartbreaking; she rivaled Philippe for who had deteriorated the most.

Maddie said it best: "She looks like she's just been dug up." She was beyond thin; her face was gaunt and her body frail. She looked like if you touched her, she would just fall apart. Her long hair was totally gray and so thin you could see her entire scalp through the broken strands. Despite our advances and support, she kept to herself the entire time. We tried to make small talk, like offering her coffee or lunch. But she just sat with her shoulders slumped and a blank stare, slowly shaking her head from side to side. I worried how Lisa would handle her on the stand.

Lisa came in to reassure all of us—as if that were possible—and to give us an idea of when our testimony was expected. The jury consisted of eight men and four women, plus an alternate. I would have preferred more women, but hoped those on the jury would be fair to us nonetheless. The first witness would be Dr. Checo—verifying that Philippe knew he was HIV-positive and had been told to use protection—then our first investigator, Tom Presley. Of the victims, Susan would be up first. Lisa told Susan to be prepared to be called in after about two hours, and then Brittani would follow shortly after that. She advised me that I would be up right after lunch, and then Dr. Kuo, another physician Philippe had visited. Then it would be Laura, Maddie, and Sophia. I popped a couple of Xanax for good measure. It didn't touch my anxiety.

I knew I couldn't talk to Susan about her testimony and that was killing me. Everyone else was nervous as well, and we all handled it in different ways. Sophia had agreed to pick up Maddie, and they argued all the way to the courthouse, then all the time in the victim advocate room. Part of the problem was that the room, although it was rather large, was very crowded, just from our case alone. Susan's boyfriend and daughter were there, along with the rest of us, Debbie, and sometimes Tonia. Tonia was a godsend. She held our hands and spent a good bit of time talking one or the other of us down off the ledge.

Then there were the others in the room: a family of six or seven connected with a different case. The dad struck up a conversation with me by asking if we were those women who "put that HIV guy in jail." Without waiting for an answer, he went into a tirade about "what an ass that guy is," and I finally politely excused myself. I really was in no mood to chat about it with strangers. But to make matters worse, I could hear him loudly discussing with his family what he had seen in the news about our case— "Yeah, those women there? They all got HIV from this French guy! He was screwing around with all of them at the same time!" Before I blew a gasket, I had the good sense to go get our victim advocate to find them another room, mainly because I didn't want to be arrested for duct-taping a stranger's mouth closed. I figured it might look bad for our case. In five minutes, they were ushered to another area. Whew! Everyone was relieved.

While all these shenanigans were going on, Philippe pled "not guilty," and the prosecution made their opening statement. The defense passed, and then Dr. Checo was called to the stand. According to his testimony, September 2005 wasn't the first time he had treated Philippe. The first visit was actually in September 2004, and Philippe had gone back and forth for several months with a recurring diagnosis of chlamydia.

Dr. Checo testified that Philippe had refused an HIV test, stating that he had tested negative the year before. In 2005, when he gave Philippe the news that his HIV test was positive, "he remained passive, maintained eye contact, and had no reaction one way or another."

I hoped the jury would realize that it didn't sound like the first time he had heard that news. He told Dr. Checo that he had multiple sexual partners but had never provided names. The doctor spent thirty-five minutes explaining the critical nature of using protection during any sexual activity, and said that he would give Philippe's name to the health department.

Tom spoke to the jury about the case, then Susan was up. I held my breath for the entire two hours she was on the stand, wondering how she would detail all our detective work and all the horror of these past two years in a compelling but matter-of-fact way for the jury. When she got back to our room, Susan looked at me and rolled her eyes.

"What was that for?" I asked.

"You won't believe it. On my way to the witness stand, I glanced over at Philippe, and he *winked* at me!"

My turn for the eye roll.

I steadied myself, knowing I would be up next. But not so fast: Lisa had switched her strategy. In order to hammer home just how many times Philippe had been tested and treated for STDs, she brought in Dr. Kuo next. Dr. Kuo was the parent of a couple of my black belt girls, so when Philippe needed a doctor for the flu or whatever, I suggested him. Dr. Kuo gave even more damning testimony.

It turned out that Philippe had seen Dr. Kuo in 2003 for a discharge and groin pain, which turned out to be a recurrence of chlamydia, which he acknowledged having when he was in the service. The doctor advised him to have an HIV test, but Philippe said he'd just been tested a few months ago and was negative. He was also treated for a urinary tract infection shortly thereafter, and then came back in early 2004 for antibiotics because he'd been exposed to *trichomoniasis*, another STD. Again the doctor asked about HIV testing, and again Philippe claimed that he'd been tested in December and didn't need another test. December. When he was in Guadeloupe and then detained in Puerto Rico almost the whole month.

On July 4, he again asked for antibiotics, and his last visit with Dr. Kuo (yet again asking for antibiotics because he'd been exposed to trichomoniasis) was on October 5, 2005—three weeks after he had seen Dr. Checo. Geez, he was even seeing more than one *doctor* at a time! It's a wonder he had time to brush his teeth and comb his hair, what with all the getting laid and getting treated for STDs. I wondered if there were other doctors, too.

Thinking back, I tried to remember what he told me to explain the doctor visits and antibiotics. He didn't talk about STDs. All I remember were a couple of times when he claimed to have a yeast infection and suggested he wear a condom so we wouldn't pass it back and forth.

On his October 5 visit, he didn't bother telling Dr. Kuo that he'd been diagnosed with HIV.

"Going through your records, do you know how many times you counseled him or talked to him about HIV and HIV testing?" the prosecutor asked.

"About five times," said Dr. Kuo.

⌒⌒

When Lisa came into the room, I again jumped up out of my seat, but she called Laura Sumner instead. Now I was really aggravated. I had been told to prepare to testify three or four times in just that one day, but every time someone was called, it wasn't me. No one explained to me that the witness order was a fluid process, and sometimes testimony comes out that makes someone else a better next witness. My old counselor Carol used to say she'd rather be depressed than anxious any day, and I was right there with her.

Laura's testimony was, for the most part, lucid and factual. She acknowledged being HIV-positive and that Philippe had never told her of his status. She also said that she'd not been with a man for a "long time" before Philippe—more than fifteen years. But I'm sure the jury started to understand that something wasn't quite right with Laura when Lisa began asking about her HIV symptoms.

"Has your health deteriorated since your HIV diagnosis?"

"I seem okay."

"Have the doctors advised you to go on medication?"

"I think that's coming up."

"Okay. And they discuss that with you when you go to see them?"

"Yeah."

"The meds are coming or that you should be on meds?"

"They are thinking about it."

"You don't want to go on meds, do you?"

"No."

"Have you lost weight since the HIV diagnosis?"

"Yes, I have."

"Have you seen a change in your skin?"

"Yes."

"And because of the HIV, you understand that your immune system is compromised?"

"Yes."

"And, therefore, because of a compromised immune system, you are susceptible to a whole host of things, correct?"

"Yes."

"So what do you do to prevent that so—to not get sick? Are you doing—are you taking any kind of vitamins? Are you just staying away from people? What are you doing?"

"I really am not sick yet. I mean, I don't feel real sick."

"How much weight have you lost since your diagnosis, do you know?"

"Maybe twenty, twenty-five pounds."

"And I think we talked about that your skin has changed?"

"Yes."

"Tell us about that."

"Doesn't look that good."

"Okay. Do you have marks on your skin—"

"Yes, I do."

"—that you didn't have before?"

"Yes."

"Has the HIV affected your hair or anything else about your physical appearance?"

"My hair is thinner."

Even on the stand, though, she wouldn't talk about her numbers, except to say that her T cell count had gone down since the initial diagnosis.

It was getting late, and it was evident that Laura would be the last witness of the day. The prosecutors popped in to the victim advocate room before we all left. Curtis was all sunshine and roses, telling us that the defense witnesses were dropping like flies.

In the morning, Lisa again passed me over, calling Brittani instead. She testified that their sexual relationship started after Philippe e-mailed her to offer a private lesson because of an earlier class that he had canceled. She noted that no other student received a similar e-mail. It was February 2006, and he met her at noon on a Sunday. He told her the dojo would be clear because everyone else would be at the school's annual awards banquet.

When she described the scene later, when I caught them at the school, she said that even though I went ballistic, he convinced her I was angry about the after-hours use of the school and not their affair—he claimed that we were platonic and had only a business relationship. Because Philippe was working for me at the school, I had tried hard to keep business and personal life separate for my students, but Brittani caught a glimpse of him giving me a peck on the cheek afterward, so she knew what was really up. Nevertheless, she said on the stand that when "things got rolling," Philippe would come to her house several times a week for sex while her husband was at work and the kids were napping. For two to three hours a day. Those kids must've been some sleepers!

The lab technician who drew our blood for the forensic analysis was called up next, and then Maddie.

Are you kidding me? My testimony was postponed yet again, and I was running out of Xanax.

Maddie talked about the women at his house, mentioning a time when she spotted a very young woman walking in.

"I knocked on the front door. I was surprised he answered," she said. "He opened the door, I could see the girl standing off into the dining room, and I just hollered it out: 'I'm HIV-positive and used to date him, too. You better get checked.' He slammed the front door in my face. I walked home."

The defense's strategy seemed to be to get the women to admit that we were just a bunch of bitches and that our support group was out for revenge. They asked each woman questions along those lines, though none of them bit.

"How many of these meetings did you say you all went to?"

"Numerous times . . . we became more friends and we'd talk on the phone, and we were supportive of each other. Particularly after the HIV-positive diagnosis, we knew it was very difficult for all of us and our families."

"And I can see this, but some of these women became extremely bitter, did they not?"

"I would think that everybody goes through different stages of anger, upset, sadness, denial, and embarrassment. At different times everybody has probably gone through a little bit of all of that. It's a horrifying thing."

"Was this a concentrated effort to make sure that you all file charges against Mr. Padieu?"

"It was a concentrated effort that he stop."

Try as he might, House couldn't get a single witness to say that those meetings constituted a hate group.

During the entire ordeal, I had worried about how Maddie would handle herself on the stand, given the high stress load, but in fact, she did really well and got the best laugh.

House asked questions about Jane Logan, who would pull into his driveway and honk the horn, and then the garage door would go up. Then she'd pull into the garage and the garage door would go down. Like she didn't want her car—a hideous orange station wagon—to be seen in his driveway.

Maddie related that once, just for fun, she pulled into Philippe's driveway and beeped the horn. "Didn't work for me," she said with a shrug. The entire courtroom erupted in laughter.

Up next was Dr. Reuben, an infectious disease physician. He was there to give a primer about HIV. First, he verified that having herpes increased the risk of transmitting HIV. Then Lisa fired off a host of difficulties that having HIV might cause. It went like this:

"Dr. Reuben, can HIV contribute to: Cancer?"

"Yes."

"Pneumonia?"

"Yes."

"Dementia?"

"Yes."

"Loneliness?"

"Yes."

"Isolation?"

"Yes."

"Financial hardship?"

"Yes."

Then she asked him the last question: "Dr. Reuben, if the definition of a deadly weapon is something that could cause serious bodily harm, would you agree that HIV-infected fluids are a deadly weapon?"

"Oh, yes. By definition, HIV causes serious bodily injury, and HIV fluids are a deadly weapon."

When Lisa came into the victim advocate room after Dr. Reuben's testimony, I barely looked up. I was so tired of getting my hopes up and then being crushed that I just wasn't up for it one more time. Good thing; Lisa called for Sophia next.

Sophia's testimony was short but certainly not sweet. She had met Philippe at yet another Addison bar in January 2006. She testified that he claimed he owned a martial arts school. He also claimed that he had just broken off an engagement after five years with his girlfriend.

After dating him for three months, she broke it off because he obviously just wanted sex instead of what she was looking for—a real relationship. Less than a month later, she was diagnosed with HIV. She had slept with a total of three men in her entire life. Before the end of her testimony, several of the jury members were crying.

Finally, at 3:30, Lisa called me. I hobbled up the aisle to the witness stand on my crutches. I could see Philippe and his lawyers at the defense table and my heart leaped into my throat. This was it—my one shot to tell my story and ask for justice.

The bailiff didn't make me raise my right hand to be sworn in because I was using it to hold on to my crutch. When I sat down, the jury was on my right, and I began sizing them up immediately. A man in the front row wore a striped shirt and smiled when I glanced his way. There were a couple of women around him with reddened eyes from crying. The rest of the jury was somewhat nondescript, except for the two men in the far corner. The one in the upper seat was a short, thin man who looked Middle Eastern, as well as sort of disapproving of the whole affair. The other was a large older man who looked like he'd kill his own mother if it would just get him out of there. Those were the only two I worried about.

Lisa took me through essentially the same process as everyone else: Where, how, and when did you meet? Did you have unprotected sex? Did he use a condom? What kind of sex did you have and how frequently? Did you discuss STDs? Did he agree that you were in an exclusive relationship? By that time it was obvious that every one of us had a similar experience with him. He had a pattern that worked, and he stuck to it.

Not only did she have a foam board with my driver's license picture (ugh), but also quite a few pictures of Philippe and me together over the years, usually on one of our trips. She wanted to make the point that we had spent a lot of time together, and that we looked like "a couple." License pictures of the other women and a time line were on the same foam board. I'm sure by that time, it was hard for the jurors to keep all the players straight.

The weird thing about testimony is that it's not purely chronological. It might start out that way, but then the attorney will jump back and forth from one incident to the other. It's confusing. And it's degrading to be up in front of a courtroom full of people who don't know you and realize they're getting a picture of a lonely and foolish woman who fell for a guy, let him take her to the cleaners, caught him cheating more than once, and continually took him back. Even though it was all true, I wanted to say, "I'm more than that. I'm really not pathetic." Philippe preyed on our loneliness. He conned us. Anyone who trusts can get conned, yet we have to trust if we are to experience love. This could have happened to anyone, and did.

Sometimes the questions would come so fast and so out of context it was hard to be clear. What's more, Lisa was hammering me—almost what you'd expect from the other side. *You're a nurse, and you don't think to get tested for STDs?* Because I loved him and I trusted him. Because when he told me he was "clean," I believed him. And really, this just isn't in the mind-set of the over-fifty crowd.

There was no emotion to it, no picture of the handsome man that made me feel like I was the only woman in the world, no video of him carrying me down a mountain. Nothing that showed the quiet moments, affectionate teasing, or the countless kind little gestures that make a relationship take root. No explanation for why I—or any of the other women—fell so hard for this guy that we put all reason aside. Surely some of the jurors had done things they regretted because they were in love. Statistics show that it takes an average of seven times for an abused woman to leave her husband for good, and these are women who get the crap beat out of them. We get in over our heads. Wanting to love and be loved makes us fallible and human.

Then I took a deep breath as cross-examination began.

"Ms. Sutherland, I'm not trying to be rude, I'm just going to ask you dead out, is some of this out of vindictiveness, revenge?"

Again with that. What difference did it make? It was impossible to quantify in my head just how pure my intentions were, though I knew my main objective was to get this guy behind bars before he infected and killed anyone else. Regardless, even if I was just straight-out after vengeance, like some demented Inigo Montoya from *The Princess Bride*, how did that in any way influence whether or not this man had knowingly committed a crime? "Yeah, he did infect a bunch of women with a deadly disease, but they're too mad about it, so let's set him free." What?

And sure enough, between the prosecution and the defense, they dissected every inch of my sex life—the who, what, where, when, and hows of it all. How often and how we'd had sex, ins and outs of bladder infections, and whether or not I'd previously been treated for an STD (I hadn't; he thought my acne medication was for chlamydia). I couldn't wait for it to be over—and when it was, I didn't even feel a sense of relief. The anxiety stayed with me. Had I done a good enough job? Did the jury get it that this was a very bad man, and that I wasn't a terrible woman?

It's weird trying to sell yourself on the stand, knowing that your future rests in the hands of these strangers and not knowing what any of them think. What if they were a bunch of Rush Limbaugh fans who agreed that we deserved what we got?

We were a somber group in the elevator that Thursday afternoon. We were all exhausted. Even though Curtis told us there would be only three or four defense witnesses, I still knew there would be a long road ahead of us. Samme took us back to our cars through the back of the courthouse to avoid the media. All I could think of was getting to my car to let go and have a good cry.

But when we got to the parking lot, I had a problem. "Hey guys, I can't find my keys."

I looked. They looked. I looked some more. And before I knew it, I was having a full-blown panic attack and turning into a raving lunatic. As we continued to search for my keys, I screamed, cursed, and wailed. Everyone tried to help, but I just came unglued.

And then Susan, with a hint of a smirk on her face, reached into my pants pocket and pulled out my keys. Wow. I felt even more humiliated than I had been in court. The next day Samme told me with a laugh and a wink that she had to take the Jeep to a priest to have all the bad language residue removed.

I tried to clear my mind on the thirty-minute drive home. The sun was low enough in the sky to turn the billowy clouds a beautiful shade of pink with a dash of purple. Everyone told me that I did well on the stand, but I was afraid I had shared too much, talked too fast, and just generally not presented well. Nobody could kick their own butt like I could.

Shana, our ABC producer, came to the rescue. I guess after spending almost a year working on our story, she knew me well enough to figure out that I would be beating myself up. So she took a few minutes just to tell me I did great and that the jury was riveted by my testimony. She said she got very little, if any, negative vibes from them. I thanked her profusely—and she had the perfect ending.

"You are a rock star . . . and don't forget it." She had used that phrase with me before. She had written those same words on a little piece of paper the first time we met, and I had kept it with me for so very long (in fact, I still have it!). Maybe she said that to everybody, maybe she was lying—but if it was a lie, it was one I wanted to believe.

CHAPTER 22

The Verdict

We were allowed to sit in the courtroom the following day, which was an unexpected treat. It was nice to finally have all of us women together in court now that the pressure was off—we were all done testifying. Except . . .

"I intend to recall Barbara Sutherland, Susan Brown, and Megan Smith, and maybe Sophia Brissan," House said.

There wasn't enough Xanax in the world.

Recall us? For what? It was so unnerving that it made it very difficult to sit through the rest of the testimony. Every muscle in my body was taut.

Today was primarily about Dr. Metzker and his blood sample analysis. He started by explaining how HIV is an unstable virus that mutates frequently. He likened it to a tree with many branches, explaining that you have to look to the trunk of the tree to see what the virus looked like at the time of infection. From there, you can compare it to the other samples to see if they are more closely related in their sequencing than other samples in public databases, or to other control samples. If they are, then you can look further and figure out a direction of transmission: which one gave the virus to the other.

In this case, he explained, there was one sample that was not only related to all the others in the case (and not related to the control samples) but was the source of the transmission for all of them with nearly 100 percent accuracy: sample one.

"And were you aware, Dr. Metzker, that sample number one belonged to the defendant, Philippe Padieu?"

"Not until you informed me just now."

There. See? Why did we even have to go any further? To me, we now had all the evidence a jury could need—we now knew that Philippe was intentionally sleeping with women without protection while lying about his status, even after being ordered not to, and we had proof that he infected at least six women. It should've been time for me to go out for ice cream, not time to get back into the witness chair. But I had no choice.

God, what could they possibly want to ask me about now?

I'd have to stew on it for days; this was the Friday before Memorial Day, and they already had their witnesses lined up for the day, so I wouldn't be back on the stand until at least Tuesday —enough time for me to really lose my mind.

One good bit of news came when the prosecution announced that they wanted to fly Lauren and Rhonda in for the punishment phase, and the judge agreed. It was a very good indication that there likely would *be* a punishment phase.

⋯

Nikki the romance author was one of the few defense witnesses who showed up. She was there to talk about what a bully I was, of course. And how Philippe always used a condom with her when they had sex three or four times a week from March to June 2007. She said they broke up in June (before his arrest in July) but remained friends.

It got interesting on cross-examination.

"Isn't it true that you're writing a book called *The French Man*?" asked Lisa.

"Yes."

"And . . . this would be loosely based on this man, correct, and all the stories he's told you?"

"Some of the stories, yes."

"And, in fact, you wrote him many, many, many letters while he was in jail asking him to give you information for your book."

"Some letters, yes."

"Yes, a lot of letters, and he would write you back, right?"

"Okay."

"A lot of letters—you would agree, right?"

"That would be interpretative; but, yes, we'll go for that."

"And you're hoping to sell that book, aren't you?"

"Yes."

"You're shopping for a publisher right now."

"Not right now."

"But you have been."

"No, I'm shopping it to an agent."

"To an agent. You just can't—you can't find anyone right now that wants that book, correct, but you're still working on it?"

"Yes."

"Pass the witness."

We're talking about a *romance novel*. This batshit woman was writing a romance novel starring a man who was currently on trial for intentionally infecting multiple women with HIV while he was having sex with anyone with reasonably good vital signs. I couldn't imagine why every agent in New York wasn't clamoring to represent such a fine love story. Why, it was like *Gone with the Wind* all over again.

We all wondered what kind of a deal she'd struck with Philippe and if he was going to profit from his crimes. Or if this was their tradeoff—she'd be his character witness if she got to keep whatever money she made from his story. In any case, it was good to hear that it hadn't gotten off the ground yet.

(To our great relief, Andy was able to shut down the book project. It is illegal in Texas for criminals to profit from their crimes. How grateful we all were to Andy for that!)

That wrapped up Friday, and before we left, Lisa came in to tell us some very important news: She had received a call from another victim who spotted Philippe on the news! This one said she had dated Philippe for nine months, and the prosecutors were scheduled to meet with her that night. Lisa promised to give her my and Susan's cell numbers.

Susan and I couldn't wait to discuss this turn of events. It had been such a long and difficult week, but once Lisa tipped us off, my whole thought process changed. I forgot about the hand-wringing, claustrophobic cage-in-a-zoo feeling and was able to pull myself back into a broader perspective. It reminded me of why I was doing all this: to save lives.

The ones who were already infected and didn't know it, the tens or hundreds more he would've infected in the future, and the ones who didn't even know Philippe but who heard our story and now might get tested or insist on protection when otherwise they wouldn't have.

Susan and I, however, talked of none of that. We fired "I wonder" statements back and forth at each other on the phone for more than an hour that night: I wonder how she met him. I wonder where. I wonder when. I wonder if she'll be able to file charges.

The following day, Susan called and excitedly announced, "I talked to her!"

Susan said that Iris had called her and they talked about all those questions we had discussed the night before. And before we knew it, I was on the phone with Iris, too. We talked for at least two hours, pouring out our stories to each other. She told me that she'd been on only three dates with him. That certainly didn't jibe with Lisa's initial statement that they were together for nine months, but I bit my tongue. She couldn't join our case because she had never been to his home and their dates had not been in Collin County, so there was no jurisdiction there. But she would testify during the punishment phase, like Lauren and Rhonda. Iris didn't want to file, anyway—she wanted nothing to do with the media circus that was sure to ensue.

We agreed to meet at my favorite brunch locale. I invited the rest of the group, but Laura declined and Nena was back in the hospital with another MS flare-up, so it was me, Susan, her boyfriend Len, Maddie, and Sophia and her new boyfriend Charlie. Iris was in her early fifties and had a great personality. She fit right in. It didn't get overly personal because Len and Charlie were there, but the symbiosis that was so characteristic of our group remained intact. I was sorry that there was a new member of a club that no one would want to be in, but I was grateful for a new friend who could really understand how we all felt. It felt good to go home and snuggle up with Tiger to take a nap that afternoon.

Monday (Memorial Day) was by far the longest day. Things seemed to slow down, like trying to run underwater, but I finally found a welcome distraction when Lauren flew in and the Reeve Hotel was open for business. It was supposed to be a favor for her, but really, it was at least as much a favor for me—I loved having her at my house, and it was great to have someone to talk to during this intensely stressful time, other than my dog (who, to be fair, is an excellent listener).

We stayed up talking until almost 1:00 AM. She was very street-wise and opinionated, and we put more of the pieces together as we compared notes that night. In 1997 when she dated Philippe, he would stand her up or not call when he promised. This was part of why they broke up. By the time he got around (and I do mean got around) to me in 2002, he had learned that to keep a woman, you had to keep your promises.

We jumped in the car around 8:00 Tuesday morning and met the group at the old hospital building to have Samme again drive us to the back of the courthouse so we could avoid the media. The victim advocate room was now even more crowded, and I knew I had one more hurdle to cross before the finish line—time for me to take the stand once more. But I couldn't be prepared for the low blow the defense was about to make.

"I don't mean to get real personal, but during this period of time, you had an abortion. It's spontaneous; what does that mean?" asked House.

"A spontaneous abortion is when you get pregnant and it doesn't work out inside and it just comes out. And that wasn't during that time; that was in 1977."

"I'm sorry. I didn't mean to say during this time. I apologize for that, okay? That was in when?"

"1977."

"Did you ever have any other abortion?"

"Does that have anything to do with this?"

"Yes, it does."

Lisa King broke in with an objection, but I decided to answer anyway.

"No, sir, I had no other abortions."

"Okay. Um . . ."

"I didn't do anything to terminate the pregnancy; the pregnancy went away on its own."

"I understand."

"It was very hard."

What in the absolute hell was this bullshittery? They were bringing up my miscarriage and D&C from thirty years ago when I was married, an incredibly painful time in my life, as proof that I was a bad person who deserved AIDS? I thought my restraint was pretty phenomenal, to be straight. I wanted to pie him in the face. Or kick his butt till his nose bled. One of those . . . okay, maybe both. And why were the prosecutors not objecting to this? I can only think now that the prosecution let it go because they knew it would backfire on the defense. That the jury would see the total lack of regard they had for a woman's heartbreak, and hate them for it. But part of me still has a hard time forgiving them for letting such a mockery be made over the loss of my child.

There was more, of course. More digging into my sexual history, trying to get me to say that I was with other men while I was dating Philippe. I wasn't. When they'd wrung me out as much as they could, they dismissed me and moved on.

One more woman testified for him, though I couldn't figure out how she was supposed to be helpful. It was Candace Wilkins, the woman I'd met with for drinks when Philippe was being held in Guaynabo.

The defense attorney was trying hard to get her to paint a picture of me as a crazy, hateful woman, but Candace didn't bite. In fact, she called me "pleasant" and "cordial," even though I had made it clear to her that I was with Philippe and I expected her to back off. The defense's whole approach seemed to be an exercise in futility, but who was I to argue with that?

Closing statements began on Wednesday morning with ABC's cameras quietly rolling. All the women sat side by side in the back two rows of the packed courtroom, clutching hands and tissues, as we listened to the final arguments the jury would hear.

The defense had nothing of substance to say, so they just tried to confuse the issue.

"Basically you've been asked to follow the law. My question to you today, this morning, my question to Austin, my question to the DAs, what law? Where is the law Philippe knew and understood to follow? The law of aggravated assault? How could you read that and understand it has any application to having sex unless you believe he's not a predator, he's a rapist? You've got to believe that, because that's where they applied this law: rape. Think about what the ladies said. They all loved him. He's romantic. He's this. He's that. Two, three, four ladies a week. Sometimes two, three, four times a day. Sound like a rapist to you? Does that really, really, really sound like a rapist to you?"

What the . . . ?

Nobody had said a word about rape, nor did the charge insinuate anything like that. The law was made pretty damn clear to him when the police arrived with the cease and desist order. Then it just got stupider.

"Think about H1N1, swine flu. It's much more deadly than this disease. You catch that and you infect somebody else and you didn't have a mask on, they'll argue you were reckless. You didn't wear a mask? You go to the drinking fountain and you infect that and you infect a whole bunch of people. You didn't bring your little spray bottle of Clorox and clean down the water fountain?"

I hoped the jury wouldn't be thrown off by this smoke and mirrors game. It wasn't an apt comparison at all—unless the person with swine flu was intentionally infecting the drinking fountain and lying to everyone who used it, saying, "It's clean! I just got tested for swine flu and I'm fine!"

Halfway through his closing argument, House came out with this gem: "He's not a predator—he's a polygamist!"

Luckily, the prosecution gave a solid closing.

Lisa pulled out some facts that were hard for us to hear—like that, even if all goes well, HIV cuts your life expectancy by ten years.

But her closing statement is perhaps best summed up with the following line.

"It's as if he took a gun and shot all of them," she said.

Then there was nothing left but to let the jury make their decision. They began deliberating at 11:30 AM, but after only thirty minutes, they broke for lunch for an hour and a half. We sent the guys to bring back some lunch, but for me it was a waste. Who could eat at a time like this?

Lisa and Curtis visited with us and were confident and encouraging, but I knew how juries work a great deal of the time. In general—not always, but often—the shorter the deliberation, the higher chance of a guilty verdict, which meant that every passing minute felt disastrous.

To keep our minds busy while we waited, we all began writing a joint statement that could be delivered to the press if we got a guilty verdict. We fairly quickly all agreed on something poignant yet powerful to say. Rhonda, in an uncharacteristically bold move, volunteered to read the statement to represent us all.

At 4:30, Curtis told us that the jury was going home for the day. All they had asked for was a part of one doctor's testimony, and it had taken the court reporter a while to find it.

"We'll see you guys in the morning. Get some rest," he chirped.

Yeah, right.

I was crestfallen. Yet another long night of not knowing. I knew I wouldn't get any rest at all, but what I would get was comradery, and a large frozen margarita—no salt.

Lauren and I, friends bound by an invisible but very real bond, climbed into my car and headed south on Central Expressway. Within five minutes, we walked into a quaint little seafood restaurant and bar in North Texas to have a drink and maybe a small bite to eat before heading to my house. It was late afternoon and we both knew neither one of us would sleep well that night.

Lauren had never been to Texas before. Originally from Detroit, her classy appearance didn't jibe with the typical motor city stereotype. She was in her midforties and had married a chiropractor. She was so pulled together, to the prim and proper end of things, which made her an unlikely companion to my sparring ways.

The smell of the Texas Grill greeted us as we navigated our way through the peanut shells strewn about on the cement floor of the restaurant. We found a small booth near the front and slid across the heavy and dark wooden bench, making ourselves comfortable on the hard seats.

I sat facing the door, in my usual state of alertness, briefly noting an escape route in case anything went down (just a thing that martial artists do). The neon dry erase board listed the specials of the day, but we hadn't had time to even consider the choices before the tall young waiter was at our side.

"What can I get you lovely ladies to drink?" he drawled amiably.

"Frozen margarita, no salt." I was a woman of decision. I had been thinking about that margarita all day long, needing something to take the edge off what had consumed me for so many months I had almost lost count.

"I'll have the same, please," Lauren said.

We picked up our menus and began studying them, lost in the same but separate thoughts. We had both hoped this would be a celebratory meal, but we weren't there yet. I stared at the menu mindlessly for a long time.

"You want some nachos?" I finally said to Lauren.

"Sure . . . sounds good."

As soon as the waiter took our order, though, my cell phone rang. I didn't recognize the number.

"Diane, this is Curtis Howard."

"Hi, Curtis. What's up?" I was surprised to hear from him because it had been less than an hour since we had all been sent home for the day.

"Can you get everybody back into the courthouse right away? We have a verdict!"

His statement hung in the air like the pregnant pause of all pregnant pauses.

"What?" I shrieked. "I thought they went home for the day." I reached for a sip of that long-awaited margarita, but I couldn't swallow because my heart was suddenly in my throat.

Lauren's widened eyes were glued to me as the conversation continued.

"They tried, but they changed their minds and decided to go ahead and finish it. Can you reach everyone quickly? How far away are you?" He had hope in his voice that we weren't so far away that the jury's decision would have to wait until tomorrow.

"We'll be there in five minutes, ten tops. I'll get the rest of the group back ASAP."

I almost tripped in my haste to get up on my crutches. There was no way I was waiting on our nachos. I hobbled to the door with my credit card in hand as I flagged down the waiter for the check. I left him a nice tip even though I'd barely had two sips of that coveted margarita. Somehow I knew that today would be the best day I'd had in a long time.

Our ragtag group of cosurvivors needed to be corralled back into the courthouse right at rush hour. Sophia had taken off with Maddie immediately after we were cut loose, and I knew they would be the farthest away of everyone.

"Get back to the courthouse now!"

"Why?" Sophia moaned. "I'm already halfway home."

"We have a verdict!" That effectively ended the conversation.

Tracking down Susan was harder. There was no answer on her phone or her boyfriend's, or at their hotel room.

"Dammit! Where the hell *are* they?" I spewed as I left messages frantically. Then the phone finally rang.

Yay! It was Susan!

"Susan! We got a verdict!"

"Holy crap! We'll be there in ten minutes." And the phone went dead.

The next seven minutes were equivalent to an eternity for all of us. It was about as long as the two-and-a-half-year eternity we had already endured together—the one that had brought us here in the first place. I contacted the remaining women and pulled into the parking lot at the back of the courthouse, avoiding the crowds and media that were surely aware that the end was here. I hoped it was the end for Philippe.

We filed silently into the courtroom, positioning ourselves in two rows. I really had no clue who was beside me; I just knew I'd never squeezed anyone's hands or had mine squeezed as hard in my life. We had to wait another ten minutes for Philippe to be brought back into the courtroom.

"All rise!" the thoroughbred Texan bailiff boomed. Cameras rolled everywhere, and Judge Henderson reminded the courtroom that there could be no outbursts or show of emotion from anyone or he would clear the courtroom.

"Be seated!" the bailiff called.

The judge wasted no time.

"Have you reached a verdict?" he asked the jury foreman, the guy who always wore the horizontal striped shirts.

"We have, Your Honor."

Henderson asked him to pass up the paper, and it was the judge who read the verdicts to the courtroom, in the order we had testified. We all held our breath.

"In the matter of the state of Texas versus Philippe Padieu, for case number 0721976: guilty."

Philippe hung his head and shook it side to side very slowly, as if in disbelief. After that, I knew what was coming, but I didn't want to let myself believe it until the last verdict was read.

0721977: guilty.

0721978: guilty.

0721979: guilty.

0721980: guilty.

That was me! *Thank you, God, thank you, Jesus!*

0721981: guilty.

We all went nuts hugging one another and crying and trying to be quiet. We were led out of the courtroom to avoid the media, but Rhonda took care of reading our statement on the courthouse steps while the rest of us filed into the victim advocate room. But this time, the air was considerably lighter.

Philippe before.

Philippe after.

CHAPTER 23

The Sentence

I couldn't call enough people fast enough: everyone who had helped us along the way. We were all on our phones, positively buzzing. Then we all went out for Tex-Mex. There was a huge table set up in the back for all of us women, plus several significant others, friends, and family members. It was a chaotic, exuberant mob scene. In an instant there was a frozen margarita, no salt in front of me, and I was darn well going to finish this one. We had just won the Super Bowl, the World Series, and the lottery! For the first time in almost two weeks, I was going to have something for dinner besides Xanax and mashed potatoes.

One by one, we raised our glasses in the air. Quite a while before the trial, our support group had adopted a theme song, which I couldn't help but bring to everybody's mind. I started very softly at first . . .

"Na na na na,
Na na na na,
Hey, hey, hey,
Good-bye."

And again a little louder as the others joined in. As the last syllable of the "good-bye" died away, the entire restaurant went dead silent. I wondered what everyone was thinking, but I really wasn't concerned about social graces at the moment. The final time was the loudest.

"NA NA NA NA,
NA NA NA NA,
HEY, HEY, HEY,
GOOOOOD-BYYYYE!"

We all laughed, clinked our glasses, took a sip, and burst into applause—as did the rest of the room. They didn't know what we were celebrating, but they were right there with us. That's Texas for ya!

Lauren and I talked a bit before bedtime, but we were both exhausted. Even though the hardest part was over, I knew there were still a few hurdles to clear. At this point, the jury believed the crime that had been committed was a second-degree felony, punishable by two to twenty years. What they wouldn't know until tomorrow was that because of his prior conviction, the DA bumped the charge to a first-degree felony. Philippe was looking at five to ninety-nine years for each count. Sentences in criminal cases can be concurrent (served at the same time) or stacked (served one at a time). Because all our cases were tried together, Philippe would serve his sentences concurrently. Obviously, all of us would have preferred stacked. But our primary hope was just that he would not be able to get out and harm another person ever again.

On May 28, the prosecution began their opening statements for sentencing. They started with the non-filing victims: Rhonda, Iris, Lauren, and Nena. I can only imagine what that jury was thinking: "Not six, but *ten* victims? And since 1997?" Plus, with Nena's videotaped deposition tugging at their heartstrings, they couldn't help but be disgusted, right?

Then Lisa had the pleasure of introducing the evidence of the prison record. I could see Philippe scrunching down in his chair.

That's right, asshole, you're going down.

I was up next to discuss the personal details I knew about his prison experience. I still haven't figured out why I was the only one he ever told about his prison record. Because he was with me longer? Because he needed someone he could confide in? Or maybe he was playing me because he thought it might appear exciting, albeit a bit dangerous to me.

Finally, Lisa asked, "Ms. Sutherland, this jury has to decide the appropriate punishment in this case. Would you be concerned for your safety if the defendant was given a light sentence?"

"I would be in fear of my life. He's already tried to kill me once."

"And by that you mean . . . ?"

"He gave me AIDS."

Maddie, Susan, and Sophia also spoke during the punishment phase. Notably absent were Laura and Brittani, who disappeared once we had a verdict.

Then there was a bit of an odd occurrence. During the trial, we had all noted that House and Philippe spent a lot of time heatedly arguing with each other at the defense table. It was increasingly obvious that House was none too happy with his client.

At 4:00, House requested a hearing. He wanted to be sure it was entered into the court record that he strongly advised his client not to testify on his own behalf. There were several emphatic requests that his advice be recorded, and soon thereafter, Philippe took the stand—and let his crazy flag fly high.

I have really never heard such maniacal rantings on the witness stand, and I avidly watch *Law and Order* and *Law and Order: Criminal Intent.* He talked about the "hate club." He blamed the whole thing on me. Then he blamed it all on Sophia. Really? Sophia? She was one of the last to join the group and had only learned about us after the initial media.

Numerous times, he went off on long tangents about how we were suppressing evidence, or that the judge was putting a "gag on justice." His lawyer was positively exasperated trying to keep him on track, but Philippe just kept blaming everyone he could, including the two prosecutors.

"Obviously this is a historical case, and they're going to get well known by this case. They are going to be famous, promotions. This is overkill and they want you, the jury, to believe that I'm a sexual predator. Where is the data? Where is the facts?"

There was a lot of eye-rolling and sighing going on in the jury box. Finally, he finished whatever it was he was trying to do. Prosecution and defense rested. Closing arguments were set for the next morning.

The closing arguments were about what you'd expect, except that when it was House's turn to speak, he told the jury that he believed his client deserved twenty years in prison.

Wow.

Question: How do you know when you're a truly evil son of a bitch?

Answer: When your own defense attorney wants you in for twenty years.

But the final kudos went to Lisa. "Mr. Padieu, it seems that every time you get in trouble, it's always a conspiracy. You were sent to prison because your friend set you up and your girlfriend 'dropped a dime on you.' And then in prison, when they found drugs in your cell, that was a setup, too. Next, it was the weapons charge when you were in an altercation with one of your conquests' ex-fiancé.

"Now Mr. Padieu, the prosecution is conspiring against you. We've gathered all these women together to make our case so we can be famous. You poor thing. Nothing is ever your fault, is it?" The jury foreman let out a quick chuckle.

The jury went off to deliberate, and I'd later learn that it was a bit contentious. Two jurors wanted Philippe to serve just five years. Luckily, the foreman put his foot down in favor of the other jurors, who were not quite as eager to let a predator off.

In less than two hours, they came back with their determination: the sentences of forty-five years for each case were to run concurrently, and he wouldn't be eligible for parole for twenty-two and a half years; he'd be seventy-four by then. Curtis looked over his shoulder at me with his big boyish grin and a thumbs-up.

Sure it wasn't my biggest hope, but it was a good sentence. Forty-five years meant that he would almost certainly die in prison and never infect another woman. Then it was all over—more than two years of hell all bottled up and packaged with a bow. *Forty-five years.* It meant I was finally free.

It's over, I had to keep repeating to myself. *Really, really over! We won! The good guys won!* If I hadn't been on crutches, I would've twirled in a circle with my arms in the air.

We all gathered in the lobby, where eight of the jurors stayed to talk. All of the women were crying in sympathy for us, and the foreman told us that it was a painful trial and he felt a lot of sadness for what we were going through. I appreciated the gift—not only of their verdict but of their kindness afterward.

Those of us who remained headed back to the victim advocate room for a final moment—a sort of debriefing with one another before we all went our separate ways. We sat down on the couch and chairs while Shana filmed us. We grasped one another's hands tightly once more as we bowed our heads and Susan said a very nice prayer. As we looked up at one another, tears were streaming down every face, and we started our little refrain that had become our theme song. In some ways it was as cathartic to sing that song as anything we had ever done in our support group meetings.

Lauren went back home that night and I crashed hard. It was the best sleep I'd had in months.

⚭

Philippe was transferred from the Collin County Jail to the prison in Tennessee Colony, Texas, where he quickly filed an appeal (of course). I heard that House had declined to represent him on appeal, which wasn't surprising.

That summer, ABC added a little cherry to the top of our sundae when they paid to have Dr. Metzker analyze Lauren's blood work, which the county never did because her case was too early to be included in the trial. Sure enough, Philippe was the source of her infection, too, confirming that he'd been spreading HIV since 1997.

On September 18, the *20/20* episode was set to air, and a local ABC news reporter asked to come to my house for a "post-*20/20*" interview. Right before 8:00 PM, the group gathered in my living room and watched. It was one of the most surreal experiences in my life. The first segment was me: doing karate, on stakeout, in his driveway, at the computer, and with the cell records. The tension of the story mounted as every woman added to the story. I was on the edge of my seat, even though I had lived it! It was compelling, powerful, moving, and bittersweet. It was viewed by more than 6 million people.

Seeing that part of my life being played out on national television was visceral, and I did a great job beating myself up about the way I looked and my karate technique. Then I started to beat myself up for being self-critical. Finally, a sense of pride started to wash over me—I was grateful for the opportunity to step up and help people. It was such an outstanding portrayal of what we had been through.

I got more validation when I went to the school the next morning. There were lots of kudos and "atta girls," and then the Facebook and e-mail messages began pouring in. They were overwhelmingly positive, poignant, and caring.

Only three days after *20/20* aired, I was on a plane to Chicago to shoot *The Oprah Winfrey Show*—a true mountaintop moment. I could barely contain myself. "I am going to meet Queen Oprah" spun around and around in my head like one of those melodies that you just can't shake. I was incredulous that I was finally living my dream of making an impact on the world.

Oprah's team put us up in beautiful hotel suites, and I felt like royalty. Tired royalty, but royalty nonetheless. Harpo Studios was an amazing labyrinth of cubicles, offices, a workout room, and a locker room, in addition to the makeup room and greenroom. But the most spectacular thing was the red marble stairway that hit you immediately as you walked in the door. It was complete with a landing and a split at the top, with additional stairways going to the left and right of the one at the bottom. It was like something out of *Gone with the Wind*.

Before I knew it, I was walking out onto the stage and hugging Oprah Winfrey! I was certain that I had died and gone to heaven. I was even more thrilled to sit next to her, and when she held my hand during a sad moment, I was electrified. The show went off without any major hitches.

There was a minor hitch, however. Toward the end of the program, there was an angry woman in the audience whom Oprah referred to as the "Neck Lady" because of the animated way the woman was moving her head and neck to get Oprah's attention

to make a comment. She started out in an accusatory and judgmental tone.

"If he don't wear a condom, he don't get any." And that was
just the opening I needed.

"I know there are quite a number of people out there who try
to say it is our fault for not protecting ourselves—but we trusted
someone who lied to us." I started picking up anger and intensity.
"You can't blame the victim. Do not blame the victim!"

There was wild applause from the audience, and it was satis-
fying. *That's for all those assholes who want to point fingers and
say "I'm too smart for that,"* I thought. I also got to spring the
information about Lauren being infected in 1997, which drew an
audible gasp from the audience.

And then, like waking up from a dream, in an instant it was
over. We posed with Oprah for a group picture, which now hangs
in my office next to the one with Elizabeth Vargas from *20/20*. An
hour earlier, Oprah had entered the stage barefoot with her quintessential red-soled Christian Louboutin shoes dangling from her
index finger. After the group picture, she again took her shoes off
and *POOF!* the entire scene evaporated. After the show, we talked
to a few audience members who were very supportive.

The show aired in December and resulted in a lot of support
from both friends and strangers. Susan and I kept checking the
comments section on the website, and our final analysis was that
the comments ran about 90 percent in our favor. I had phone
calls and e-mails from guys who said I was still nice-looking at
fifty-something, and women who came forward to tell me that
their experience had been similar to mine. I was incredulous that
so many of them came forward to tell me that their husband or
boyfriend had knowingly infected them. And then there was this
very interesting phone call.

A woman left a voice mail on my home phone one evening shortly after the *Oprah* segment aired. She explained that she had seen me on television and wanted to let me know about her connection to Philippe.

She had known him when he was in the navy, stationed at Virginia Beach. She had dated him for a while, not knowing he was married at the time—but then again, so was she. She also said that her husband was seeing Philippe's wife at the same time and that both marriages fell apart because of it. I knew she wasn't making it up because he had told me the same story.

She also mentioned Philippe's old dance rival, Pablo. I knew from Philippe that they were both good dancers, and they were always after the same women. This woman had a juicier version: she told me that it was rumored that Philippe and Pablo were lovers.

I'll be darned.

CHAPTER 24
The View from Here

Here are the things I want to tell you: I want to tell you that once the trial was over, I became a magnanimous sort of person who learned to forgive her enemies, and that I also developed a Zen-like sense of patience. I would also like to tell you that a handsome prince came along and carried me off to his castle far, far away, and that I'm now fabulously wealthy and spend my days cavorting on the Spanish Riviera and doing charitable deeds. But fairy tales are for little girls and schmucks—and I'm certainly neither.

It was exciting doing the talk show circuit (there were several more shows and documentaries after the first two), and I got a high from knowing that I'd done something really important. But real life was still real life: I still had AIDS, my business was in the toilet, and my daughters were not happy with me and my quest to go public. The stress of the diagnosis, trial, and aftermath took its toll on our relationships, and we've had to build them back up little piece by little piece. I'm delighted to say that both of my girls now strongly support what I did and what I do. I couldn't be prouder!

I haven't found true love again, though I've dated a bit. My rule now is to disclose on the second date, and if I ever decide to have sex with anyone to use condoms every time. A good turn of events: my viral load is now undetectable thanks to the medications, which means it's virtually impossible for me to transmit the virus. Even so, I'm not taking any chances!

Our support group is scattered around quite a bit, with two of the women (Susan and Maddie) now happily remarried, and we were all saddened by the passing of Rhonda's husband. There are new grandkids for some of us, and lots of new adventures and jobs. Nena is still struggling with her MS, Laura finally went on medication, and—I know this will shock you—I haven't heard from Brittani. I suspect she's joined a convent. Or something. I recently had an opportunity to help Sophia with a health issue. She is much better now, and we're both happy about that!

We don't meet regularly in person anymore, though several of us still talk on the phone or by e-mail. I miss our closeness, but I am so thankful that we all had one another at a time when we all so desperately needed it. Every so often, Rhonda still calls me and just says, "Thank you for saving my life," and it brings me to tears every time. If we hadn't pushed the case forward and she hadn't seen his picture in the media, she might never have gotten tested and never realized that she had AIDS. Any opportunistic infection could've taken her out. That humbles me and makes me appreciate the journey—it reminds me of why I bothered.

The easier road would've been to shrink away and do nothing, to feel so ashamed of my own mistakes that it would prevent me from holding a predator accountable and warning others. I wouldn't have had to worry about his reaction to the investigation, or had to deal with public scrutiny, or devote so much of my time and energy to finding the other women, building the case, and preparing for court. But the easier way is rarely the right way.

So here's what I've *really* learned:

1) I am not defined by living with HIV. I am a mother, grand-mother, friend, business owner, and seventh-degree black belt—aka a *badass bitch*. I am not an HIV victim, as I described myself when I walked into the Dallas County Health Department STD clinic that first time. I am a *survivor* who acquired HIV through an intentional transmission. I am a living, loving, and vibrant human being who is an unwilling host to one particular virus. It lives with me; I don't live with it. And I have learned the importance of terminology—using words to describe people who have this virus rather than reducing us to just a bunch of letters, and using "acquired" and "transmitted" rather than that defamatory word "infected." Plus, it's rarely necessary to label a person as having AIDS—such an inflammatory acronym—rather than HIV. What difference does it really make if my CD4 is 199 or 201? A person shouldn't be denigrated because of their cell count. I am a living, breathing human being with all the accomplishments and difficulties that accompany it.

2) I now believe I am fine just as I am, thank you very much. I was so desperate for companionship when I met Philippe that it created weakness; I was willing to accept nearly anything in a bid to attract him and keep him.
I believed then that I *needed* a man for me to be whole. Now I know that I'm already whole, and I manage quite well on my own. Would it be nice to have "backup" at some point in time? Well, I'm not looking for it, but it's not beyond the realm of possibility. For now, I'm happy just being me. I will never again be so desperate for companionship that I am willing to take less than I should. I won't settle.

3) Echoing what my doctor (Louis Sloan, if you ever need the best doctor on the planet!) told me when I interviewed him for this book: If you are a person living with HIV, take your meds! Every stinking day! No ifs, ands, or buts! And even if you think you haven't acquired HIV, get tested (just to be sure) now, and once a year if you've had unprotected sex since your last test. HIV is not a death sentence if treated, but it can kill you if you don't know you have it.

4) If you decide on an exclusive relationship, get tested together, get the results together, and continue to verify. It won't keep you from getting HIV if he cheats, but at least you'll be starting out on an even playing field. You may find it awkward to ask, but it's a lot less difficult than spending the rest of your life fighting a disease that keeps trying to do you in.

5) No matter how much you may want to please a partner or stay "in the mood" yourself, protecting your life and health have to come first. You have to take the best precautions you can: always use a condom in nonmonogamous relationships. And if that supposedly monogamous partner cheats and you stay with him? Right back to condoms—and STD testing for six months afterward. Of course, no one should live their life in constant fear, and there comes a point in a monogamous relationship where you'll probably both want to stop using condoms. I can only suggest, based on what I've learned, that you take whatever precautions you can (asking about exclusivity and risky behaviors, getting tested together) and trust your gut and your observations. If you have any suspicion at all that your partner may not be monogamous, then you need to protect yourself no matter how much he tells you he's

changed, or that you just need to trust him. There are too many stories of women who acquire HIV from their husbands or long-term boyfriends after believing they knew everything that was happening in their relationship. We're all human, and it can be hard to follow this advice—but do your best.

6) I didn't deserve HIV and nobody else does, either. I didn't do anything your mama didn't do to get you here! All I did was trust the wrong guy—and I'll bet there are only a handful of you out there who couldn't say the same.

7) Trust your instincts! Pay attention to those red flags and that little small voice inside that says "something isn't quite right." I will never again be so needy that I ignore my own good judgment. *Never*.

8) I've learned the importance of having support. I would never have come through this in one piece had it not been for the group. We did save one another's lives.

9) If you have a problem, a difficult situation, an obstacle, or heartbreak, or if your "get up and go" got up and went, do something. Stand strong. Don't wallow in self-pity. It will only make you old and miserable and dried up as a prune. There is no healing as powerful as finding a purpose. My mission has always been to help people, and I have done that in martial arts for years. That basic purpose, however, didn't serve to heal me in this situation. I needed more. Getting a predator off the streets and saving countless lives, reducing stigma, and educating others sure as hell did help to heal me.

10) Two words: *indomitable spirit*! This is the hallmark characteristic of a black belt (at least a good one). When I broke up with the man I'd been sure was the last great love

of my life, and I had a myriad of mysterious symptoms,
I didn't give up. I had AIDS, no insurance, no medicine,
and I was losing my livelihood—but I kept going. I was
sick and tired, and then I was sick and tired of being sick
and tired, but I did what it took to put away an evil man.
I was terrified of ridicule, stigma, being an outcast, and
losing my business—but I did what I knew was right. I did
that and then some! I did it so I could look myself in the
mirror every day and be proud of what I did and what I'm
doing. I didn't crawl into a hole like I wanted to. I held
my head up high, moved forward, and got the job done. I
did it so that my yesterdays wouldn't become anyone else's
tomorrows.

I gave up using a pseudonym shortly after the trial. It's scary
sometimes knowing that I'm "out" to the world, but if I'm going to
do something to serve a greater good, I'd like to do it as me. I can't
speak about reducing stigma if I'm going to perpetuate the problem
by cowering to it. There are still some people in the world who will
be afraid to hug me or sit next to me on a plane. I can't let that get
to me. I have to do the best I can every day to show people what it
is to be a person living with HIV—a real person who is more than
just a diagnosis.

In 2014, I was inducted into the martial arts Masters Hall of
Fame—a huge honor! I still run Vision Martial Arts Center, where
I've trained more than 170 black belts and thousands of other kids
and adults.

The romantic betrayal and the disease both took their toll on me,
and I'm not the same person I was before, but I've learned to like
the new me—imperfections and all. The new me has a perspective
that I never would've had otherwise, and an understanding that I

need to share. I've done so by speaking to people at conferences, seminars, and schools; by writing articles, starting a website, and reaching out to women who are in similar situations. It's a gift to know that what I do matters.

As I have told my story, many people have asked, "Have you forgiven him?" There is no simple answer to this question.

I know that it is in my best interest to forgive because holding onto anger only poisons the soul. As a Christian, I also believe that God wants us to forgive others, as He forgives us. But God requires that we ask for forgiveness, and I'm certain Philippe cares not one iota whether or not I forgive him.

That's not what's important to me. I am working toward that goal anyway, and in writing this book, I have come closer than ever before at letting go of the anger. I now come from a place of peace, of kindness. But never mistake my kindness for weakness because I am still standing strong! We all are, I believe.

Lately, I've thought a lot about the quote from Christine Mason Miller given at the beginning of this book: "At any given moment, you have the power to say: 'This is not how the story is going to end.'" Wrestling against victimhood takes effort. You really get two choices when your lifeboat is about to sink: get swept under or jump off and fight your way to higher ground. I decided not to let my story end with HIV, so I jumped out of the boat of despair and fought to live with purpose again.

I didn't start the deadly chain. Philippe was the one who caused the disease to spread unabated for years, to countless women and maybe men. But by God, I stopped that chain.

And that is something worth living for.

Epilogue

I've been brokenhearted to see more "Philippes" in the news again and again in the last few years: a preacher who knowingly transmitted HIV to women in his congregation under the guise of spiritual healing, a college wrestler, a Michigan man who claims to have transmitted to thousands of people because he enjoys causing women pain, a police officer who didn't get caught for seven years . . . gay, straight, black, white. Predominantly men, but a few women, too. A woman in Kenya who announced on social media that because a man gave her HIV, she was going to get back at all men by attempting to have unprotected sex four times a day (she actually kept a tally of how many people she had potentially transmitted to—it was in the hundreds).

Every one of these perpetrators is a sociopath: people who come across as charming but who are totally lacking in empathy. They care about their own pleasure, not about you. They get off on the power they have to cause suffering.

We need to do a better job of getting people tested. We can start by changing our choice of words, and educating people about what is and is not a risk of transmission. Despite CDC recommendations that all people under 65 get tested for HIV, a recent study found that only 5 percent of people over age fifty have been tested.[1] Then, those who have acquired it must be placed and kept in treatment, regardless of side effects, costs, stigma, or any other concerns. With better screening and improved linkage to and retention in medical care, it is estimated that over half of new transmissions and almost two-thirds of AIDS-related deaths would be prevented. Would that cost a lot of money? According to AIDSmap.com, the estimate over 20 years is $96 billion. Sounds like a whole lot. But the cost of the projected increase over the next twenty years without these interventions? A staggering $256 billion.

There is a small but vocal minority of folks in the HIV world who want to decriminalize all transmission—meaning that they want all the Philippes of the world to get away with it, no matter how egregious the circumstances. Their viewpoint is that no one should be required to disclose or be responsible for anyone else's sexual health. Maybe some are rabid about this because they feel that disclosure will put a damper on their sex lives. Well, of course it will! *As it should!* Any decent human being would want to keep their intimate partners as safe as possible—but not all people *are* decent. That's basically the point of the criminalization laws. Just because you have HIV, you don't get a pass to do anything you want. HIV doesn't make you a criminal, but for those who are criminals to start with, they can and will use whatever means necessary to carry out their evil.

---

1 Ford, Chandra L. et al. "Recent HIV Testing Prevalence, Determinants, and Disparities Among U.S. Older Adult Respondents to the Behavioral Risk Factor Surveillance System," *Sexually Transmitted Diseases*: (August 2015): 42 (8), 405–410.

Here's the scary truth: In a 2015 study published in the *Journal of the American Medical Association*,[2] researchers broke down how new infections are transmitted:

30% are transmitted by people who don't know they have HIV

61% are transmitted by people who know they have HIV and are not in medical care

6% are transmitted by people who know they have HIV and are in medical care, but are not virally suppressed

2.5% are transmitted by those who are virally suppressed

The majority of cases are transmitted by people who know they have it and are not being treated for it. It's not a lunatic fringe. It's not the outliers. It's the majority.

Of course, this doesn't mean that *all* of them are spreading it intentionally or recklessly, but it suggests that an awful lot of people are far too casual with both their own lives and the lives of others. It's hard for me to imagine that in that 61 percent of cases, the person with HIV is disclosing before having sex and the partner living without it is intentionally choosing to have sex without a condom. It seems far more likely to me that people are not disclosing and are knowingly putting others at risk. Some transmissions are through means other than sex, of course. The CDC states that 8–10 percent of transmissions occur through needle sharing.

We need to do better. We don't need to take away the laws meant to protect people from intentional transmission; we need to make those laws stronger. In some states, Philippe would have gotten a maximum of five years in prison and then been right back out there transmitting to others.

---

2 J. Skarbinski et al., "Human Immunodeficiency Virus Transmission at Each Step of the Care Continuum in the United States," *Journal of the American Medical Association* (April 2015): 175 (4) 588–96,.

We also need to make sure that the older generation is as educated as the younger generation: HIV does not care how old you are, what race you are, what your socioeconomic status is, whether you've had one partner or a hundred; if you've ever had unprotected sex, you're at risk, and you should get tested every year at minimum—more often if you have new partners.

There are 1.2 million people living with HIV in the United States, and 50,000 new diagnoses each year. Lots of people (1 in 8 according to a 2015 CDC report)* are out there undiagnosed, without knowing that they're spreading the virus. So even if you *have* found someone wonderful who you're sure you can trust, that doesn't mean he or she knows.

In addition, while the number of new cases in the United States each year has remained steady at about 50,000 since the 1990s, it's not balanced: women accounted for just 15 percent of the HIV population from 1981 to 1995, but now it's about 25 percent, with black and Hispanic women affected in far greater proportion than Caucasian women. Despite the fact that African Americans make up only 12 percent of the U.S. population, they make up over half of the people in this country who have died of AIDS.

Women over fifty are increasingly at risk. According to HIV wisdom.org, the rate of AIDS diagnoses in women over fifty has tripled in recent years. The CDC reports that 84 percent of new HIV infections in women are from heterosexual contact. It can happen to your mother, your grandmother, your aunt, your sister. It can happen to you. Women are fighting the double stigma of ageism and sexism. We don't talk about our sexuality, and neither do our doctors. Less than 5 percent of the over-fifty population

* Centers for Disease Control and Prevention HIV in the United States: At a Glance, Sept. 29, 2015.

gets tested for HIV each year, yet in 2013, that demographic accounted for 27 percent of new AIDS diagnoses in the United States.

The Centers for Disease Control reports that just 45 percent of all people who are diagnosed with HIV are on medication, and only 32 percent are virally suppressed.[3] This is one of the reasons why it's still so dangerous: we could reduce new infections by 94 percent if everyone with HIV had it under control with medications—but poverty, abuse, unwanted side effects, lack of public and private discourse, shame, and willful noncompliance all play a role. The new hope is PREP—pre-exposure prophylaxis—a daily pill to prevent you from acquiring HIV. This could be a game-changer for both men and women.

In the meantime, I will keep fighting to educate women about preventing and treating HIV, and I hope to see this disease eradicated within my lifetime.

3 "HIV among Women," CDC fact sheet, *www.cdc.gov/hiv/group/gender/women/index.html.*

Resources for
People with HIV/AIDS

AIDS Healthcare Foundation (*www.ahf.org*): The largest provider of HIV/AIDS health care in the United States.

AIDS.gov (*www.aids.gov*): Government-sponsored website providing links to services, latest information from the FDA and other federal sources, information about funding and grants, statistics, a history of AIDS, and advice for the newly diagnosed.

International Community of Women with HIV in North America (*www.iamicw.org*): Global network by and for women with HIV. Campaigns, personal stories, news, and advocacy.

Poz (*www.poz.com*): The online site of a print magazine dedicated to helping people with HIV/AIDS. Advice and information about treatments and side effects, social issues, criminalization, and more, along with a dating section and job listings.

The Body (*www.thebody.com*): A significant resource for people with HIV/AIDS, including discussion forums, an "Ask the Expert" section, blogs, treatment options, information about prevention, and personal stories. Includes a special section of resources about violence against women and its relation to HIV: *www.thebody.com*

*/content/76307/resources-on-the-intersection-of-women-hiv-and-vio
.html.*

The Well Project (*www.thewellproject.com*): A nonprofit "global hub for resources that help women and girls overcome the inequalities, barriers, and stigma that contribute to the epidemic among women."

We Make the Change (*www.wemakethechange.com*): Videos documenting people's experiences with HIV and AIDS.

Women Organized to Respond to Life-threatening Diseases (*www.women hiv.org*): Peer advocacy services, outreach, a speaker's bureau, client and community retreats, and a policy/advocacy department.

About the Authors

Diane Reeve has been called "the new face of HIV." Her gripping life story has been the subject of many TV specials and magazine articles, including *20/20, The Oprah Winfrey Show,* the *Ricki Lake Show,* and *The Guardian Weekend* magazine. She owns and teaches at Vision Martial Arts Center in Plano, Texas, and in 2014 was inducted into the martial arts Masters Hall of Fame.

Her passion for HIV advocacy and education has become a mission and she is a popular speaker who delivers inspiring messages to diverse audiences nationwide, from corporate events to health conferences. She also loves gardening and spending time with her children and grandchildren.

Her newest venture is *datestronger .com,* a nonprofit organization empowering women to make strong, smart dating choices. Her message is one of inspiration, hope, and courage. And, of course, standing strong.

Jenna Glatzer is an award-winning full-time writer who's written twenty-six books and hundreds of articles for magazines and online publications. Her latest release is *Who's the New Kid?* with Heidi Bond. It's the story of how Heidi helped her daughter beat childhood obesity. Prior to that, Jenna wrote *Never Ever Give Up: The Inspiring Story of Jessie and Her JoyJars* with Erik Rees —the true story of eleven-year-old Jessica Joy Rees, who started a foundation to help kids with cancer even as she battled the disease herself. She also wrote *The Pregnancy Project* with Gaby Rodriguez, who faked her own pregnancy as a senior project in high school. She worked with Celine Dion on the authorized biography *Celine Dion: For Keeps*, which was one of Jenna's favorite life experiences.